It Was, It Was Not

IT WAS,
IT WAS NOT

*Essays and Art
on the War Against Iraq*

Edited by
MORDECAI BRIEMBERG

1992
New Star Books
Vancouver

To the memory of friends, Saghir Ahmad and Kathleen Aberle

New Star Books Ltd.
2504 York Avenue
Vancouver, B.C.
V6K 1E3

Printed and bound in Canada by Gagné Printers, Louiseville, Que.
1 2 3 4 5   96 95 94 93 92
First printing, January 1992

We wish to express our thanks to the following authors and publishers for permission to reprint:
"High-Death Weapons" by Michael T. Klare, *The Nation* magazine/The Nation Co. Inc., June 3, 1991. "Christian Misconceptions of Islam" by Dr. Hanna Kassis, *The Ecumenist*, Volume 25, No. 6, September-October 1987. "From the Hebrew Press" by Dr. Israel Shahak, *Washington Report on Middle East Affairs*, August-September 1991. "The Next Phase – Problems of Transition" by Dr. Salim Tamari, Palestinian Academic Society for the Study of International Affairs (PASSIA), *Palestinian Assessments of the Gulf War and its Aftermath* (East Jerusalem, 1991). The poems of Heather Spears, Wolsak and Wynn Publishers Ltd., publishers of *Human Acts* (Toronto, 1991). Heather Spears' drawings are reproduced from *Drawn from the Fire* (1989) and *Massacre* (1990). "A Cold Coming" by Tony Harrison, Bloodaxe Books, publishers of *A Cold Coming – Gulf War Poems* (Newcastle upon Tyne, 1991).

Cover illustration by Carel Moiseiwitsch.
Cover design by David Lester.
Editing and production: Jean Kavanagh, Audrey McClellan, Rolf Maurer

The publisher is grateful for assistance provided by the Canada Council and the Cultural Services Branch, Province of British Columbia.

Canadian Cataloguing in Publication Data

Main entry under title:
It was, it was not

  Includes bibliographical references.
  ISBN 0-921586-21-3.
  1. Persian Gulf War, 1991. 2. Petroleum industry and trade – political aspects –
Persian Gulf Region. 3. Middle East – Politics and government – 1945- 4. Middle
East – History. 5. Arab countries – Foreign public opinion. I. Briemberg, Mordecai.
DS79.72.I82 1991   956.05'3   C91-091681-0

Contents

Part 4: **HARD CHOICES**

The Iraqi people are being killed by epidemics and starvation in the tens of thousands. "Surgical" bombing created the conditions for major epidemics and starvation. The still enforced comprehensive sanctions against the people of Iraq magnify and multiply the disaster. The U.S. and its allies are ruthlessly blocking equipment and supplies necessary to halt the spread of deadly diseases and hunger.

George Bush has said sanctions will remain until Saddam Hussein is replaced, replaced by a military coup, a new dictatorship. Bush is prolonging the victimization of the Iraqi people, literally holding the Iraqi people hostage and cold-bloodedly killing them for his own political agenda.

There is an urgent need to lift the sanctions and to provide the Iraqi people with desperately needed assistance.

Authors' revenues from the sale of this book will go to help meet the health needs of the Iraqi people, via the charitable organization International Development and Refugee Foundation, 100 McLevin Avenue, # 2, Scarborough, Ontario M1B 2V5.

Preface

Kan wa ma kan – it was and it was not. With these traditional words Arab folk-tellers begin their stories.

It was and it was not...a war. The massive weapons of armies were used but where were the battles? The uninterrupted sorties and exploding missiles made this a slaughter, not a contest.

It was and it was not...in the Gulf. Certainly that body of water, that environmental casualty of conflict, was one front of the confrontation. But the invasion of Kuwait, like the assassination of Archduke Ferdinand in Sarajevo in 1914, was only one event in a far larger set of global calculations.

It was and it was not...a television spectacle. In North America it was: the wide western screen, malignant with its infotainment, enveloped, excited, and calmed us with sanitized surgical strikes and clinical comment. In Iraq and Kuwait, the consequences were burned flesh and spilled blood.

It was and it was not...a new world order. This much was new: the United States stood militarily rampant over its prostrate super-power rival, while its economic nemeses, Germany and

Japan, gaped from the sidelines, politically paralyzed. But the vast millions of humanity still remain ground between the old hard stones of imperial order.

It was and it was not...43 days long. The coalition bombing of Baghdad spanned 43 days and culminated a central phase of the United States war against Iraq. But in the regional game of tilt, in the imperial game of controlled destabilization with its on-going wars between foreign-armed dictators and an Israeli Sparta, the starting date precedes Iraq's invasion of Kuwait. And the war continues still: as sanctions reinforce the massive bombing to ensure continuing death for countless Iraqis; as Bush manoeuvres for a military coup to provide a new dictator to replace Saddam; as the restored Kuwaiti emirate pursues its pogrom against homeless Palestinians; as Israeli generals already discuss the next war with Syria; as Turkey invades Iraq to kill Kurds; as the environmental disaster resonates with uncalculated consequences.

This volume of essays and art on the war against Iraq is intended to surface your memories, to stimulate a recalling of events and personal responses, to summon these for reconsideration, so you can extend reflection beyond the 43-day definition of "reality." This book is an alternative to the media crucible: the crucible where "understanding" and "feeling" are forged in briefly intense moments of pre-fabricated presentation, then instantly congealed and shelved; where thought is drained of the contradictions that make it dynamic, on-going, honest.

When we cannot sustain thought beyond the television's flicking focus – this country today, that region tomorrow, this second's hot issue replacing last second's dead issue; when we do not precede the cameras with our own alternatively generated information points of reference, then unavoidably we become the accomplices of someone else's agenda. Addicted to the sensational, disconnected from the actual, we are guided, blinkered and gagged, into the darkening future.

The British journalist, Sir Peregrine Worsthorne, writing in the

Sunday Telegraph three days after the bombing of Iraq began,
honestly expressed the future the war-makers dreamt:

> . . . if the Gulf war ends as it has begun, there can be no doubt who
> are the masters now – at any rate for another generation. We have
> the laser beams and they have not. And the we who matter are not
> the Germans or the Japanese or the Russians but the Americans.
> Happy days are here again. Bliss it is in this dawn to be alive; but to
> be an old reactionary is very heaven.

This book is compiled for those who reject this chauvinist cant,
this gloating, this delusionary triumphalism. This book is compiled
for those whose decency and intelligence have survived the test of
this war. It aims to bring to the fore human realities and to nourish
practical desires for a world in which humanity is not ranked,
dominated and denied.

Contributors to this volume are from Canada, England, the
United States, Palestine and Israel. They generously gave their
time and knowledge to this project. Several of the Canadians are of
Middle Eastern ancestry, as one of the aims was to enlist the
co-operation of those with attachments to the peoples and societies
of the Middle East. In the course of opposition to the war, their
knowledge and insight were increasingly sought out and valued, as
they should have been earlier. Perhaps one good day their
welcomed participation no longer will be remarkable.

Some contributors are poets, singers, artists, some academics,
some journalists, some activists, some combinations of these. My
hope is that readers likewise will vary, with a capacity to enjoy the
different voices mixed together, and an energy to respond to them,
particularly when you find yourself at odds with an interpretation,
emphasis or emotion.

The contributions are arranged in four sections. But unlike a
story or poem, a chronological history or biography, you may
discover interplays between the contributions that lead you to
"jump around" in your reading.

The first section of the book is called **War Fronts**. Four essays, and poems and photos and songs, examine the war on each of these fronts in turn: the political, military, propaganda and environmental. Obviously war is a military endeavour, but as Clausewitz made explicit long ago, armed conflict also is an extension of politics. Propaganda is essential to those who wage war, and they devote important efforts to it. We also came to recognize, this time with vivid abruptness, that war is fought against the environment as well.

The second section of the book is called **Rediscovering The Middle East,** for while most of us know little about this region our minds are not *carte blanche*, and we have to rediscover the Middle East, self-consciously this time.

Ten-year-old boys may memorize the teams, players, and performance records of an entire hockey league, recalling, comparing and evaluating them with comfortable familiarity. But for most adults in Canada, the many fewer countries and leaders of the Middle East seem unmanageably complex. Need this be so? During the course of this war, a goodly number of Canadians realized they could understand important elements of the geography, culture, history and politics of the Middle East once they had the desire to do so. Through public forums and private curiosity, they began to rediscover.

Propaganda presented Iraq as a land of sand and Saddam, depopulated; but the curious searched for the "disappeared" people of this ancient and modern society. George Bush drew his line in the sand; but the curious were eager to learn who drew the many boundaries down rivers, mountains and valleys, when and why, sometimes dividing a shared Arab culture into many countries. We were told: the Palestinians are unconnected to the war against Iraq, there is "no linkage." We were told: Israel is innocent, restrained, and uninvolved. We were told at the end of the bombing: the U.S.-led coalition was there, magnanimously, to protect the Kurds. We were told all along: the Canadian government was upholding international law and organization. In this section writers and artists critically explore each of these fairy-tales.

The third section of the book is called **Obstacles To Understanding**. Do you remember that short-lived sensation, the 3D movie? Everyone who entered the theatre was given special glasses to view the screen. The tacky cardboard-framed plastic was indispensable: no glasses, no thrills. In our culture, there have been special glasses for viewing the "thrills" of the Middle East. We too have been fitted with tacky, cardboard-framed plastic that matches what is projected for us to see. This section explores some of the distorting stereotypes and double standards which have been entrenched obstacles to seeing the Middle East for ourselves, closer to what it is, and discovering "conversations" it otherwise would be hard even to have imagined. In this section there are essays and cartoons, calligraphy and a short excerpt from an untranslated novel.

The fourth and last section is called **Hard Choices**. It examines the opposition to the war, and explores future possibilities for peace and justice. Opposition to the war did not forestall it, nor change its course. But a vital question remains: has this war changed our course? Do we better understand our old commitments to peace and justice? Are our responses becoming geared to the challenges of the "new world order"? Have we discovered new voices with whom we can make common cause? This concluding section reflects on some of the hard choices before us.

I want to thank all those who so willingly contributed their work to this project. The ideas and their expression in individual contributions are those of the identified author and artist, and they retain copyright. Responsibility for the selection, editing and arrangement of pieces is mine. All otherwise unattributed sections of writing are the editor's, as is responsibility for errors.

I want also to thank Elizabeth. Her encouragement, independent comment, patience and practical assistance were, for me, an essential contribution.

It Was, It Was Not

Rick McCutcheon, coordinator for the Canadian Friends Service Committee, visited Iraq in March and in September 1991. This photo was taken by him in the Adhamiya neighbourhood of Baghdad which was hit by U.S.-coalition bombing.

War Against People

The human face of this war – the killed, the maimed and the displaced – rarely was visible. The numbers too were kept from us, though the tonnage of bombs and total of sorties were recorded with precision. And in this war, civilian casualties began to multiply even more rapidly *after* the bombing.

"Surgical precision destroyed the brain of Iraq and the body has been left to die. A new level of inhumanity, brought about by the development of weapons of precision, has been achieved."[1] This is the predictable result of a conscious two-pronged strategy. First, the bombing destroyed the essential infrastructure of Iraq – turbines for electrical power, water purification plants and pumping stations, oil refineries and storage facilities, seed and animal vaccine warehouses, telecommunications, and transportation networks. Then, continuing sanctions have prevented the importation of what is necessary to reconstruct the devastation, to halt the spread of resulting disease and malnutrition, epidemics and starvation.

> The new world order is one in which disease and starvation can be induced where they did not exist, in a relatively short period of

3

time, by the products of human creation. It is one in which entire
populations can be rallied behind a lie, while at the same time
believing they live in a free and democratic society; where
intelligent people can be convinced that wearing yellow ribbons
and waving flags are more important than human life; and where
children are intentionally left prey to disease and starvation while
those, unable to see with their own eyes, are told that lives have
been saved.[2]

43 days...plus

American casualties always were counted, precisely: 144 killed, 479
wounded, though the ratio that were victims of mistaken assaults
by the American military itself is minimally controversial.[3] Equally
precise: two Israelis died directly from Iraqi Scud attacks. At least
eight Palestinians in the occupied territories died directly because
Israel imposed confinement to their homes, preventing them from
receiving emergency medical treatment.

Kuwaiti deaths at the hands of the Iraqi military have been
revised downward from an early estimated 4,000 civilians. Middle
East Watch now reports 300 were killed, of some 7,000 to 9,500
Kuwaitis taken out of Kuwait by Iraqi forces during the course of
the occupation. Some 2,000 to 2,500 Kuwaitis still are
unaccounted for, so the death toll may rise. About 100 Iraqi
soldiers were killed by the Kuwaiti opposition during the
occupation.

But there are no precise figures for Iraqi military casualties at the
hands of the U.S.-led allies. That country which has been so
concerned to know the fate of its missing in action in Vietnam
callously buried alive Iraqi soldiers in their trenches, and bulldozed
thousands of Iraqi dead into mass graves, without even the respect
of taking identification to notify next of kin.[4]

Unofficial U.S. government estimates of Iraqi soldiers killed as a
direct consequence of the 43-day air and ground war range from
75,000 to 105,000: 60,000 to 80,000 killed in bunkers during the
sustained air assaults, 15,000 to 25,000 in the 100-hour ground

offensive. But an Iraqi doctor working in Basra told relief workers that between 60,000 to 70,000 Iraqi soldiers were killed in the flight from Kuwait, half of whom could have been saved had medical supplies and facilities been available.

How many were maimed? There are no estimates, only a military rule of thumb, three wounded to each death – 300,000? And Iraq's total population is 18 million, one-quarter less than that of Canada.

Kuwaiti civilian deaths from the bombing campaign are a reported 28, though the oil fields remain sown with hundreds and hundreds of U.S.-dropped cluster bombs.[5] According to Louise Cainkar, Director of the Human Rights Research Foundation who visited Iraq in March, "a good estimate of the total number of Iraqi civilians immediately killed by coalition bombing is between 11,000 and 24,500."[6] This estimate does not account for indirect deaths, like the infants in incubators who died in a Baghdad hospital when bombing cut off electricity.[7] In the U.S.-promoted and then abandoned popular uprising in southern Iraq, estimates of dead begin at 6,000. In the simultaneous Kurdish uprising estimates begin at 2,000, but in their squalid refugee encampments along the borders of Iraq, Iran and Turkey, some 20,000 died of disease and exposure, mainly children.

"Altogether, at least 100,000 and possibly as many as 200,000 Iraqis, civilian and military, perished as a consequence of the U.S.-led military campaign and subsequent civil strife."[8]

Disease and starvation

At the end of the bombing campaign, in early March, the Secretary-General of the United Nations dispatched a mission to Iraq led by Under-Secretary-General Martti Ahtisaari. Their report states:

> The recent conflict has wrought near-apocalyptic results upon the economic infrastructure of what had been, until January 1991, a rather highly urbanized and mechanized society. Now, most means

of modern life support have been destroyed or rendered tenuous. Iraq has, for some time to come, been relegated to a pre-industrial age, but with all the disabilities of post-industrial dependency on an intensive use of energy and technology.[9]

A 10-member Harvard medical team that visited Iraq from April 28 to May 6, stressed a direct correlation between the bombing destruction of power-generating plants, consequent inability to provide sanitary water, and the breakdown of public health. They forecast a minimum death toll of 170,000 additional children under the age of five from infectious diseases in the 12-month period following the cessation of bombing. "These projections are conservative," said an overview to the study.[10]

In July, Prince Sadruddin Aga Khan led another U.N. mission to Iraq.

> As for the food supply, the position is deteriorating rapidly in virtually all parts of the country...this year's aggregate cereal production will be around one-third of last year's. Current retail prices for wheat and rice – the two normal staple food items – remain 45 and 22 times their price levels of last year...The government rationing system can only provide about one-third of the typical family's food needs.
>
> Several independent studies and direct observation by the mission, confirmed the high prevalence of malnutrition among children. This clearly demonstrates a widespread and acute food supply crisis which, if not averted through timely intervention, will inexorably cause massive starvation throughout the country.[11]

But the permanent member countries of the U.N. Security Council refuse to implement the report's recommendations, sabotaging "timely intervention."

Displacement

Displacement of people is another calamity of this war.[12] There have been two massive waves of uprooted humanity. More than 2.6

million people were displaced in the first wave, August 2 to
January 17. Among these: 1.6 million refugees fled Kuwait, a
million of whom were foreign nationals who lost jobs, homes and
savings, 200,000 of these Palestinians and 600,000 from the Indian
sub-continent; the Saudi government deported some 700,000
Yemeni people because the Yemeni government did not support the
U.S. plans for war; and some 400,000 foreign nationals, mainly
Egyptians, fled Iraq before the bombing campaign.

In March and April a second wave of displacement uprooted as
many as 2.5 million Iraqis, 14 per cent of the total population. Of
these some 210,000 were civilians from the south, and 2.3 million,
mainly Kurds, from the north. In Kuwait, the remaining 150,000
Palestinians are being forced out by the restored emirate, as are
thousands of *bidun* tribespeople.

> This war has been an unmitigated disaster for millions of people in
> the Middle East and beyond. The many tens of thousands killed,
> the billions of dollars of property destruction, the millions of
> displaced persons and disrupted lives, the uncounted thousands
> with permanent physical and psychological scars, and the badly
> damaged economies are far more devastating than anything that
> has happened in the region in this century.[13]

This omits the environmental effects on the health and life of
people in the region and beyond. At an international conference
on this problem, a Harvard physicist and specialist in risk analysis
estimated 50,000 people in Kuwait alone "will have their lives
shortened in some way" due to pollutants.[14]

In an interview with the English newspaper *The Guardian*,
Richard Reid, UNICEF's Middle East regional director said: "We
can speak with alarming, grave assurance of a lost generation"
because of the war's effects on 5 million children of Kuwait, Iraq,
Jordan, Yemen and the occupied Palestinian territories.[15]

An event so momentous, so catastrophic, lives in the
consciousness of generations and assuredly will endure longer than
Canadians and Americans can keep their heads buried in the sand.

Notes

[1] Cainkar, Louise, "Desert Sin: A Post-War Journey Through Iraq," p.18. This article will appear in Moushabeck, Michel and Phyllis Bennis (eds), *Beyond the Storm: A Gulf Crisis Reader* (New York, Olive Branch Press, 1991).

[2] *Ibid.*, p.20.

[3] "Iraqis buried alive in war," *The Globe and Mail*, September 13, 1991.

[4] An excellent compilation of the human consequences of the war is "The Other Face of War" by Eric Hooglund, *Middle East Report*, No.171, July/August 1991.

[5] This was reported on the CBC Radio "Morning Show," July 16, by Mike Miller of Safety Boss company, Calgary, who was working in Kuwait fighting oil well fires.

[6] Cainkar, *op. cit.*, p.24.

[7] *Ibid.*, p.10.

[8] Hooglund, *op. cit.*

[9] *Report to the Secretary-General on Humanitarian Needs in Iraq in the Immediate Post-crisis Environment*, by a mission to the area led by Mr. Martti Ahtisaari, Under-Secretary-General for Administration and Management, Dated 20 March 1991.

[10] *The Globe and Mail*, May 22, 1991.

[11] *Manchester Guardian Weekly*, August 4, 1991.

[12] Hooglund, *op. cit.*

[13] *Ibid.* There also have been reports of depression and increased family violence among returning Iraqi soldiers.

[14] *The New York Times*, August 14, 1991.

[15] Hooglund, *op. cit.*

Desert Sin: A Post-War Journey Through Iraq

Louise Cainkar

This civilian bus was hit by U.S.-coalition bombs on the highway between Iraq and Jordan, about 100 km from the Jordanian border. Louise Cainkar initiated a project to assess the effects of the war on civilians, and spent several weeks in Iraq during March and April 1991. She took this and many other photos, commenting: "The successful achievement of the mission to destroy Iraq's infrastructure had not only thrown Iraq back at least 100 years, it had forced every single Iraqi to search for a new way to cope with the new circumstances of life: no electricity, no running water, reliance on contaminated water, food shortages, fuel shortages, transportation problems, for many no work, no income and thus no food, unreliable access or the total absence of access to medical care and medicine, massive inflation, and a real severing of human relations. . . . Iraq had been a highly developed, technologically sophisticated, and self-reliant country. Now most Iraqis appeared to be in silent shock, trying to figure out how to accomplish the day's tasks."

LAURIE TORMEY HASBROOK/FOLKLENS

All the female members of a Palestinian family living in Baghdad were killed by the U.S. missile attack on the Ameriyeh bomb shelter February 13, 1991. Abir Khader (17), Ghana (10), Adiba (the mother, 47), Ghada (21) and Ghaida (14) were survived by the father Mohammed and one brother, Ghassan (18). This memorial photo was taken in May 1991.

A residential neighbourhood of Basra, Iraq, where a U.S.-coalition bomb destroyed eight Iraqi homes.

LOUISE CAINKAR/FOLKLENS

The water tower in the Ma'kel neighbourhood of Basra was bombed. Women and children try to gather water from the ground, while a man uses the same supply to cool off.

LOUISE CAINKAR/FOLKLENS

Men are collecting contaminated water from a broken water pipe in the Ma'kel neighbourhood of Basra.

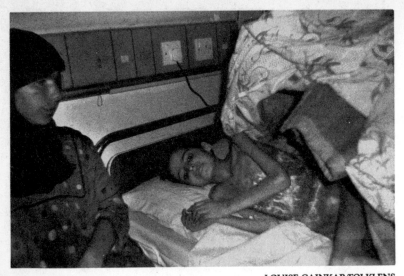

LOUISE CAINKAR/FOLKLENS

This young Iraqi boy in a Baghdad hospital was burned by a kerosene lamp fire. The lack of electrical power means many Iraqis resort to kerosene fires to boil contaminated water.

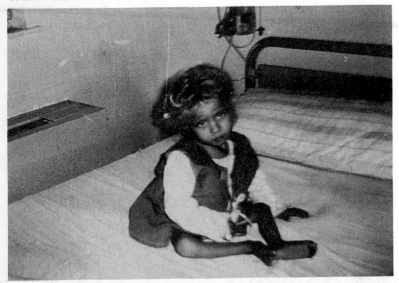

LOUISE CAINKAR/FOLKLENS

This young child is a victim of malnutrition. This photo was taken April 11, 1991 in a Baghdad hospital.

Like Hiroshima survivors

Close to one million children are malnourished and 100,000 are starving and at risk of dying in the near future, according to Dr. Eric Hoskins. He presented a report in late October 1991 that was written by 87 international professionals from a wide variety of disciplines. They had carried out investigations in Iraq's 30 largest cities and in rural areas across that country (*Health and Welfare in Iraq After the Gulf Crisis: An In-Depth Assessment*). A Harvard team of lawyers and public health experts played a leading role. Dr. Hoskins said it was "a definitive assessment of the impact of the Gulf crisis on children" and "the most comprehensive study ever done of the impact of conflict."

Professor Magne Raundalen of the University of Bergen, a member of the team of academics, reported that some children were "like living dead. They have eradicated all their feelings and have no joy in their lives." They reminded experts of Hiroshima survivors.

According to the child psychologists who were part of the international study, psychologists with a decade of experience of the wars of Uganda, Sudan and Mozambique, the children of Iraq are "the most traumatised children of war ever described."

"We must not keep this a secret, what has happened to these children. The international community must fulfil the promise made in the UNICEF summit just a year ago that children have the right to be looked after and brought back from despair and trauma," said Professor Raundalen.

Part 1: WAR FRONTS

Rødby-Puttgarten Crossing

August 25, 1990

Heather Spears

Presumably even a small
jellyfish is thoughtful, is happy,
floating in the calm water,
greenly, under the surface,
warm in August.
The wake pulls them softly, and rolls them
they bell and extend
they are almost passive
they extend to their boundaries
and are content
conscious
of light and its direction,
of their centres,
and their extension to their boundaries.
They lift in the wake,
candles, smocked muslin
muscle in two dimensions,
pink parody of lungs,
thought-bubbles from the comics,
solar discs – floppy ones,
storing, out of all we have in common
what seems moral and good to them

The huge prow of the ferry
is stubby, it does not slice them
they are far from the grit of beaches

and Puttgarten there low on the horizon
they drift in their hundreds
unurgent, blameless, baffled
by a wavery line of weed and ruck

When war was declared, Mother told,
"It was the most beautiful, late summer day,
at the end of summer, 1939 – "

And now
this light,
calm dermis of the water,
stretched, puckered like a zwieback
clouded with submergent, happy thought –
it is my skin I am crossing
this is my ignorant body
these are my happy cells

Negotiations or War

Mordecai Briemberg

LUIGI PIRANDELLO ONCE WROTE A PLAY TITLED *SIX CHARACTERS IN Search of an Author*. Pirandello was reversing the common understanding that it is authors who create their characters. In the case of warmaking there is a shared pretence that the publicly offered rationale for war precedes the decision to wage war. But in fact it is usually the other way round; wars are decided upon in closed quarters and then the war makers go in search of publicly acceptable justifications. What was peculiar about the war against Iraq, however, was the awkward fumbling before the war makers settled upon their public justification for what they already had decided to do.

The search for a rationale

The dilemma in finding a compelling rationale stemmed from the collapse of the old order with its ready-made justifications. The U.S.-U.S.S.R. superpower rivalry was over. Not only was the Soviet Union now in full public retreat as a world power, its capitulation already had proceeded so far that it positioned itself as an ally of Washington against Iraq. This war in the making therefore hardly could be promoted as a war against the "communist menace."

At one point Secretary of Defense Cheney, part of Bush's inner circle, floated the idea that this was a war "for jobs." That rationale faded with the short laughter that greeted it. As late as October 21, 1990, James LeMoyne of *The New York Times*, after interviewing more than 200 troops, reported that U.S. soldiers in Saudi Arabia "constantly ask what it is they are expected to do and whether their countrymen support their mission...American troops become visibly uncomfortable when discussing the thought that they are here to defend low oil prices and the near-absolute monarchies that dominate Saudi Arabia and most other gulf states." Sacrificing one's life for low oil prices and absolute monarchies lacked the classic nobility and the paranoia-fuelled hate so essential to justify a "good war."

Firstly, evil had to be matched with danger for Washington effectively to justify its predetermined massing of a truly vast offensive military arsenal in the Saudi desert. Saddam Hussein, yesterday's regional ally, villainous like so many other U.S.-allied regimes, had to be inflated into a world-scale demon of Hitlerian proportions. Iraq's military capability also had to be greatly exaggerated. In mid-November, stopping Saddam Hussein from manufacturing nuclear weapons became the sole reason a majority of Americans would support making war.[1]

Then to complement this generation of a hateful paranoia, the war makers also advanced a noble cause for war: the vision of a "new world order." The demonic invader of Kuwait would be driven back, the legitimate government of Kuwait would be restored, and international law would be advanced through the cooperative resolve of a united world, symbolized by the United Nations.

After the total and rapid devastation of Iraq's military by the U.S.-led coalition, in a war without battles, is it plausible to still believe that "the fabulous tale of Iraqi military power" was honestly intended?[2] Lt. General Walter Boomer, commander of the U.S. Marines, acknowledged after the ceasefire: "We made them [the Iraqi military] into something they weren't. The whole thing was blown up."[3] Don't misinterpret this as hindsight. French reporters for *L'Express* newspaper wrote on October 19, 1990 that in the Pentagon

American military leaders have all sized up Saddam Hussein: he's a paper tiger. With calm assurance, tinged with condescension toward the Iraqi dictator, an advisor to Secretary of Defense Dick Cheney revealed to *L'Express* the broad outlines of [the operation]. "The most murderous attack in history in such a short period of time."[4]

Were the noble rationales any more plausible? Restoration of the "legitimate government" of Kuwait: only 68,000 males out of 800,000 Kuwaitis, themselves well less than half of the 1.9 million resident population, sometimes had a vote for an elected assembly which itself remained subordinate to the Emir and was totally suspended in 1986. The principle of inviolability of international law was trumpeted by the state that only recently had invaded Grenada and Panama, and openly defied the International Court ruling against its intervention in Nicaragua. The enhancement of coordinated world action through the United Nations was heralded by the state that continued to default on its $700 million in U.N. back dues; by the state whose longtime ambassador to the U.N., Daniel Moynihan, wrote that his government "desired that the United Nations prove utterly ineffective in whatever measures it undertook," as Indonesia killed 10 per cent of the East Timorese within a few weeks of its invasion of that country; by the state that had vetoed 58 Security Council resolutions from 1970-1990, blocking united action. By comparison, in the same 20-year period the Soviet Union had exercised a veto eight times.

But, it was countered, this is carping about "the old order": the old order in the Middle East where Turkey occupied Cyprus, Syria occupied Lebanon, and where Israel occupied Lebanon, Syria and Palestine, in clear defiance of U.N. resolutions. Now we had started a new game, a new order. Presumably the message conveyed to Saddam Hussein by the U.S. Ambassador to Iraq, April Glaspie, only one week before Iraq invaded Kuwait, also was a remnant of the old order. That message was: "we [the U.S.] have no opinion on your Arab-Arab conflicts, like your border disagreement with Kuwait."

But even were we to be born again and believe that a new order arrived instantly, one week after Iraq's invasion of Kuwait, why in the new order did the U.S., with nods and winks, give the Syrian military latitude to kill without hindrance in Beirut and consolidate a client regime? Why, with the same nods and winks, did the U.S. give the Israelis the latitude to invade the territory of a foreign country, Lebanon, to regularly bomb and kill villagers there? And with those nods and winks, the U.S. let Saudi Arabia torture several hundred resident Yemenis, according to Amnesty International, and deport 700,000 of them only because their government did not endorse the impending war. All this happened in the dawn of the "new order": after the cold war, after the August 2nd invasion of Kuwait, precisely with the now, today, this moment, instant U.S. promulgation of respect for international borders and human rights. Yes, the war against Iraq found its public rationales, but ones so opportunistically manufactured and so inconsistently adhered to that they disintegrate upon initial examination.

Avoiding diplomacy

Compared to the many voices that questioned why the U.S.-led coalition escalated so quickly from the policy of sanctions to the initiation of armed war, there were too few voices that posed any critical questions about negotiation. Obviously sanctions were not introduced as an alternative to armed war, but as a stepping stone toward it. Indeed the war makers never have abandoned their sanctions; they still are in place multiplying human disaster among the innocent Iraqi people. Meanwhile by swallowing the war makers' demonization of Iraq and concentrating attention on sanctions as *the* alternative to war, significant parts of the anti-war movement underplayed the possibilities for negotiation.

In the fall of 1990 U.S. and Israeli administrations, speaking "off-the-record," acknowledged they were apprehensive Iraq would find a way to withdraw from Kuwait. They called this their "nightmare scenario." But if *the* issue was Iraq's invasion of Kuwait and *the* remedy was to end that occupation, why should Iraqi withdrawal be called a "nightmare"? It could be a nightmare only if there were other objectives, objectives that would be derailed by a diplomatic, negotiated, peaceful resolution of the dispute.

"There will be no negotiations," President Bush explicitly and consistently said. In all the months prior to the U.S.-initiated bombing of Iraq, Washington met only once with a major Iraqi representative. At that meeting in Geneva, U.S. Secretary of State James Baker again emphasized: "I met with Mr. Aziz today not to negotiate, as we had made clear we would not do." As early as August 22, 1990, on the front page of *The New York Times*, Thomas Friedman, chief diplomatic correspondent and an intimate of James Baker, outlined the U.S. position: diplomacy would "defuse the crisis at the cost of a few token gains for Iraq." The tokens Friedman was referring to were the Rumaila oil field, already 98 per cent inside of Iraq but with a tiny part straddling the disputed British-drawn Iraq-Kuwait border, and two uninhabited islands in the Gulf that the British allocated to its Kuwaiti protectorate in the 1920s in order to keep Iraq land-locked.

Because the U.S. did not want the crisis defused, it had to and did block all diplomatic efforts to resolve the conflict. Iraq made several and varied diplomatic proposals. On August 12, 1990, ten days after its invasion of Kuwait, Baghdad proposed a settlement "on the same principles" linking Iraq's withdrawal from Kuwait with withdrawal of occupying forces from other Arab lands: Syria from Lebanon and Israel from Lebanon, Syria and Palestine. The editors of London's *Financial Times* wrote the next day that it might offer "a path away from disaster...through negotiation." The editors called on the West "to seize the initiative and harness diplomacy," but the U.S. dismissed the proposal out of hand.

On August 23, 1990 a different proposal from Iraq was personally transmitted to National Security Advisor Brent Scowcroft via a former high-ranking U.S. official returning from Iraq. This proposal made no link between the resolution of Iraq's occupation of Kuwait and the resolution of other occupations. Instead Iraq offered to withdraw from Kuwait in return for the lifting of sanctions, guaranteed access to the Gulf, and full control of the Rumaila oil field. The proposal also referred to negotiating an oil agreement "satisfactory to both nations' national security interests" and developing a plan for "stability in the gulf " and "to alleviate Iraq's economical and financial problems." Iraq's motivations for invading Kuwait were pre-eminently economic.[5]

After this Iraqi memorandum was quoted in the New York newspaper *Newsday* (August 29), *The New York Times* conceded it was accurate but "had not been taken seriously" and was "dismissed" by Washington.

On January 2, 1991, U.S. officials revealed that Iraq had made another diplomatic proposal in late December: "to withdraw from Kuwait if the United States pledges not to attack as soldiers are pulled out, if foreign troops leave the region, and if there is an agreement on the Palestinian problem and on the banning of all weapons of mass destruction in the region."[6] This time Iraq dropped its claims to disputed islands and oil fields. Still the U.S. "immediately dismissed the proposal," even though Yasser Arafat made clear in a report carried in next day's *New York Times* that "Mr. Hussein's statement August 12, linking an Iraqi withdrawal to an Israeli withdrawal from the West Bank and Gaza Strip, was no longer operative as a negotiating demand." Instead what was necessary was only a promise, a "strong link to be guaranteed by the five permanent members of the Security Council that we have to solve all the problems in the Gulf, in the Middle East and especially the Palestinian cause."[7]

France made two major diplomatic proposals the U.S. scorned and rejected. On September 24, 1990 President Mitterand personally put forward a four-point proposal at the U.N.: an Iraqi declaration of intent to withdraw from Kuwait; U.N. supervision; restoration of Kuwaiti sovereignty and the opportunity for the people there to democratically choose their own government; an international peace conference on the Middle East. On January 14, in a last minute effort to avoid war, France proposed that the Security Council call for a "rapid and massive [Iraqi] withdrawal" from Kuwait and commit itself to an "active contribution" to the settlement of other regional problems, particularly the Palestinian problem, by "convening, at an appropriate date, an international conference." Belgium on the Security Council, as well as Germany, Spain, Italy, Algeria, Morocco, and Tunisia supported the proposal. Britain and the Soviet Union joined the U.S. in rejection.

It is clear now the U.S. was prepared to organize its own international Middle East conference only after it had made war, but not to avoid it. An international conference to avoid war would have been a conference based on the United Nations resolutions on the Middle

East, and on the widely shared international consensus on the question of Palestine, a consensus rejected by the United States and Israel but one shared by Washington's two main economic rivals, Europe and Japan. In a conference to avoid war the U.S. would find itself diplomatically isolated with its ally Israel, whereas its economic rivals would be important participants. But a conference after the U.S. waged its war is a conference where, by contrast, the U.N. and the European roles have been explicitly marginalized, where the international consensus on Palestine has been unabashedly discarded, and where the U.S. is the sole decisive power in orchestrating arrangements.

There were many other diplomatic efforts to forestall war, particularly from within the Arab world, which required Iraq's withdrawal. Efforts were made by Jordan's King Hussein among others, as early as a day after the invasion of Kuwait, but these too were scuppered by U.S. pressures.[8] President Chadli of Algeria, a country whose diplomatic skills had been used by the U.S. and Iran to end the hostage crisis, visited Baghdad in December and planned to proceed to Saudi Arabia, until under U.S. pressure Saudi Arabia refused to receive him. On the morning of January 13 reporters were summoned to Algiers airport to accompany President Chadli on a negotiating mission to Washington, to try and avert the impending war. But as the President's motorcade arrived at the airport, he received the message U.S. officials would refuse to meet him when he arrived in Washington. There were visits to Baghdad to meet with Saddam Hussein by former German Chancellor Brandt and former Japanese Prime Minister Nakasone. *The New York Times* Tokyo correspondent Steve Weissman reported that the president of a large Japanese energy corporation "close to" Prime Minister Kaifu told him it would be "best if some sort of inter-Arab solution were to be found, giving Saddam some concessions on territory or oil prices or freedom of waterways." Why then, if so many thought there were real possibilities of negotiation, did the U.S. dismiss them untested, block and indeed fear them as a "nightmare"?

Goals of war

General Schwarzkopf, commander of the U.S. forces in the Gulf, told *The New York Times* on November 1, 1991 that the "ultimate objective is to make sure that we have peace, stability and a correct balance of power in the Middle East..." Though the "correct balance of power" was not part of U.N. resolutions, it certainly was key to U.S. calculations.

U.S. control of the oil resources of the Middle East is one crucial element of its "correct balance of power." In 1945 a U.S. State Department report referred to Middle East oil as "a stupendous source of strategic power and one of the greatest material prizes in world history." There was a period, from 1973 to 1985, when the percentage of world-wide production of oil that came from the Gulf states and OPEC declined as oil exploration capital shifted to the U.S. and the North Sea. That trend now has been reversed and the OPEC share of world production is expected to rise to 50 per cent by 1995 from a low of 30 per cent in 1985. Similarly since 1985 U.S. oil imports have been ballooning, with 28 per cent of these now coming from the Gulf. Japan and Western Europe, America's global economic rivals, are even more dependent on imported oil, 92 and 65 per cent respectively, and the Gulf provides 59 per cent of Japan's imports and 29 per cent of Western Europe's. Perhaps most important, the Gulf area accounts for 62 per cent of the world's known oil reserves. "In the absence of serious efforts to enhance energy efficiency and to develop renewable sources of energy, oil demand is set to grow; only the Gulf states seem able to satisfy that demand."[9]

In addition to access to the oil, the U.S. is concerned with oil pricing and profits from the sale of oil. Both the Saudis and the Kuwaitis have pursued a policy of co-operating with U.S. pricing needs, but even more important they have recycled their petro-dollars into the U.S. and British economies particularly, providing massive infusions of much needed capital to companies and banks. Kuwaiti rulers were so integrated into the Western economies that since the mid-80s they apparently derived more revenues from their $100 to $150 billion investment portfolios than from the sale of oil.

Control over access to oil, its pricing and profits depends upon the establishment and maintenance of client-regimes. These surrogates defend U.S. interests in the region against the people who live there, particularly should they be so presumptuous to think the oil could be used to meet their own pressing economic and social needs, to end vast inequities, and to develop and advance independent political objectives. Iran under the Shah, Israel and Saudi Arabia were America's key surrogates. In 1979 the Shah was overthrown. Israel remained the key defender of U.S. interests against Arab nationalism, but was unable to fill the Shah's shoes in the Gulf. To compensate for the "loss" of Iran, in addition to promoting Iraq's war against Khomeini, the U.S. Carter administration developed plans for a direct U.S. military presence in the region. The first major step in this direction was the military escort the U.S. provided Kuwaiti tankers in 1987, to demonstrate Iran would not be allowed to win its war with Iraq.

Iraq was massively indebted at the end of its U.S.-backed war against Iran, and wanted an increase in the price of oil, to which U.S. interests did not seem to have major objections. But already a modernized and scientifically advanced society, Baghdad over the previous eight years of war also had increased its military capacity to an extent that might *begin* to challenge Israel's predominant position in the region. The invasion of Kuwait, in the absence of a client Iran, also highlighted the "need" for direct U.S. military presence. The military destruction of Iraq's infrastructure, returning it to a pre-industrial state, would re-establish the "correct balance." However a negotiated end to the invasion of Kuwait would not. Iraq's social and military capacity would survive and an opportunity for a direct U.S. military presence would be lost. Similarly, any diplomatic connection between Iraq's withdrawal from Kuwait and Israel's equally illegal occupations, any connection between Iraq's disarmament of non-conventional weapons and Israel's disarmament of its functional and significant nuclear arsenal, would only reduce the predominance of the key U.S. surrogate which helps maintain the "correct balance" in the region.

There also was a global consideration in the U.S. decision to wage war. The prosperity of U.S. capitalism, what Eisenhower called the "military-industrial complex," has for decades been linked to world war and cold war. Now the rivalry with the Soviet Union is over; simultaneously the political constraints that rivalry placed on Washington's major economic rivals have been loosened. An economically weakening U.S. faces growing challenges from German-dominated European and Japanese capitalism. However the U.S. stands unchallenged militarily.

Well before Iraq's invasion of Kuwait, U.S. policy circles were debating how to maintain supremacy in this new world order. Some argued for increased social expenditure to remedy the predicted serious shortage of skilled labour, to rehabilitate a deteriorating education system, in short to transform the U.S. economy and improve its competitiveness. Others argued the best option was to maintain a military-driven economy, guarding trade routes and access to raw materials, with the economic victims of the system implicitly offered the career of mercenary. The choice of war against Iraq was one watershed in this debate. In September 1990, in the rush to war against Iraq, the financial editor of the conservative *Chicago Tribune* proudly enthused about the U.S. becoming "the world's rent-a-cops," who could charge Japan and Europe "a fair price for our considerable services." The U.S. could forego the role of enforcer, he concluded, "but with it would go much of our control over the world economic system."[10]

It is no wonder that, conversely, Germany and Japan were opposed to this military strategy for U.S. global dominance. They were very reluctant financial contributors to the war-making, a reluctance that often turned to and lingers as resentment. They were marginalized by the U.S. sabotage of diplomacy, and by the orchestration of a Middle East conference under its aegis; besides, the U.S. military directly sits astride oil resources so vital to their own economies.

In short, the U.S. rejected diplomacy in the Gulf not because the principles were too noble for compromise, nor because the threat posed by Saddam Hussein was so imminent, cataclysmic and irresolvable by negotiation. Rather U.S. ruling circles calculated the best chance to maintain their "correct balance" of regional power and global predominance. They concluded it lay in the ruthless use of military power and the cultural and political affirmation, both at home and abroad, of the continuing necessity for wars, what Bush calls ending the "Vietnam syndrome." So it is not surprising that the U.S. soldiers in the desert were instructed to salute with the shout: "Total Victory. Total War."

Notes

[1] See "Nuclear Threats and Nuclear Realities," pp.34-38, for the misleading propaganda on this subject.

[2] *Monthly Review*, May 1991, p.8.

[3] *Boston Globe*, March 6, 1991, quoted *ibid.*

[4] Quoted *ibid.*, p.9.

[5] In his conversation with U.S. Ambassador Glaspie before the invasion, Hussein accused Kuwait of waging "economic war" against Iraq. Kuwait was undercutting oil prices, thereby reducing Iraq's oil export earnings, and pressing for massive debt repayment in the aftermath of the economically disastrous war Iraq had waged against Iran for eight years. The U.S. encouraged Iraq's invasion of Iran and the Gulf states fully backed it because both feared the spread of the Iranian revolution.

[6] Royce, Knut, *Newsday*, January 3, 1991.

[7] Tyler, Patrick, *The New York Times*, January 3, 1991.

[8] Emery, Michael, "How Mister Bush Got His War," Open Magazine Pamphlet Series (New Jersey, April 1991). This includes an exclusive interview with King Hussein.

[9] Aarts, Paul and Michael Renner, "Oil and the Gulf War," *Middle East Report*, No.171, pp.25-29. Also see an interview with Lebanese oil expert Pierre Terzian in *Journal of Palestine Studies*, No. 78, Winter 1991, pp.100-105.

[10] Neikirk, William, "We are the world's guardian angels," *Chicago Tribune*, September 9, 1990; quoted in Noam Chomsky, *Deterring Democracy* (London, Verso, 1991), p.5.

News of War

Heather Spears

The phone, and we're out of sleep
one of the young men
saying irreparable things.
How did I get into this?
You fling yourself against my arms
as if I were a coat
you fling off. Floor, walls, furniture
are as much use. Your face
pulled into its exaggerations, hideous.
Shit, you say in your infallible woman's voice,
Shit Denmark, shit Bush, shit the people.
You run from room to room, switching on lights.
I'm trying to get the BBC and you're screaming.
*[During the war an Iraqi woman refugee, Hind, lived with
Heather Spears in Denmark]*

School Parent Council Meeting Under the George Bush Controlled Choice Plan

Susan Eisenberg

The first half-hour we sit mute, until
someone reads an agenda.
Slow-motion robots, words
shuffle from our mouths. **Item:**
given textbook funds insufficient for students in
all grades, for which grades must funds
definitely be set aside? Numbed we listen, argue
scrambling to control a pencil mark on a
line item. **Decision: grades 3 through 5**
definitely **need one textbook per child.** Tonight we
gag over this task, war blitzkrieging
across television screens as we left our homes.
a billion dollars a day to carpet bomb Iraq
a billion dollars a day to uphold monarchy
Our children: beggars for books and
don't ask for art supplies next year.
How many candy bars how many 5 cent deposit on bottles
how many grocery stubs to collect cookies to sell
pizza slices: cut them in half to make extra!
A billion dollars a day to carpet bomb Iraq?
A billion dollars a day to uphold monarchy?
A mother's curse on you George Bush!
We spit on your choices, your mocking of us.
Yellow ribbon down your throat!

Nuclear threats
and nuclear realities

The Middle East is the major Third World market for arms merchants. For years the U.S., the U.K., France and the Soviet Union have sold more arms to this region than to all of Latin America, Africa, South Asia and the Far East combined.[1] In the build up to the beginning of its bombing campaign against Iraq, increased arms sales to the region boosted the U.S. to the world's top seller for the first time since 1983.[2] But the Middle East is not just a market for arms, it also produces them. Israel's arms industry, intimately tied to that of the U.S., is one of the world's largest, and Israel is the Third World's top arms exporter.[3]

In addition to purchasing and producing weapons, the Middle East has been the major battle-testing ground for the most modern instruments of death and destruction.

> If you are selling textiles you can hire a big auditorium and display your wares. The U.S. is not selling textiles. It hires the Sinai and the Iraqi desert to show off in; that's basically our showroom. Every Israeli war and every U.S. war in the region is part of an export promotion device.[4]

The end of one war becomes the occasion for the sale of that war's "proven" weapons, as well as the impetus for research and development of the next war's "improved" weapons. In the words of an Iraqi housewife during the bombing of Iraq:

> The United States, Great Britain, and France made huge profits by selling us weapons. Now they are killing our people, ruining our homeland, and destroying those weapons they sold us. Believe me, when and if this bloody war ends, these countries will once again sell us their merchandise of death. I have no education and I just say what I think is common sense. Weapons are meant for war.[5]

In the aftermath of the U.S. bombing of Iraq, George Bush announced an initiative to curb weapons sales to the Middle East by the five top suppliers. Then he added this linguistically revealing qualification: "That doesn't mean we're going to refuse to sell anything to everybody."[6] True to those words, the U.S. made new arrangements to stockpile weapons in Israel and has sold $15 billion of arms to Middle East countries since the Gulf conflict began.

Most peace activists think no state power can be trusted with nuclear, chemical and biological weapons. Most peace activists might agree with the suggestion that arms proliferation, particularly proliferation of non-conventional weapons, "can only be resolved in the Middle East, in the same way that it is being resolved in Europe: by mutual, balanced force reductions, growing out of negotiations on the basis of equity, in the context of a regional security regime."[7] But how many peace activists were aware that the possibilities for this were foreclosed?

Well before the invasion of Kuwait, on April 12, 1990, U.S. Senators returned from Iraq with an offer from Saddam Hussein, then still an ally. Iraq would destroy its chemical and all other non-conventional weapons if Israel agreed to eliminate its chemical and nuclear weapons. After its invasion of Kuwait, in December 1990, Iraq repeated the offer. The Iraqi ambassador to France said "Iraq would scrap chemical and mass destruction weapons if Israel was also prepared to do so."[8] The U.S. administration chose to dismiss peremptorily Saddam Hussein's proposals, rather than to test their sincerity. De facto they opted to keep a destabilizing imbalance, in Israel's favour, of horrifying armaments.

But to single out one power and demand the destruction only of its arsenal "is based on assumptions that are...deeply racist: in essence, non-European peoples cannot be trusted with these kinds of weapons."[9] Thus the public threat by Israeli cabinet minister Yuval Neeman, before the invasion of Kuwait, to use chemical weapons against Iraq, was tolerated as civilized; only Iraq's threat to use chemical weapons, if first attacked by Israel, was treated as barbaric.[10] George Bush assembled a thousand nuclear weapons for possible use against the people of Iraq, a possibility he never publicly renounced. That threat entered our political culture neutered and unperturbing. When instead Bush resorted to a range of "conventional" weapons developed explicitly to be the equivalent of tactical nuclear weapons, something Michael Klare details in the following article, Bush was praised as righteous and reasonable, a "surgical" warrior.

In contrast, a great deal was made of Iraq's nuclear threat. A sweeping campaign to exaggerate Iraq's military capacities tapped the paranoia so central to our political culture, and a majority were led to believe the whole world was threatened by a madman with the worst weapons of all, nuclear ones. In the aftermath of the swift and overwhelming U.S. military victory, which proved the Iraqi military and arsenal to have been no challenge to "the world," it is difficult to recapture the pervasive and intense fears that gripped Canadians and Americans in the months leading up to the bombing. Mid-November 1990 polls showed the U.S. public was prepared to endorse Washington's war plans if that would "stop Saddam Hussein from developing nuclear weapons." The majority of Americans did not think any other reason could justify war.[11] So we were fed more and more speculation about Iraq's nuclear program. Critical and reputable scientific opinion deflating this speculation appeared only in out-of-the-way places.[12]

A short time after the U.S. victory, we witnessed a sequel campaign, Nuclear Threat Two. Diverting attention from the starvation and epidemics that are killing Iraqi people because of continuing comprehensive sanctions, U.S. administration officials filled the cooperative media with speculation about secret Iraqi stores of nuclear grade uranium. They raised the spectre of Iraq rising like a military phoenix from the ashes of its now pre-industrial state.

Nuclear Threat Two then faded amidst a buried reference to a U.N. inspection team finding no more than three grams of secretly processed plutonium. This was far from the predicted 40 kilograms and certainly insufficient for a single nuclear warhead.[13] Nonetheless Nuclear Threat Two, like Nuclear Threat One, and like the false story of Iraqis pulling Kuwaiti infants out of incubators, served to rally the public behind Washington's policies as both necessary and noble.

There is no doubt Iraq wanted to make nuclear weapons. However it was using a system for enriching uranium that the U.S. had abandoned in 1945 as inefficient. Nor did Iraq have a nuclear-capable missile delivery system. Most important, there were other ways than the massive slaughter of Iraqis to forestall further nuclear development. Not the least of these ways would have been to welcome, publicize, and push for the implementation of Saddam Hussein's own offers in April and December 1990 to eliminate his non-conventional weapons parallel with Israel eliminating theirs. After all, Israel's nuclear arsenal is controlled by a prime minister who proudly defended on Israeli radio the "terror" of the Stern Gang, a group he had led. "From a moral point of view, there is no difference between personal terror and collective terror. Here and there blood is spilled, here and there people are killed," said Yitzhak Shamir.[14] But that set off no alarm bells.

Notes

[1] *Middle East Report*, January-February 1987.

[2] *The Globe and Mail*, August 12, 1991, summarizes the annual U.S. Congressional Research Service report showing U.S. arms sales went from $8 billion in 1989 to $18.5 billion in 1990.

[3] "Arms Industries of the Middle East" by Joe Stork, "U.S. Military Contractors in Israel" by Sheila Ryan, and "Israel's Private Arms Network" by Bishara A. Bahbah, *Middle East Report, op. cit.*, discuss Israel's arms industry.

[4] Chomsky, Noam, "Arms to Order," *New Internationalist*, July 1991, p. 20.

[5] From "Iraqi Women's Chronicle of War," a collection of comments dating from late January to early February 1991, prepared and translated by the Committee for the Defence of Human Rights in Iraq, Spring Valley, California.

[6] *The New York Times*, March 18, 1991.

[7] Khalidi, Rashid, "Arms limitations must include all parties," *Middle East Report*, January-February 1991, p.11.

[8] Chomsky, Noam, *Deterring Democracy* (London, Verso, 1991), p.208.

[9] Khalidi, *Ibid.*

[10] *The Globe and Mail*, July 28, 1990, reports the threats issued by Israeli Cabinet Minister Dr. Yuval Neeman, a scientist central to his country's nuclear weapons program.

[11] Only 31 per cent thought protecting the source of much of the world's oil was a "good enough" reason for making war.

[12] See the articles by Richard Wilson, Mallinckrodt Chair of Physics at Harvard University in the *Journal of Palestine Studies*, Spring 1991, and David Albright and Mark Hibbs in *The Bulletin of Atomic Scientists*, March 1991.

[13] Albright, David and Mark Hibbs, "Iraq's Nuclear Hide-and-Seek," *The Bulletin of Atomic Scientists*, September 1991.

[14] It is noteworthy that Shamir frankly defends both "collective terror" and "personal terror." Among the Stern Gang's victims of personal terror was the U.N. Mediator Count Bernadotte, who was sent to Palestine in 1948. *The Globe and Mail*, September 5, 1991.

An Act of Conscience

Mordechai Vanunu, an Israeli nuclear technician who worked at his country's Dimona facility, confirmed with photos and testimony Israel's clandestine manufacture of nuclear weapons. Vanunu gave his information to *The Sunday Times* of London where it was cross-checked by an American and a British nuclear weapons scientist. Vanunu suddenly and mysteriously disappeared from London on September 30, 1986, only days before his revelations were printed October 5. It later was learned that Israeli Mossad kidnapped Vanunu from Europe and forcibly transported him to Israel. There, in a completely closed, secret trial, barring all observers, he was sentenced to 18 years imprisonment. One day on his way to court in a police van, Vanunu outsmarted his captors and shoved one palm against the window. The message he had written on it was photographed by international television. Thereafter Vanunu was transported to court in a sealed van. This prisoner of conscience, nominated for a Nobel Peace Prize by many parliamentarians around the world, has been languishing in solitary confinement since October 1986.

Israel always has refused to sign the Nuclear Non-Proliferation
Treaty and to open its facilities to international inspection.
Israel's Dimona reactor was constructed with French assistance
and clandestinely converted to weapons use with that
government's knowledge. Israel is purchasing a new nuclear
reactor from Hungary. South Africa collaborates closely on
Israel's nuclear program. South African scientists and technicians
have worked at Dimona; Israel has been monitored preparing a
test for nuclear capable missiles in the South African Kalahari
desert; Israel and South Africa test fired a nuclear device in the
south Atlantic September 22, 1979.[1]
According to the latest U.S. National Intelligence Council
"authoritative" estimate, Israel has accumulated an arsenal of at
least 60 to 80 weapons.[2] This is lower than other previous,
expert estimates. To demonstrate its willingness to use this
arsenal, Israel test fired one of its nuclear capable missiles across
the Mediterranean waters, in the very midst of the bombing of
Iraq.[3]
According to Seymour Hersh, Israel also moved its nuclear
missile launchers into the open during the war against Iraq.
Hersh's book, *The Samson Option*, is filled with vital new
information on Israel's nuclear arsenal, including the revelation
that Israel has produced hundreds of low-yield neutron warheads,
and used them in landmines on the Syrian Golan Heights, which
Israel has occupied since 1967.[4]

Notes

[1] The *London Observer*, December 28, 1986, reported Israeli-South African
preparation of a possible new site for nuclear weapons testing.

[2] Along with Canada, Australia and Japan, Israel was exempted from
provisions of Section 1701 of a U.S. defense authorization bill that requires
the president to report annually on "developments in the transfer of weapons,
technology and materials that can be used to deliver, manufacture or
weaponize nuclear, biological, or chemical weapons. . . ." See *Israeli Foreign
Affairs*, August 21, 1991.

[3] *Israeli Foreign Affairs*, *op. cit.*

[4] Hersh, Seymour, *The Samson Option: Israel's Nuclear Arsenal and American
Foreign Policy* (Toronto: Random House, 1991).

High-Death Weapons

Michael T. Klare

THE TRUE HORROR OF WHAT THE MILITARY AND ITS PROPAGANDA ARM, the U.S. media, sold as a clean, high-tech war in the Persian Gulf now has become evident. An estimated 85,000 tons of non-nuclear, "conventional" bombs were dropped on Iraq and Kuwait during the conflict. Together, these munitions produced a destructive power equivalent to five Hiroshimas. Comparable quantities of rockets, missiles and artillery shells also were fired during the Persian Gulf war, making it the most firepower-intensive conflict since World War Two. Many of these munitions, designed for use against Soviet forces in Europe, first were used in combat during Operation Desert Storm. While unaccompanied by radiation or radioactive fallout, their use against Iraq's civilian infrastructure produced high levels of death, disease and starvation.

To inflict those damages on Iraq, the United States and its allies used a vast array of munitions, ranging from highly touted "smart" weapons like the Tomahawk and the laser-guided Paveway-II missile to ordinary "dumb" bombs of the sort used in Korea and Vietnam. What made the Gulf war so distinctive, however, was the widespread (and

41

often experimental) use of a new breed of munitions designed to dupli-
cate the destructive effects of tactical nuclear weapons. These
munitions – fuel-air explosives, penetration bombs and wide-area
cluster bombs – were dropped in great profusion to destroy fortifications, demolish underground bunkers, disable tanks and vehicles, and
kill or maim military personnel. Many casualties were also produced by
"collateral damage" – bombs or missiles that missed their intended
targets and exploded among civilians instead.

Although the effects of these attacks may never be fully known, a
frightening impression is provided by the report of a United Nations
observation team that visited Baghdad shortly after the war. "Nothing
that we had seen or read quite prepared us for the particular form of
devastation which has now befallen the country," the team reported on
March 21. "The recent conflict has wrought near-apocalyptical results
on the infrastructure of what had been, until January 1991, a rather
highly urbanized and mechanized society. Now, most means of modern
life support have been destroyed or rendered tenuous."

Baghdad, moreover, was spared the heaviest bombing – far heavier
loads of ordnance were dropped on Iraqi troop positions in Kuwait and
along the Saudi border. Most of the heavy bombing by attack planes
and B-52s, as well as all of the rocket and artillery barrages, were
directed against these frontline positions. In the final hours of the war,
U.S. aircraft systematically bombed and strafed a 30-mile column of
fleeing Iraqi troops on the "highway of death" from Kuwait City to
Basra, killing thousands. "It was close to Armageddon," said one U.S.
Air Force officer who witnessed the slaughter.

This carnage was necessary, U.S. officials argued, to cripple the Iraqi
Army and to prevent Iraq from ever again exerting a hegemonic role in
the Gulf area. As President Bush stated on January 16 in the first public
announcement of the air campaign: "We are determined to knock out
Saddam Hussein's nuclear bomb potential. We will also destroy his
chemical weapons facilities. Much of Saddam's artillery and tanks will
be destroyed."

In accordance with these edicts, U.S. and allied forces conducted a
systematic bombing campaign against military installations, munitions
plants and research laboratories in Iraq. Also attacked were facilities

that would be needed to rebuild Iraqi military capabilities after the war: electric power plants, highways, factories and oil refineries. And, of course, the human element of the Iraqi war machine was targeted for destruction, especially senior military officers and the elite units of the Republican Guard.

The concentrated use of firepower had another strategic objective: to break the will of Iraqi resistance quickly, and thus avoid a long, drawn-out war like Vietnam that would generate widespread opposition at home. In this sense, the relentless pounding of Iraqi positions was as much a response to the still-potent "Vietnam syndrome" as it was to military conditions in the Gulf.

"This will not be another Vietnam," Bush pledged on November 30, 1990. "If one American soldier has to go into battle, that soldier will have enough force behind him to win...I will never, ever agree to a halfway effort."*

In line with this outlook, General Norman Schwarzkopf and his associates were instructed to employ whatever force was needed to produce a rapid and conclusive victory. And while the use of nuclear arms was excluded, Schwarzkopf was allowed to use any other weapons in the U.S. arsenal, including powerful new munitions designed for an all-out war with the Soviet Union.

* One of the big lies of this war was the pretence that the war against Vietnam was a halfway effort. "Not counting napalm and defoliants, fifteen million tons of bombs and shells were used [by the U.S. military], three times the quantity in all theatres of operations during World War Two. In South Vietnam, 9,000 out of 15,000 hamlets were destroyed or severely damaged by 1975. Ten million hectares of cultivated land were devastated; five million hectares of forests...In a detailed analysis, E.Z.Herman, an American researcher, estimated civilian losses in South Vietnam at one million killed and 2 million injured between 1961 and 1970...In North Vietnam three industrial cities were razed to the ground and the other three severely damaged...All the railways, bridges, industrial centers, main roads, irrigation systems, and sea and river ports were destroyed or seriously damaged ...Vietnamese authorities say that they do not know how many were killed throughout the country during the anti-U.S. war, but estimate them at least 3 million, with another million crippled or seriously injured. More than 15 million lost their homes...More than 100,000 tons of these [toxic] chemicals were dropped on South Vietnam alone." See Kathleen Gough's *Political Economy in Vietnam* (Berkeley, Folklore Institute, 1990), pp.3-7. [editor]

In a war in Europe against the U.S.S.R., the United States and NATO very likely would have drawn on their stockpile of tactical nuclear weapons. But the use of nuclear weapons against a Third World country in 1991, in the absence of a demonstrated nuclear threat, would have produced international revulsion and undermined U.S. strategic objectives. Hence the decision by the Bush administration to rely on a new generation of conventional weapons and to eschew the nuclear option. The fact that U.S. and allied forces were equipped with conventional weapons with near-nuclear destructive capabilities made it far easier, of course, for President Bush to order a ban on nuclear weapons.

The development of conventional weapons of near-nuclear destructiveness grew out of a critical paradox that confronted U.S. and NATO officials in the late 1970s and early 1980s. On the one hand, European and American voters were unwilling to shoulder the immense costs of enlarging the NATO ground forces in order to match improvement in Warsaw Pact capabilities. On the other, Europeans and Americans were calling for diminished reliance on the nuclear weapons that had long constituted the West's counterweight to the superior numbers of eastern bloc conventional forces. This contradiction left U.S. military planners with but one choice, as they saw it, to develop conventional weapons with an impact comparable to tactical nuclear weapons.

Such weapons were especially needed, in the military's view, to attack "high value" targets in the enemy's rear: such facilities as command-and-control centers, radar stations, air bases, river crossings and tank formations. To destroy these capabilities, NATO officials called for the development of two types of advanced munitions: first, highly accurate "smart" bombs and missiles capable of striking critical "point" targets (radar sites, underground bunkers, bridges and so on) with great precision, and second, wide-area munitions capable of engulfing large facilities (airfields, vehicle parks, railroad yards) with deadly shrapnel and explosives.

At a time when European and American public opinion was turning more and more strongly against NATO's reliance on nuclear weapons, the introduction of such weapons was seen as a major priority. "A series of conventional initiatives resulting from U.S. investment in research and development offers the opportunity to reduce reliance on nuclear weapons," the House Armed Services Committee affirmed in 1983. "These initiatives, based upon newly developed technologies, provide the capability to engage military targets with conventional weapons that *previously could be effectively engaged only with nuclear weapons.*" [emphasis added]

The upshot was that in January, when Desert Storm commenced, U.S. and allied forces were able to draw on an impressive arsenal of extremely potent conventional weapons developed or improved for NATO operations against the Soviet Union. Some of these weapons, never before used in combat and still considered experimental, were rushed to the Gulf in order to be tested under battlefield conditions. Among the most awesome were:

Multiple-Launch Rocket System (MLRS): Introduced in 1983 and first used in battle in the Persian Gulf, the MLRS is a mobile, boxlike container that can hurl a dozen rockets armed with hundreds of individual "bomblets" up to 20 miles. According to the Defense Department: "A single launcher can fire its load of 12 rockets in less than a minute, covering an area the size of six football fields with approximately 7,700 grenade-like submunitions effective against both personnel and lightly-armored targets." During Operation Desert Storm, dozens of these launchers were often used simultaneously, spewing a lethal shower of explosive bomblets – dubbed "steel rain" by U.S. soldiers – over city-sized areas. First produced in the United States, MLRS is now being "co-produced" in France, Germany, Italy and Britain (prime contractor: LTV Aerospace; cost: [U.S.] $100,000 per missile, or [US] $1.2 million per 12-shot salvo).

Army Tactical Missile System (ATACM): This system was developed by the Army in the 1980s to provide frontline NATO forces with a surface-to-surface missile capable of striking Warsaw Pact bases and facilities deep inside enemy territory. ATACMs are designed to be fired from a MLRS launch canister, have a range of approximately 65 miles and carry a payload of some 950 anti-personnel bomblets. Although still in their test and evaluation phase in late 1990, the missiles were rushed to the Persian Gulf and used for strikes against rear-area Iraqi forces and installations (prime contractor: LTV Aerospace; cost [US] $615,000 per missile).

Tomahawk: This is a sea-launched cruise missile designed for attacks on ships and high-value inland targets. The land-attack version of Tomahawk that was used in the Gulf has a range of about 700 nautical miles, carries a 1,000-pound warhead and can be fired from surface ships and submarines.

According to the [U.S.] Defense Department, approximately 240 Tomahawks were fired at Iraqi forces during the first two weeks of the war, representing one-fourth of the total U.S. inventory of these missiles. Although described as highly effective in strikes against heavily defended "point" targets such as nuclear reactors, power stations and military headquarters, several Tomahawks reportedly missed their targets and hit civilian structures in populated areas. A more advanced version of this type is now in development (prime contractors: General Dynamics and McDonnell-Douglas; cost: [US] $1.4 million per missile).

Standoff Land-Attack Missile (SLAM): An aircraft-fired missile with a range of 60 nautical miles and a 500-pound warhead, SLAM carries a "Walleye" video data link in its nose cone, allowing a pilot to manoeuver the missile directly toward its target while remaining at "standoff" distances beyond the range of enemy air-defence systems. Like ATACM, SLAM was still in its final test and evaluation phase when Desert Storm commenced and was rushed to the Gulf on the eve of war. SLAM was used for strikes against Iraqi naval bases and power stations (prime contractor: McDonnell-Douglas; cost: [US] $1.1 million per missile.)

Laser-Guided Bomb (LGB): Familiar to millions of Americans because of the extensive television coverage of its effects, the GBU-10 "Paveway-II" laser-guided bomb was aimed at Iraqi military bases and facilities, including some in downtown Baghdad. The 2,000-pound bomb carries a "laser seeker" that homes-in on a laser beam directed at the target by a crew member on the launching aircraft or an accompanying plane. Other LGBs used during the war include the 500-pound GBU-12 and the 2,000-pound GBU-24. Although U.S. officials boasted of their pinpoint accuracy, the LGBs frequently missed their targets, striking nearby structures and producing many of the civilian casualties suffered during the war.

Fuel-Air Explosive (FAE): One of the most potent weapons used in the Persian Gulf conflict, fuel-air explosives have come to replace tactical nuclear munitions as the preferred weapon for attacking dug-in troops and heavy fortifications.

Essentially FAEs are large bombs filled with highly volatile fuels (ethylene oxide, propylene oxide, butane and propane, among others) and an explosive charge. When dropped over the target area, the fuels are released in a cloud over the target. When the charge is ignited, the vapour cloud explodes in a massive fireball that engulfs everything within several hundred square yards. Any human caught in this area is likely to be incinerated by flame, asphyxiated from lack of oxygen or crushed by falling structures.

An impression of these weapons' awesome potential is provided by a recent CIA report: "When detonation occurs, an overpressure is created that can reach 420 pounds per square inch in the cloud's center. As the explosive wave burns toward its fringes, it is accompanied by a supersonic pressure front that moves at up to 1,825 meters per second – about six times the speed of sound [creating a force sufficient to crush fortified bunkers]. . . When the fuel is burned, the wave front travels on, creating overpressures of enormous destructive potential over considerable distances. *The pressure effects of FAEs approach those produced by low-yield nuclear weapons at short ranges.*" [emphasis added]

The most potent weapon of this type is the BLU-82/B "Daisy Cutter," a 15,000-pound bomb filled with an aqueous mixture of ammonium nitrate, aluminum powder and polystyrene soap (as a binder). Too heavy to be carried by conventional aircraft, the BLU-82/B (also known as "Big Blue 82") had to be pushed out of specially fitted C-130s flown by Special Operations personnel.

Cluster Bomb Unit (CBU): Other than ordinary high-explosive iron bombs, the most widely used air-delivered weapons in Operation Desert Storm were cluster bomb units of various types. Typically, CBUs consist of a large bomb-like metal casing that splits open over the target, spewing out dozens or hundreds of anti-armour and/or anti-personnel bomblets or submunitions. By releasing these bomblets in a controlled manner, a single CBU can inundate a very large area (several football fields in size) with a lethal deluge of razor-sharp metal fragments. Soldiers and civilians unfortunate enough to be caught in this volley are literally cut to pieces.

According to one Air Force official, the CBU-87/B combined effects munition was the "weapon of choice" against dug-in Republican Guard units because each of its 202 bomblets contains an explosive charge that is effective against tanks, as well as metal fragments and an incendiary device effective against humans. Other CBUs used in the Gulf war include the CBU-52 (with 254 submunitions), the CBU-58 (with 650 submunitions) and the Mark-20 Rockeye-II (with 717 anti-tank submunitions). CBUs were dropped on Iraqi troops fleeing Kuwait via the "highway of death," causing thousands of casualties.

Similar weapons were used by other members of the anti-Iraq coalition. The most common British CBU is the Hunting Engineering BL-755 cluster bomb, which fires 147 submunitions, each of which produces some 2,000 high-velocity anti-personnel steel fragments. French CBUs include the Thompson-Brandt BM-400 (which can inundate a 60,000 square-metre area with lethal steel fragments) and the smaller BLG-66 Belouga. Also worthy of note is the British JP-233 runway attack CBU system, which was targeted on Iraqi airfields.

Penetration Bomb: In an effort to cripple enemy defences, U.S. forces attempted the "decapitation" of the Iraqi military by killing senior officers through bombing and missile attacks on underground "command and control" centers in Baghdad. A family of specialized weapons known as "penetration bombs" because of their ability to punch through thick layers of earth and concrete before exploding was employed. At least two new bombs of this type were used in the Gulf war: the 2,000-pound GBU-17 and the 4,700-pound GBU-28. The GBU-27 has a Paveway-III laser guidance unit and an I-2000 penetrator warhead; designed specifically for the F-117 Stealth bomber, it was involved in the February 13 attack on an underground shelter in Baghdad that killed hundreds of civilians. The heavier GBU-28, made up of eight-inch howitzer tubes, was developed during the course of the war and rushed to the Gulf in the final days of combat. It was used in attacks on an underground command center on the outskirts of Baghdad.

In light of the Persian Gulf experience, many countries, including the Soviet Union and China, have begun to develop new high-tech weapons like those used by the U.S. and allied forces during Desert Storm. Several Third World countries, and Israel and Brazil, have also begun to manufacture high-tech conventional weapons, and others are likely to follow in the coming years, sparking a new conventional arms race.

For those nations with access to the critical technology – the United States, Britain, France and Germany – such a context may not appear particularly threatening. But as the technology spreads to other countries, which it surely will, the proliferation of high-tech conventional weapons will pose significant risks to many nations. Future wars fought between comparably equipped high-tech forces are likely to result in terrifying levels of death and destruction on all sides, irrespective of the outcome of the conflict.*

While the world has placed strong moral inhibitions on the use of nuclear and chemical weapons, few restraints govern the newer conventional weapons. Yet, as demonstrated by the Gulf conflict, they can produce levels of death and destruction comparable to that wreaked by low-yield tactical nuclear weapons. Recognizing this potential, British historian John Keegan wrote in a 1983 article on the new NATO strategy that "a high-intensity conventional war and a low-intensity nuclear war might inflict very much the same level of damage on any given piece of inhabited landscape."

Although some U.S. and European leaders have expressed qualms about the one-sided nature of the slaughter in the Gulf, most Americans approved the use of high-impact conventional weapons against Iraq and seem willing to support the continued development and procurement of such munitions. In order to get people to confront the moral issues raised by the introduction of high-tech conventional weapons and their use in defence of a "new world order," these weapons must first be stripped of their geewhiz appeal and seen as what they truly are – highly effective killing instruments that are designed to produce nuclear-like levels of destruction without arousing popular revulsion.

* As we have seen in the war against Iraq, even when only one side uses these weapons the results are terrifying. [editor]

Map 1

Heather Spears

Taleb has xeroxed a map of Baghdad,
he brought it today and left,
about A3, the lines grayish,
there on the kitchen table
Hind's hands on it, her face
bent over it, she is not here,
not crying right now, her finger moves and touches:
Look, this is Palestina Street, here
we lived, this is our house, at this corner.
All that was hit, all that area.
And this is the power plant, all that area
finished, burning. Her voice is almost inaudible.
She is silent, staring,
the weight of her hands gentle,
her finger unfists, traces the looping river.
See, she begins again,
how the river turns, it is beautiful really,
see how beautiful it is
she is silent
the map, under her hands
before I can prevent this,
bandages, death, a death.

Map 2

Heather Spears

No high-tech laser
sees what she sees

up against a simplistic truism
that truth
is the first casualty of war

or do people actually nod
as if there is wisdom in this
permission

as though nothing in us dies
each time we reassure our children
over maps and globes

we are safe: here, riddled
with off-beat stories of war
there: that's where weapons shred lives

for whose comic relief do we
wonder at gas masks for poultry
condoms to protect gun barrels from sand

Occupation

Barbara Coward

In early February, while visiting my parents on Galiano Island, I came upon the remnants of an innocent accident. Oregon Juncos had flown into an illusion of space, high windows, painted with dark green images of the forest beyond. The two birds lay in their feathery embrace (no, they can't embrace, they're birds after all) but it seemed so, as if protecting one another from a threat more ominous than the pane of glass that rendered them finally still, eyes bright with false life.

Another image, another island, a crater of unspeakable horror. It was a charred corpse, legs folded up in a gentle encirclement of the second smaller, body – her child (I want to write non-child because this bit of blackened bone and skin was no longer a child, anymore than the peace declared is peace). Her – because she was an Iraqi mother, not just a body, perhaps still asleep at the moment of incineration. Cradled in the illusion of safety like the birds? In this concrete oven, what heat they must have felt. Did their ears burst with the roar? Did the mother have a second of recognition, of raw terror before the inferno, of helplessness for her helpless child? Or had dreams carried them off to some reality more benign? What was the smell like? Did flesh melt in a torrent, blood vaporize? Were their eyes open or shut? Was this "clever" concussion more merciful to the dying than a dumb one?

I feel we have been occupied. The pores of our skin are complicit – the lies enter our cells without a fight, deceit infects us with statistics, technical miracles, folksy truisms. Clichés click

off our tongues like a religious creed. Our retinas record the
military smirks, mechanical geometry, endless, meaningless
maps. We hear the steady drone and hum of falling percussion,
regular rhythm of revenge. ("Kiss the big one, Saddam" reads a
graffiti outside the library). The language resonates through our
flesh: the "peace" of starvation and sickness, the "silence" of
dead enemies, the "restored calm" of broken life. No blood, no
mothers, no scared eyes, no cries in the desert-bright light.

We have been occupied by this decay, feelings giving way to
an emptiness. The men in suits march in. Their briefcases are
full of crisp orders and portfolios. Their eyes gleam like an oil
slick, and their palms are warm with dollar bills. They mean this
occupation to be permanent.

Not All the Yellow Ribbon in the World

Anton Kuerti

Not all the yellow ribbon in the world can hide the fact that bestial massacre has been perpetrated on the Iraqi army in the Gulf war; nor can all the vainglorious self-congratulation about the "stunning victory" obscure the fact that more than 100,000 air sorties have demolished a country with a viciousness no less odious than that of a nuclear attack.

For purely political reasons, a horde of starving, demoralized, frightened human beings, fleeing chaotically (mostly in non-military vehicles) and no longer capable of harming anyone, was essentially exterminated. Heroic airmen, drunk with their apparent omnipotence, spewed forth their miraculous explosives on orders from their brave super-hero, no longer a "wimp" and still comfortably safe in Washington.

While this savagery was taking place, another group of heroes watched the neat crosshairs on their video screens as they were given a final chance to trash Baghdad – one more gratuitous and obviously unnecessary assault on the Iraqi people. The reports about the young soldiers' attitudes were nauseating: "It was a fun mission, seeing trucks blown apart into bits"; "When we returned we sat on the wing of the plane and laughed"; "Blowing up bunkers was sexy."

The U.S. military was extremely adept at counting the number of missions flown, the number of tanks and personnel carriers demolished, the number of oil wells set on fire, the amount of oil spilled into the Gulf. No doubt they could also give us the number of meals served and the number of condoms

distributed. But the number of Iraqi dead? Not even an order of
magnitude was hinted at. Was this figure of no interest to them;
or was it just too horrendous to contemplate?

Imagine a single bombing raid on your own city; even imagine
that it seeks out a genuine military target, not civilian ones such
as power plants, water-supply facilities, bridges and public
buildings, as was the case in Iraq. Is it plausible that several tons
of explosives dropped on a city could avoid killing even one
person? While many of the 100,000-plus sorties were patrol,
support or reconnaissance flights that didn't kill anyone, we
know that one bombing mission killed as many as 500 people, so
an estimate of one death per sortie is probably low.

Is no one embarrassed and ashamed of a death tally of 100,000
compared with about 200 combat deaths for the U.S.-led
coalition? Does not this ratio of 500 to 1, whether caused by
disparity in equipment, training and/or morale, incontrovertibly
prove that the amount of force used was criminally excessive?

On one hand our leaders tried to personalize the conflict,
constantly demeaning Iraqi President Saddam Hussein by
referring to him as "Saddam" and by painting him as the
ultimate Satan at fault for the whole situation. But by destroying
much of his country and almost his entire army, full of 17-year-
old conscripts, our actions seem rather to assume a collective
guilt and resemble scenes from the recent past when whole
villages were destroyed because one or a few individuals were
engaged in resistance activities.

It is bad enough when a cruel despot like Mr. Hussein
commits atrocities, spurred on by some mania, be it religious,
nationalistic or purely personal; but for the world's leading
democracies, ceremoniously draped in the flag of the United
Nations, constantly in consultation with each other, endlessly
spouting unctuous moral homilies (as though they had never
invaded an innocent country) to commit such an unspeakable
assault is the global equivalent of a gang rape.

Without a murmur of dissent, the tragically weak Secretary-General of the United Nations gave President George Bush *carte blanche* to make every decision, to reject every Iraqi move to end the war as always "falling far short" of what was required, and to go far beyond victory to achieve the abject humiliation and dismemberment of the "enemy." Who can ever trust the UN again?

Mr. Bush, British Prime Minister John Major and Prime Minister Brian Mulroney have droned on about the lessons we must teach would-be dictators and aggressors. But what we have really taught them is this:

- We are just as ready to commit atrocities as they are.
- They must have the most modern weapons, including nuclear weapons, if they are to stand a chance.
- We will arm them indiscriminately with our hand-me-down weapons and silently ignore all their violations of human rights as long as they don't threaten our selfish and narrow political interests.
- Our thirst for cheap oil and our determination to prevent Third World forces from shaping their own future will always take precedence over our moral and humanitarian considerations and our sense of proportion.

By all means let Mr. Hussein be tried for his war crimes; but only if the same court provides for at least the possibility of indicting and convicting the so-called "coalition" leaders for the colossal, unconscionable scale of the killing that has been done under their flags.

[February 26, 1991]

More than Censorship, More than Imbalance

The media endorsed and promoted Washington's war policies. Those who reject the argument that there was a "manufacturing of consent,"[1] an orchestration of reporting to activate popular support for prior elite decisions, should offer an alternate framework to explain the following.

The media systematically ignored investigating and reporting the many proposals for and possibilities of a negotiated solution to the conflict, promoting the notion that war was unavoidable.[2]

U.S. television news coverage from August 8, when the U.S. committed its troops, until January 3, spent 2,855 minutes on the impending war and only 29 of those dealt with grass roots dissent, even though public opinion surveys found half of the U.S. population opposed war.[3]

Acts of the gravest moral nature went almost unreported: a 48-year-old Vietnam veteran in California burned himself to death on December 9, 1990 to protest U.S. action in the Gulf, as a man in his 20s did in Massachusetts on February 18. Nor did the media choose to publicize the suicide protest January 23 of a decorated

MOIR/SYDNEY MORNING HERALD

"The propagandist will not accuse the enemy of just any misdeed; he will accuse him of the very intention that he himself has and of trying to commit the very crime that he himself is about to commit." Jacques Ellul, Propaganda: The Formation of Men's Attitudes

Vietnam veteran who, dressed in his uniform and medals, wrote a note saying, "This war has brought up too many nightmares of the last war."

Most media uncritically and prominently presented the story that 300 premature Kuwaiti babies died when Iraqi soldiers removed them from incubators. Yet after the end of the occupation when Kuwait medical personnel said the story was incorrect, media reported this inconspicuously, if at all, and certainly without self-criticism of how the story originated and came to be so widely broadcast.[4]

There was a correlation between heavy media viewing and an increased belief that the emirate of Kuwait and the Kingdom of Saudi Arabia were democracies, a belief in defiance of all facts but consistent with Washington's rhetoric about restoring "legitimate" governments and "liberation."[5]

Granted, many citizens were sceptical of media reports because they knew TV, radio and print had blandly accepted the limits imposed by overt military censorship. But such scepticism, even cynicism, of media omissions, exaggerations and outright lies, remained compatible with tacit acceptance of the media's way of labelling the good and the evil, the just and the unjust.

How was Washington successful *so quickly* in demonizing Saddam Hussein, in emptying Iraq of its people and bypassing its history, elements that were the essence of U.S. wartime propaganda, as Mason Harris explains?

Media, as an integrated part of the military-industrial centres of power, prepares public opinion to accept these labels as reality, to defer to patriotic authority, well before the first missile is fired. War propaganda depends for its effectiveness on successful peace-time propaganda. Concomitantly, effective opposition to the media requires exposure of that continuity, and the presentation of alternative information before the crises.[6]

Notes

[1] Herman, Edward S. and Noam Chomsky, *Manufacturing Consent: The Political Economy of the Mass Media* (Pantheon, 1988).

[2] See "Negotiations or War," pp.21-31.

[3] *Extra!*, May 1991, p.19, a publication of Fairness and Accuracy in Reporting (FAIR). On the CBC radio show *Media File*, a program whose precise mandate is to examine the media's role critically, host Jim Nunn dismissively referred to the "anti-war rhetoric" of the "peaceniks," while he told us the generals provided "technical analysis." See James Winter, "Truth as the First Casualty," *Canadian Dimension*, June 30, 1991, p.33.

[4] Alexander Cockburn, writing in *The Nation*, February 4, 1991, cited Kuwaiti medical personnel who said the babies still were in incubators in September, and that empty incubators had not been taken by the Iraqis. When *The New York Times*, February 28, 1991, retracted its false report of the incubators, it was only a brief mention near the end of another article, saying "Some of the atrocities that had been reported, such as the killing of infants in the main hospitals shortly after the invasion, are untrue or have been exaggerated, Kuwaitis said. Hospital officials, for instance, said that stories circulated about the killing of 300 children were incorrect." (February 28, 1991) David Chiu, a biomedical engineer who visited Kuwait in June on behalf of the World Health Organization to assess damage to medical machinery, reported that the incubators for neo-natals in the specialist hospitals were still there. Nor was expensive dialysis and nuclear medical machinery taken. Aside from low-technology polyclinics which were ransacked, 90 per cent of the major hospital equipment was undamaged, according to Mr. Chiu in personal communication.

[5] Lewis, Justin, Sut Jhally and Michael Morgan, *The Gulf War: A Study of the*

Media, Public Opinion and Public Knowledge (Amherst, Center for the Study of Communication, University of Massachusetts, March 1991).

[6] See Part Three, "Obstacles to Understanding," for discussion of the on-going peace-time propaganda about the Middle East.

Mad Dogs and Englishmen

The Manchester Guardian Weekly *newspaper, February 3, 1991, printed examples of the different language used for "them" and "us" in British war reporting. Here are some of the examples.*

We have	**They have**
Army, Navy and Airforce	A war machine
Reporting guidelines	Censorship
Press briefings	Propaganda

We launch	**They launch**
First strikes	Sneak missile attacks
Pre-emptively	Without provocation

Our boys are...	**Theirs are...**
Professional	Brainwashed
Lion-hearts	Paper tigers
Cautious	Cowardly
Confident	Desperate
Loyal	Blindly obedient
Resolute	Ruthless
Brave	Fanatical

Our missiles cause...	**Their missiles cause...**
Collateral damage	Civilian casualties

George Bush is...	**Saddam Hussein is...**
At peace with himself	Demented
Resolute	Defiant
Statesmanlike	An evil tyrant
Assured	A crackpot monster

The Language of Dwarf-Killing: Orwell and Victory in the Gulf

Mason Harris

TO PERCEIVE THE TRUTH ABOUT THE WAR, WE MUST FIRST BREAK AWAY from the carefully crafted set of vocabulary and images which dominated our media during the bombing campaign. To my mind, George Orwell's criticism of the reporting – or non-reporting – of war in the 1930s and 1940s provides the best guide.

Orwell's critique of political language has the great virtue of focusing intensely on the specific meaning of words and phrases. In his famous essay on style, "Politics and the English Language" (1946), Orwell, looking back at the Second World War, explains why bad writing has political significance.

> In our time, political speech and writing are largely the defence of the indefensible. Things like the continuance of British rule in India, the Russian purges and deportations, the dropping of the atom bomb on Japan, can indeed be defended, but only by arguments which are too brutal for most people to face, and which do not square with the professed aims of political parties. Thus political language has to consist largely of euphemism,

question-begging and sheer cloudy vagueness. Defenceless villages
are bombarded from the air, the inhabitants driven out into the
countryside, the cattle machine-gunned, the huts set on fire with
incendiary bullets: this is called *pacification*.[1]

Thirty years after Orwell wrote his essay on language, the U.S. military and government used precisely the same euphemism, "pacification," for their practice of destroying defenceless villages in Vietnam.
In his essay, Orwell writes that the dispossession of a whole people from
their land is also called *"transfer of population."* Zionist activists, well
before Orwell wrote his essay, used the euphemism of *"transfer"* for the
policy of massive dispossession of Palestinians of their land and homes.
And there is a political party, part of the current Israeli cabinet, which
advocates *"transfering"* all the Palestinians presently resident in the
West Bank and Gaza.

I would divide the metaphors used in the war against Iraq into two
main groups, both sharing a common objective. There is the vocabulary of technological magic, words and images which imply that the
entire war consists of stages of a technical process. There are no human,
social or political consequences. A second set of vocabulary evokes a
nostalgic patriotism, creating the image of a united world facing a single
enemy – the evil dictator, Saddam Hussein.

The most important metaphor of the technical language may have
been "surgical strike, surgical operation." Surgery is a process consisting
of a clearly defined series of stages, ending with everything sewed up. It
is done entirely for the benefit of the anaesthetized patient who feels
nothing. (If a tumour is removed, the malignant Saddam, the patient
then awakes and recovers.)

The tools of this surgery are "smart" bombs guided by lasers, famous
as surgical instruments for delicate eye operations, and "Tomahawks"
(cruise missiles) with computer brains and radar eyes. The motion is
exact, "pinpoint" and "precision" bombing.

But if the explosion is larger than the pinpoint? For even "success"
was a euphemism: *The Globe and Mail* revealed that the 85 per cent
success rate claimed by the U.S. military for cruise missiles was "defined
not by targets hit but by the fact that [the missiles] had flown over the

horizon."[2] The Pentagon first claimed a 90 per cent success rate, counting as successful all missiles that left the launcher.

Of all the jargon phrases manufactured for this war, "collateral damage," meaning destruction that goes beyond the intended target, is the one that Orwell most would have appreciated. "Collateral damage" hides the debris, the blood, the corpses and the grieving relatives. The dictionary meaning of "associated" or "secondary" given to the word collateral has become rare in current usage; hence it seems colourless and technical to a modern audience. As used today collateral usually means property put up as security for a loan. Thus the word suggests damage only to real estate. "[O]nly soldiers are killed, and only buildings are destroyed. A strange country, Iraq, filled with buildings with no people in them...So the word 'kill' is the new four-letter word. Civilians have mysteriously disappeared from the language."[3]

Alongside the euphemism "collateral damage," we should place these others: "radius of concussion," the "servicing," "softening" and "degrading of the target." We were told that the air offensive would "get the work done," as the planes flew "sorties" to drop "ordnance." "Conventional weapons" sounded kinder and gentler, as did "friendly fire," when members of the coalition shot at one another by mistake. "Carpet bombing" has a domestic association, cosy and wall-to-wall; quite different from the real meaning of mass, indiscriminate bombing that put a fiery end to Hamburg, Dresden, and Tokyo in the Second World War. Defying logic, *Newsweek* combined carpet devastation with precision. It was, they wrote, a "bombing campaign that was at once surgical and earth-scorching."[4]

This war-making was presented to us almost exclusively as viewed from the air. There is a profound difference between viewing aerial bombardment from above and from ground level. For instance, among my own memories of what the Second World War looked like to North Americans, I find two segregated images: the ground-level image of the grubbiness and deprivation of life in London during the blitz defines a world apart from the stratospheric heroics of allied pilots and crews bombing Germany. No doubt Germans have a reverse imagery. From the air, the ground targets are only a technical problem. From the point of view of mass suffering, the method of delivery is irrelevant: blast and shrapnel strike at random among people who are trying to live their daily lives. We were cut off from the reality on the ground in Iraq.

Ground troops are forced to live in the war situation at the front, pilots are not. Only knight-errants can master the air; they sally forth on their high-tech steeds to joust with the enemy, then return to their bases and officers' clubs. The *Vancouver Sun* described the first combat of the Canadian airforce as a "rite of passage for the pilots," apparently a combination of male coming-of-age with an ordeal for the achievement of knighthood.

Evocation of a simple, nostalgic image of the Second World War is another major characteristic of the vocabulary used to generate popular support for this war-making. Because it wasn't fought on their territory, North Americans, alone among the major participants in the Second World War, are privileged to remember it as nostalgia without devastation. Ronald Reagan was known to confuse acting in Hollywood Second World War movies with actually being in battle in Europe himself.

The key Second World War words here are "allied" or "the allies." These were used frequently at the beginning of the air war, as in "allied air force," "allied armada." Later on "allied" tended to give way to "coalition" as the lead adjective, but then "allied" became popular again with the ground war. This evoked unity: Bush declared at the beginning of his war, "no nation can stand against a world united." (Does a majority on the 15-member Security Council unite the world?)

The Second World War paradigm casts the Hero, the Villain, and the Victim into prescribed roles and hence short-circuits the need for evidence and thinking. The allies are again the heroic Allies. The word "allied" lent substance to a situation where, unlike the Second World War, a single country totally dominated the coalition.

Saddam is the villainous Hitler. The main point of the Saddam-Hitler equation is that it facilitated personification: making one man or a small group stand for a country whose whole population disappears behind the evil giant. We now remember the enemy in the Second World War as Hitler and a few key associates dressed up in Nazi uniforms. The image was readily transferred to Saddam Hussein in a fancy uniform alone with his rockets in the desert. Once we have accepted that Saddam is really Hitler, we can easily believe the oft-repeated charge that he is a "madman," which in turn justifies the American refusal to negotiate. Reporter Daniel Goleman, in *The Globe and Mail*, asked the question: "Is Saddam Hussein Clinically Insane?" He quoted Dr. Jerrold Post, an advisor to the U.S. government. Post said Saddam Hussein is "not clinically insane but suffering from 'malignant narcissism,' a severe personality disorder that leaves him grandiose, paranoid and ruthless." Note the way this "diagnosis," made from Washington without ever meeting the man, hedged its bets. Terms like "malignant narcissism" and "paranoid" suggest psychosis, yet by allowing that Saddam isn't "clinically insane" Dr. Post avoided the burden of proof involved in calling him psychotic, and also avoided the problem of explaining how such a deficient personality could be a successful politician in a complex society.

A political figure is converted into a hate symbol representing both metaphysical evil and madness. This places him, like Satan, outside of historical time. The fact that until recently Hussein was the ally of the United States, helping them to defend the world from an earlier Satan, the Ayatollah Khomeini, is simply ignored. By responding to Saddam as pure monster, we facilitate one of those hysterical transformations, dramatized by Orwell in 1984, whereby yesterday's ally in struggle against evil becomes today's evil enemy, with no sense of inconsistency.

In his crude opportunism, Saddam seems like a garden variety brutal dictator, a typical strongman cultivated by the U.S. He only became a Satan-figure when his own pursuit of power was seen as threatening vital American interests. He is not the first to have achieved this distinction. Panamanian General Noriega was awarded it earlier, after years of U.S. support, because he threatened to interfere with American control of the Panama Canal.

A conviction that the war represents the personal actions of Saddam Hussein enables us to believe that an incredibly intense bombardment of the people of Iraq is justified on the grounds that this is the punishment which "he" deserves for "his" evil deeds. Even worse, the conviction that he is the root of all evil enables us to transfer to him all the aggression on our side, thus making him personally responsible for the results of our actions. Confronted with the horrific results of bombing the Ameriyeh shelter in Iraq, U.S. presidential spokesman Marlin Fitzwater said this happened because "Saddam Hussein does not share our value for the sanctity of human life." According to Fitzwater, unlike the U.S., Saddam "kills civilians intentionally and with purpose."[5] There seems to be a confusion between subject and object here: who bombed this bunker, "intentionally and with purpose," the Americans or the Iraqis?

To complete the Second World War replay, Kuwait is the innocent, occupied Europe, especially France. At the start of Bush's bombing campaign, the White House press secretary announced: "We are now beginning the liberation of Kuwait," paralleling Eisenhower's D-Day proclamation about beginning the liberation of Europe. "Liberation," mentioned so often in this war, was the key word in the invasion of Normandy.[6]

Newsweek laboured to fit General Schwarzkopf into the Second World War analogy. "[T]he country badly needed a victory and he delivered it, playing Omar Bradley, the soldier's soldier of World War Two, to Colin Powell's Eisenhower." Schwarzkopf is a "warrior with a soul, not a dour martinet like William Westmoreland": the Vietnam War general.[7]

Bob McKeown, a CBS (and former CBC) correspondent raced to Kuwait City ahead of the press pool. On the CBC-Radio program "As It Happens," McKeown said Kuwait City felt just like liberated Paris, except that he couldn't get a drink, and only the men would kiss him. (Throughout the interview he paraded his ignorance of local culture.) In his speech at the start of the bombing, Bush predicted: "The legitimate government of Kuwait will be restored to its rightful place and Kuwait will once again be free." What does "free" mean in a family-ruled emirate, or "legitimate" where two-thirds of the population had no political rights because they couldn't trace descent back to a Kuwaiti at least as far as 1920?

The prize for the paradoxical use of a word should go to Canadian air force chief Colonel Lalonde. At a time when our official policy was still "defensive," he had to explain why Canadian planes had been given orders to shoot down enemy planes when they didn't attack; even if, for instance, they were fleeing to Iran. According to Lalonde, attacking is still "defensive" because every attack on an enemy plane defends our side. This explanation, of course, renders the word "defensive" meaningless. It is a minor analogue to the great paradoxical slogans of Orwell's *1984*: "War is Peace," "Freedom is Slavery."

There was, however, one inadvertent echo of the Second World War in George Bush's rhetoric. In a speech before Congress he introduced his now famous phrase "new world order," to suggest a community of nations coming together to promote peace and justice. The phrase was first made popular by Hitler, anticipating the Thousand-Year Reich. But Hitler's lines were supposed to go to Saddam Hussein.

The phrases "New Order" and "New European Order" were used repeatedly in Hitler's speeches and in Nazi propaganda. Before the war Hitler used these phrases mainly as a foreign policy ploy to predict an era of harmony and equal rights between nations, which would arise once certain injustices against Germany were corrected.[8] In a concise summary of the various uses of these phrases, Raoul de Sales points out that starting in 1940 the "New Order" meant the imposition of German economic domination and Nazification of conquered territories by force.

During the war, however, Hitler continued to prophesy an era of peace and harmony in the near future, as a substitute for the "final victory" which he failed to achieve.[9] Hence, in this concept of a "New Order," an era of natural harmony, supposedly emerging in the future, becomes the justification for the use of force to maintain "order" in the present, and a justification for the social chaos and deprivation caused by war. The arrival of the "New Order" can be indefinitely postponed, but ever striven for by more conquest.

Of course Hitler's Second World War *blitzkrieg*, literally lightning war, so appropriate to the allied attacks against Iraq, had to be renamed "Air-Land Battle." *The Globe and Mail* told us that the "air-land war in Kuwait and Iraq will be an elaborate ballet in which choreography may be the key to success."[10]

Orwell wrote that the language of euphemism "is needed if one wants to name things without calling up mental pictures of them." The psychologist Robert Jay Lifton said this language generates "dissociation": a separation between knowledge and feeling which leads to "psychic numbing."

Different methods of reporting can enable the audience to identify fully with victims, to distance them, or to leave them out altogether. Coverage of the Scud missile hit of an apartment building in Tel Aviv showed the whole reality: collapsed building with objects representing the inhabitants' private life strewn about in the wreckage, bloody figures being carried out on stretchers, people in shock and weeping relatives, along with plenty of interviews. Through most of the coverage of the immeasurably more intense bombing of Iraq, people just weren't there. The startling exception to this was the bombing of the civilian shelter in Baghdad. The effect of the grieving, angry faces of Iraqi civilians starkly reminded me how these images had been excluded until then.

In announcing the heavy bombing of Basra, *The Globe and Mail* described it only as a "key transportation centre in Southern Iraq."[11] In fact, Basra is Iraq's only port, of Arabian Nights fame, and the largest city in southern Iraq. But Basra was not portrayed as a place where people lived until the focus shifted, after the U.S.-led bombing, to the Shiite revolt there against Saddam Hussein.

The towns and cities of Iraq must have been captured constantly in air reconnaissance photos, but all we got to see were fuzzy shots of "smart" bombs hitting their cross-hairs target. Official accounts of the destruction wrought by the air offensive substituted objects for people. "Citing the destructive example of Vietnam, allied Commander General Norman Schwarzkopf has forbidden anything that resembles that war's infamous body count...Instead, senior officers in the Gulf have provided estimates concerning the number of Iraqi aircraft, bridges, tanks, artillery pieces and missile launchers that have been destroyed."[12] The Pentagon wanted to spare our sensibilities.

Even referring to their own soldiers, U.S. officers at press conferences used psychic numbing techniques. They presented lists of KIAs, WIAs and MIAs. Orwell noted how the use of initials eliminates the meaning of words; here killed, wounded, and missing in action.

But the real objective was to depopulate Iraq, to suggest it is a largely uninhabited country, with its leader standing in the desert surrounded by his tanks and missiles. The code name of the entire military operation, "Desert Storm," implies that Iraq is all desert and therefore uninhabited; nothing there but sand and Saddam Hussein. So a headline from the Vancouver *Province* newspaper proclaimed: "Canadian Pilots Help Pound Saddam."[13]

After all the months in which to prepare, why was there so little on the history, geography and culture of Iraq, and so few and so poor documentaries on the political career of Saddam Hussein? There is one obvious answer: both Washington and the media colluded in preventing the population of Iraq from becoming real to the North American audience. Documentary narratives on history or politics or culture would present us with Iraqi faces, and they wanted us to see as few of these as possible.

If "dissociation" can be understood as an indirect form of dehumanization, the language of this war also showed a pattern of direct dehumanization. An American commentator referred to the desert as "an evil, barren place," and Saddam Hussein as a "scorpion." This metamorphosis of human into insect was used by Marine Lieutenant Colonel Dick White, speaking to pool reporters. Describing Iraqi troops from the air, White said: "It was like turning on the kitchen light at night and the cockroaches started scurrying. We finally got them out where we could find them and kill them."[14]

Los Angeles Times reporter John Balzar interviewed a U.S. pilot who participated in the air attack, in the final hours of the war, against a column of Iraqi vehicles and conscripts desperately fleeing north out of Kuwait City back to Iraq. The article was reprinted in the *Vancouver Sun* newspaper.

> I just didn't envision going up there and shooting the hell out of everything in the dark and have them not know what hit them.
> A truck blows up to the right, the ground blows up to the left. When we got back, I sat there on the wing, and I was laughing. I wasn't laughing at the Iraqis. I was thinking of the training and the anticipation. . . I was probably laughing at myself. . . I laid there in bed and said, 'OK, I'm tired, I've got to get some sleep.' And then I'd think about sneaking up there and blowing this up, blowing that up.

Later, he recalled, "a guy came up to me, and we were slapping each other on the back and all that stuff, and he said, 'By God, I thought we had shot into a damn farm. It looked like somebody opened up on the sheep pen.'"

The interview combines the thrill of slaughter with an admission that training provided no preparation for it. The pilot's laughter seems a bit nervous, but he appears to give full assent to the strange hunting image with which the passage ends. What kind of hunting is represented by the machine-gunning of barnyard animals? Here we see how the distancing of the violence also permits a certain enjoyment of it.

In another part of the same article, Balzar describes a video taken through the gunsights of an Apache helicopter equipped with infra-red night vision.

> Through the powerful night-vision gunsights, the Iraqi soldiers looked like ghostly sheep flushed from a pen – bewildered and terrified, jarred from sleep and fleeing their bunkers under a hellish fire.
>
> One by one, they were cut down by attackers they could not see. Some were blown to bits by bursts of 30-mm exploding cannon shells. One man dropped, writhing on the ground, then struggled to his feet; another burst of fire tore him apart...
>
> For those who try to stay in the bunkers, laser guided Hellfire missiles are launched to an altitude of a half-mile, where they then arc almost straight down on the target.

This sequence is already perceived as a TV spectacle, through one of those flat, gunsight videos where doubtless the people do look like ghosts. The journalist has picked up the sheep metaphor from the pilot he interviewed, hardly an effective image for the scene he describes. The description seems completely emotionless. We are left free to enjoy it if we want. "Death in the Dark" could be taken as instruction in how to view this war and future ones, addressed to an audience already accustomed to the mild enjoyment of violence on TV.

The characteristic aggressive phrases of both George Bush and Saddam Hussein present an interesting contrast. Bush went into Iraq to "kick ass," while Saddam Hussein prophesied that U.S. troops would

"wade through rivers of blood." Any realistic estimate would have fore-
seen the blood was to be that of the Iraqi people, but politicians who
indulge in such rhetoric are not moved by blood. On the other hand,
Bush's phrase, associated with sport, implies a bloodless assertion of
authority.

Sporting terms became prominent in war reportage, especially since
the Super Bowl was integrated with the war at an early stage. "It will be
like the Super Bowl to end Super Bowls," enthused a Marine dreaming
about the time when his unit would enter combat.[15] The paradigm can
be found in General Schwarzkopf's press conferences, presented in the
jocular but firm and manly manner of a coach whose team has just won.
A U.S. pilot described his first bombing mission: "Hey, we got to the
stadium, but the other team forgot to turn up." Another remarked: "We
scored big on that one. We did an end-run around them."[16] Military
personnel commonly linked this war to past wounds to U.S. national
prestige: "We tied one in Korea, we lost one in Vietnam, now we have
to win this one." As long as we accept the sports metaphor that Bush
was just "kicking ass," he is under no pressure to admit what he actually
did to Iraqi people.

Celebratory metaphors began with the first bombings, though they
reached a peak with the "victory" parades. The CNN reporters
described the opening bombing attacks on Baghdad this way: "Baghdad
looked like a Fourth of July celebration multiplied a hundred times." A
pilot doing the bombing remarked Baghdad was "lit up like a Christmas
tree." An American officer, anticipating the ground war, said "We
have all our tools ready, and we're going to bring them to the party."

"It's a proud day for America, and, by God, we've kicked the Vietnam syndrome once and for all," proclaimed the U.S. President.
Determined to outdo Bush in boyish enthusiasm, *Newsweek* announced
"a triumph of almost Biblical proportions" in its Special Victory Issue.[17]
In its colour foldout pages of the war, *Newsweek* trumpeted in headline
style: "A Swift Surrender: For the first time since World War Two, tri-
umphant Americans liberated an occupied nation like swashbuckling
storybook heroes – and the United States rejoiced in its military
might."[18]

A financial basis for euphoria was provided by Peter Passell in the

In the romantic-heroic style of U.S. social realism circa the 1930s and 1940s, this graphic appeared in the business section of The New York Times *under the headline "The Big Spoils From a Bargain War."*

business section of *The New York Times*. Under the headline, "The Big Spoils From a Bargain War," and an eyecatching drawing representing industry, workers, the army and the flag marching forward in the romantic-heroic style of U.S. social-realism from the thirties and forties, he tells us that even the most cautious economists are "being swept up in the euphoria of victory." Since contributions from the allies may more than cover the cost of maintaining the troops in the Gulf, "[most] likely, the Pentagon will be left with a profit."[19]

The same mood seemed to have overtaken *The MacNeil-Lehrer Newshour* which on March 1 was dedicated entirely to national self-congratulation. Looking back at the ceasefire and Bush's press conference, the four Middle East experts had only one subject: how and how soon would Saddam Hussein be done in? Who would give him "the silver bullet"? "We want him to end like Mussolini. If you string him up by his heels, then we'll do business with you." This was reminiscent of the corridor banter in the United Nations. Yves Fortier, Canada's ambassador to the U.N., told Florida businessmen in a private talk that he, and other dignified diplomats of the Security Council dedicated to international law, joked among themselves about hiring the Soviet KGB to "take out a contract" on Saddam Hussein.

Can it be that the jocular, banal, spectator-sport language of violence which has dominated the media, especially TV, is becoming the characteristic discourse of the American empire?

This thought brings me back to Orwell, who feared that the future would bring a new language of pure aggression which would appeal on a gut level to a vicarious sadism in its audience, while making abstract thought impossible – the essence of "Newspeak."

Reflecting that "Jack the Giant Killer" has traditionally been a favourite fairy tale because it sides with the underdog, Orwell suggests that since sympathy for underdogs has become so unfashionable in the "bully-worship" characteristic of modern politics, an amended tale, "Jack the Dwarf Killer," might be more appropriate for our time.[20]

Starting with Grenada, working up through Panama to Iraq, the U.S. has achieved its "glory" by killing dwarfs. As commander of the ground troops in Grenada (1983), General Schwarzkopf already was an experienced dwarf killer.

We can assume that Bush really does know what happened in Iraq, and intends it to be an object lesson to the rest of the Third World, in his "new order." A third-world country has been successfully bombed back into the "pre-oil era,"[21] and now is set up for starvation and epidemics. By all accounts, Iraq will be an "economic cripple" for years to come. Every telecommunications centre, power plant and oil refinery in the country has been destroyed. Thirty years of development must be replaced at today's costs; yet the U.N. maintains sanctions and has announced the enforcement of reparations as well.

We can take some consolation in the fact that the shallow language of this war lacked the full aggressive gusto and emotional force of "Newspeak," the imaginary language of Orwell's *1984*. In some ways, the full-voiced polemics of the Cold War, especially during the McCarthy era, resembled "Newspeak" more than the discourse of this one, with its narrow range between technological magic, nostalgic patriotism, highly abstract notions of justice, a sporting view of slaughter, and a feeling that victory somehow will benefit the economy.

Also dwarf killing presents special problems in public relations. We were told that the stomping of the tiniest dwarf, Grenada, was necessary to halt the "communist menace." Since the public collapse of the Soviet Union, this rationale has lost its force. So the Panama and Iraqi dwarfs were enlarged into evil giants through emphasis on the monstrous character of their leaders. This thinner discourse will be more vulnerable to disruption by reality when the results of war become evident.

To pause and reflect on the media ploys sold to us during the war against Iraq is to see through them. Surely this plastic imitation of the victorious conclusion of the Second World War can only be a passing mood?

Notes

[1] Orwell, George, "Politics and the English Language," *Inside the Whale and Other Essays* (New York, Penguin, 1962), p.153.
[2] February 19, A8.
[3] Fotheringham, Allan, *Maclean's*, February 18, 1991, p.56.
[4] Special Victory Issue, p.38.
[5] The *Vancouver Sun*, February 13, 1991, front page.
[6] I am indebted to Darin Barney, a graduate student in the Political Science department at Simon Fraser University, for calling my attention to the echo of Eisenhower's statement, and the importance of the word "liberation" in press coverage of the Normandy invasion.
[7] Special Victory Issue, p.32.
[8] Baynes, Norman H. *The Speeches of Adolf Hitler: April 1922-August 1939*, Vol. 2 (New York, Howard Fetig, 1969). See Hitler's speech of 22 March 1936, pp.1313-14.
[9] Hitler, Adolf, *My New Order*, edited with commentary by Raoul de Roussy de Sales (New York, Octagon Books, 1973), pp. 866-70.
[10] February 2, A6.
[11] January 18, A8.
[12] *The Globe and Mail*, February 20, A8.
[13] January 20, 1991, front page.

General Lockjaw Briefs the British Media

Leon Rosselson

Don't mention the oil.
We're fighting because this war is just,
The Bishop says so, and we must
Stand up to aggression and evil deeds from which we all recoil.
Our cause is this: to liberate
The suffering people of Kuwait,
And victory will vindicate
– our intervention.
We can't be expected not to act
Just because of the accidental fact

77

That Kuwait is absolutely packed
– with the stuff you may not mention.
So pay attention!
And don't mention the oil.

Try not to dwell on the dead.
And *kill* is better not heard or seen
Except when it's modified by *clean*.
Forget about *people* refer, if you must, to *personnel* instead.
Describe an allied bombing raid
As a kind of victory parade
And stress that our surgical strikes are made
– with great precision.
Collateral damage please employ
And *take out* rather than *destroy*
Descriptions of mangled bodies annoy
– and will need careful revision
It's your decision
But don't dwell on the dead.

Please play down the fact
That we kept his military force supplied
As long as he seemed to be on our side
But it's a different ball game now that our interests are attacked.
We knew his crimes, we made no fuss,
But now the brute has turned on us,
So what in the world is there left to discuss
– but retribution?
You're all old hands, you know the score,
Let's agree to forget what's gone before
And focus attention upon the war
– and its successful prosecution.
Your contribution
Is not to confuse us with facts.

Morale must be maintained.
Our boys are keen to do the job,
Their troops are a ruthless, fanatical mob,
And their pilots are running scared even though they may be
British trained
We're Patriots, they're skulking Scuds, Our missiles are smart,
theirs mostly duds,
Except when they're spilling civilian blood
– in a terror attack.
Make sure that the British are given their due,
They're resolute, cool and loyal, too,
While the Krauts and the Belgies play peekaboo
– somewhere safe from the flak.
Wave the Union Jack.
It'll help boost morale.

War is a serious game.
We must unite to show we're strong
One line for all, one single song,
That's why to win the war at home must be your primary aim.
Our battle plan is to neutralise
Opposing voices which sympathise
With calls for peace, for they jeopardise
– our whole operation.
Our PR firm is there to advise –
It isn't a question of telling lies,
Think of it more as an exercise
– in news co-ordination.
We need your co-operation –

So don't mention the oil, don't dwell on the dead,
Don't confuse us with facts, help to boost morale,
And play your part in the game.

Rituals of War

Sandy Shreve

far from the fighting
we are bombarded with the tangled
language of propaganda

transparent turns of phrase
twisted like cats' cradles
for us to inspect and straighten

up against a simplistic truism
that truth
is the first casualty of war

or do people actually nod
as if there is wisdom in this
permission

as though nothing in us dies
each time we reassure our children
over maps and globes

we are safe: here, riddled
with off-beat stories of war
there: that's where weapons shred lives

for whose comic relief do we
wonder at gas masks for poultry
condoms to protect gun barrels from sand

this verbal memorabilia of the absurd
is devastation's thin disguise
yet it feels like there is no end

to the appalling applause for bombs
as the curtains are drawn once more
on what we really know of war

What Would They Hide From Us?

U.S.-coalition bombing of Iraq began January 17, 1991. One week later the U.S. Department of Energy (DOE) issued a gag on comments on the environmental consequences of the war. The memorandum reads in part:

> DOE Headquarters Public Affairs has requested that all DOE facilities and contractors immediately discontinue any further discussion of war-related research and issues with the media until further notice. The extent of what we are authorized to say about environmental impacts of fires/oil spills in the Middle East follows: "Most independent studies and experts suggest that the catastrophic predictions in some recent news reports are exaggerated. We are currently reviewing the matter, but these predictions remain speculative and do not warrant any further comment at this time."
>
> If there are any doubts about appropriate comments, please refer inquiries to Office of Communications and Planning, John Belluardo.[1]

Mr. Belluardo told *Scientific American* that the memo was not to "muzzle" debate, but to keep information from the Iraqis that would hinder U.S. military operations. So why was the policy still in effect in May? Because "we are still in a transition period," Belluardo told *Scientific American*.[2]

The U.S. Environmental Protection Agency (EPA) has been researching the effects of the burning oil well fires since late February, and continually monitoring the smoke since early March. They had issued only a single report by May which concluded smoke emissions were not "at levels of concern." But requests for press interviews with the researchers were turned down. "We don't want them talking to the press," said EPA spokeswoman Mary Mears.[3]

Other DOE scientists studying the fires also have been instructed to remain silent. A U.S. observatory in Hawaii detected elevated

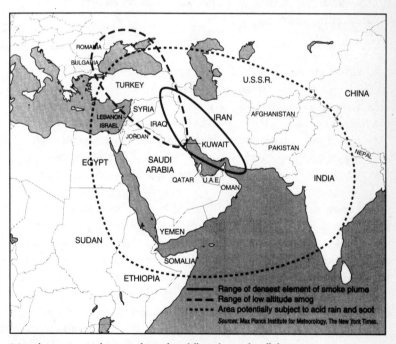

Map shows extent of areas subjected to fallout from oil well fires.

soot levels, believed to originate from Kuwait. A government official cancelled a press release which the scientists had prepared. The official denied he was trying to conceal potentially embarrassing information: "[Y]ou've got to have someone in charge of press releases and announcements, or the whole thing could get very confusing."[4]

Some scientists have suggested that there may be an attempt to hide U.S.-coalition *direct* responsibility for the undeniably profound ecological disaster that has been inflicted on a vast region, and possibly worldwide.

Lara Gundel, an aerosol specialist at the Lawrence Berkeley Laboratory, said the first "spike" of increased soot levels detected in Hawaii arrived there in early February. This is before Iraq set fire to the Kuwait wells. "The timing suggests, she says, that the soot may have resulted from Allied bombing of Iraqi oil refineries and storage tanks," according to a *Scientific American* report.

The report continues:

> Other data support the conclusion that Allied bombing caused significant pollution. A document prepared in early March by the Defense Nuclear Agency and obtained by the Natural Resources Defense Council (NRDC) through a Freedom of Information request notes that Iraq's neighbor Iran experienced "repeated black rain events starting Jan. 22." Satellite images made in mid-February by Landsat-5 and NOAA-11 reveal smoke plumes several hundred kilometres long emanating from various regions of Iraq.[5]

We know enough to say that both U.S.-led coalition and Iraqi state policies created an ecological disaster of massive proportions, and wilfully risked even more. We know that neither the U.S.-led coalition nor the Iraqi state therefore have an interest in revealing to us their knowledge of the extent of the disaster they inflicted on the environment and people of the Middle East region and beyond.

Only the laborious effort of independent researchers will uncover the scope of this environmental catastrophe, and in her article Dr. Suzanne Rose begins to collate some of the evidence presently available. Evidence will have to continue to be gathered because of the long-term implications and cyclical nature of ecological destruction. The metaphor of "surgical strikes" is no more applicable to understanding the environmental consequences of this war than it is to understanding the human consequences.

Notes

[1] *Scientific American*, May 1991, p.24. The censorship order came from the White House, according to Belluardo. A DOE spokesperson in Washington said it came from the Environmental Protection Agency (EPA) and the Department of Defense (DOD). Spokespersons for the White House, EPA, and DOD deny all knowledge of any such order.

[2] *Ibid.*

[3] *Scientific American*, July 1991, p.20.

[4] *Ibid.*

[5] *Ibid.* On August 1, the Iran news agency INRA said black, oily rain caused by oil well fires has contaminated 4.5 million hectares of forest and pasture in its western province of Fars. (The *Vancouver Sun*, August 6, Reuters report, p.A3.) A brief CBC-TV National news report in August reported astronauts saying they never before had seen the entire earth so shrouded in haze. A small report in *The New York Times*, August 13, 1991, says the U.S. has provided U.N. monitors in Iraq with U-2 spy-planes "because spy satellite coverage has been interrupted by cloud cover or haze." Information seems to accumulate like dust, almost imperceptibly.

Fallout

"This is the most intense burning source, probably, in the history of the world... There is basically no literature on this problem." *– Joel Levine, NASA Langley Research Center, is an expert on biomass burning*

"What we saw was really devastating, and I don't know why people aren't paying more attention to it, why it's a 'non-story' these days.

"The impression close up on the ground is the most vivid. You have a 30 mile per hour wind blowing which is why you can get pretty close to the fires. All around you [are] literally hundreds of burning wells – the total is still around 500 fires burning – and what is particularly worrying right now, and this is new, is that the wells that have been put out but are still gushing oil, are forming huge lakes. We saw lakes over a mile long. And on some of them the entire perimeter, or maybe half a mile of perimeter, is on fire and polluting in a much worse way than the oil fire from the original well that had been extinguished.

"As soon as you start moving around down wind, you get droplets of oily stuff falling in your eyes and on your skin. You feel it as you breathe in. You feel it on your lips. You lick your lips and wonder what's going on – it's sort of acrid stuff. You see it spotting your clothing. It gets in your eyes. It's really horrible, and what shocked me is communities living in the immediate vicinity of the fires, like Al Ahmadi which is only five miles away from the nearest fires.

"We did have access to many people who were able to tell us that hospital admissions were considerably above normal, especially in categories of respiratory problems, lung problems – even circulatory and ear problems are up – and they think these are the result of the smoke plumes and the pollution falling out from the fires."   – *James George, former Canadian ambassador to Kuwait and Iran, spoke June 24, 1991, on CBC radio after his return from a tour sponsored by Friends of the Earth.*

"Firefighters have recently called in tanks to shell crusted wells."   – *The New York Times, August 14, 1991.*

"[I]t's premature to rule out global effects."   – *Darrel Baumgartner, National Center for Atmospheric Research (U.S.A.), was quoted in Scientific American, July 1991.*

Ecological Implications of the War

Suzanne Rose

HUMAN BEINGS, ACTING AS AGENTS FOR THEIR GOVERNMENTS, HAVE devastated the Gulf region: the land, sea, and air. This devastation continues. It is making life more difficult for humans and non-humans alike.

What was the environmental impact of the military activity, biochemical and nuclear contamination, oil spills, and oil burning? I consider the implications of these on land, sea, and air; on plants, animals and humans; and on our support systems, including climate itself.

From an ecological perspective, life on the earth is a set of complex relationships among living beings, dependent on one another, on matter, and on systems such as climate. Humans are not protected by birthright, politics or religion from the effects of their intervention in the earth's systems. The earth is not a warehouse in which humans play out their dramas with impunity.

An embattled land

In this time of fascination with technological mastery, we forget that "everyday" war or "conventional" war affects a landscape and thereby its inhabitants. The military language for the destruction of the habitat, or ecocide, is "scorched earth." Vietnam's environment remains ravaged from the U.S. military's scorched earth, and much of that damage may never be repaired.[1]

The Tigris and Euphrates riverine delta forms most of Kuwait and Iraq. It is well-watered and well-cultivated. It is home to many plants and animals, including the steppe and booted eagles, Houbara bustard, crowned sandgrouse, marsh harrier, Indian gerbil, Euphrates jerboa, long-eared hedgehog and the Arabian sand gazelle.[2] This is a fertile and productive area of the Middle East: growing dates, rice, wheat, barley, fruit and vegetables.[3] There are millions of sheep and goats, thousands of camels, buffaloes and donkeys. One quarter of Iraq's population depends for their livelihood on caring for the land and livestock; the whole population depends on those plants and animals for their food.[4]

This region was intensely bombed. The U.S. coalition flew over 100,000 sorties. The bombing destroyed not only buildings but also sewers, water purification facilities, dams and underground canal systems. Of special concern in Iraq are the dams in the Zagros mountains, outside Baghdad, and the traditional underground wells called *qanat*.

In the desert, bombing and air activity can increase the number and severity of dust storms. During World War Two, dust storms increased by tenfold in Northern Africa. Such storms would hinder agriculture and grazing, and could disrupt rainfall. Military vehicles destroy the sensitive living crust of the desert: micro-organisms, plants, salt and soil. This takes decades to recover: the vegetation in the U.S. deserts displaced by the tank tracks of General Patton still has recovered only 30 per cent after 50 years.[5]

Bombs may take decades to explode, leaving some areas uninhabitable. In Vietnam, people are still injured by bombs exploding 20 years after the U.S. dropped them. Some bombs are "smart": they explode only when metal, such as a hoe, comes near them. Once exploded, bombs may release toxic metals, chemicals or depleted uranium, used in their manufacture. These destroy plant life and farmland, poisoning soil, groundwater, and the animals depending on them.[6] This, in turn, may force humans to migrate, to use new areas and encroach on wild lands.

Military forces, by their simple presence, take a toll on the environment as well. The U.S.-coalition forces consumed 10 gallons of water per day per soldier and per vehicle. They created huge garbage dumps of materiel, of human waste, and of cleaning solvents. Who is cleaning up? The toxic waste generated by the U.S. military is well known and circles the world.[7]

Seeding disease: biological weapons

In 1346, the Tartars broke the defences of Caffa by catapulting plague-infected bodies into that city. In the last century, here in North America, distribution of smallpox-infected blankets was a weapon of genocide used against aboriginal peoples.[8] During World War Two, the U.S., England and Canada worked at Grosse Ile, Quebec and at Suffield, Alberta to create an anthrax bomb. Gruniard Island, Scotland, was sprayed with anthrax and remained uninhabitable for 30 years. The Nazis experimented with typhoid at Dachau and Buchenwald. Since World War Two, the Soviets, Americans, and Europeans among others, have worked with diseases such as anthrax, plague, and typhoid.[9]

Anthrax is a bacteria which attacks cud-chewing animals and human beings through the lungs, the stomach and wounds. This irritates the tissues, causing infection, swelling, lung congestion, bloody and painful diarrhoea, fever of up to 40 degrees Celsius and, commonly, death within three days. Anthrax spores can survive for decades.

The 1972 Biological Weapons Convention banned development, production and storage of such weapons but both the U.S. and England reserved the right to use them in retaliation. So research, usually on non-humans, carries on. The University of Victoria, British Columbia, receives military funds to research tularaemia and Suffield continues to research nerve gas.[10]

Biological weapons are relatively cheap and have become popular with poorer countries. They entered Iraq only in the last decades. West

German companies, for example, helped build the laboratories and delivered biological materials, such as 200 milligrams of mycotoxins in 1986.[11] Apparently Iraq possessed anthrax as well.

U.S.-coalition bombing targets included facilities storing poisons, such as biological weapons. On January 30, General Schwarzkopf said that 31 biological, chemical and nuclear locations had been attacked: "We have absolute confirmation that we've destroyed over 11 chemical and biological storage areas." A Cairo newspaper reported that an Egyptian doctor observed 50 Iraqi soldiers die of anthrax after U.S. B-52 bombers destroyed an anthrax facility.[12]

Chemical weapons

Mustard gas was used in World War One trenches and the Germans first developed tabun, a nerve gas, from insecticide in the 1930s. The 1925 Geneva Convention prevented first-strike use but the U.S. and England, among others, again reserved the right to retaliate. Research and development continues to this day. The U.S. for example is researching weapons such as VX, one of the most potent nerve gases.[13]

Chemical weapons are the "poor country's atom bomb" and Western firms delivered the technology: Phillips Petroleum (Belgium) provided 500 tons of thiodiglycol (precursor to mustard gas) and Karl Kolb (Germany) built a facility easily modified to produce the nerve gas sarin.[14] Despite the arms embargo, the Reagan and Bush administrations allowed sales to Iraq of billions of dollars worth of scientific material even after it was clear this material was diverted to weapons production and that the Iraqi military had used them on the Kurds.[15] In fact, when the United Nations Human Rights Commission passed a resolution condemning Iraq for these chemical bombings, the Bush administration worked against its passage.[16]

U.S.-led forces were well aware of these chemical stocks. The Pentagon announced in the first week of the war that it had destroyed Salman Pak, a research site; Samarra, the main production site for mustard gas, tabun and sarin; and Bayji, a site producing ammonia, needed in nerve gas. Later, they bombed chemical weapons stored with military units.

We do not know whether chemical materials had been moved before the war started. However, there are at least two reports of contamination from the bombing. On January 21, the *Washington Times* reported that a Czech unit observed chemical agents in the air along the Saudi-Kuwaiti border, presumably coming from destroyed chemical shells. On February 3, French General Raymond Germanos said that coalition attacks had sent nerve agents into the air. He said there were traces "almost everywhere" at low levels.[17]

Chemically poisonous gases are indiscriminate. They disperse rapidly and kill unprotected civilians and non-humans more than soldiers. Mustard gas can be lethal, or in less concentrated amounts, can burn tissues, impair breathing, vision, and reproduction. It can cause cancer and genetic damage. There is no antidote. Nerve gases block nervous system activity, causing paralysis, psychosis and death due to lung failure.[18]

These gases could move with prevailing winds, travelling from the Samarra factory, for example, to the Tigris river and Lake Mileh Tharthar, used for drinking and irrigation water. The gases permeate soil or ground water, contaminating foods and drinking water for humans and non-humans alike. Fires have raged at some of the bombed chemical facilities and this creates new worries.[19] Even scientifically controlled incineration of chemical weapons could disperse toxic material: if halogenated compounds such as hydrogen cyanide and nitrogen dioxide burn, these can produce dioxin and furans, much as pulp mills using chlorine do, with carcinogenic implications. There are, in addition, long-term environmental effects. Although tabun and sarin would dissipate in a few days, nerve gases could decimate insects and thus weaken soil and make it less plant-supporting.

Trying to mitigate the damage of chemical gases is time-consuming and costly.[20] The soil would have to be dug up and incinerated. As mustard stays around for decades, breaking down and then reforming, soil could be contaminated once again. An estimated 90 per cent of Iraq's chemical weapons stock was mustard gas.[21]

Nuclear contamination

Conventional bombing was used against nuclear technology in Iraq. The nuclear weaponry was all on the U.S.-led side. To supplement the

200 Israeli nuclear weapons, the U.S. and U.K. moved over 1000 nuclear weapons into the region: 300 land-based in Turkey and 700 aboard U.S. naval vessels, including 83 Tomahawk cruise missiles. The naval vessels also housed over 20 nuclear reactors. U.S. officials declined publicly to give up the nuclear option in Iraq. (The bunkers of Iraqi soldiers in Kuwait not only had informational posters telling them how to "respond" to a chemical attack, but how to "respond" to a nuclear attack.[22])

Iraq had a nuclear weapons research program, but no weapons. It had two research reactors at Tuwaitha, and other research sites. On January 16, the U.S. attacked Iraq's nuclear facilities. The *Washington Times* reported the next day that four nuclear research sites and the two reactors had been hit. The reactors, the IRT-5000 and Tammuz-2, were about 20 km north of Baghdad. General Powell, at a Pentagon briefing, described them as "gone...down...finished."

Both the U.S. government and the Pentagon announced that they had used an unspecified method to prevent contamination. They said their bomb explosions had buried the radioactive material under tons of rubble.[23] They made no mention of the waste fuel. The IRT-5000 reactor may have produced as much as 150 to 300 kilograms of radioactive waste: strontium, iodine, cesium, etc.[24] Given the history of radioactive waste storage and reactor accidents – such as the Chernobyl explosion and the U.S. Hanford iodine leaks – the risk of leakage sounds high. Conventional bombing of a reactor also could disperse plutonium, one of the most toxic materials known. The claim of the International Atomic Energy Agency (IAEA) that the bombings would cause only "local" contamination, does not increase one's confidence.[25] The IAEA is the body designated by the U.N. to enforce the Nuclear Non-Proliferation Treaty, by inspecting reactors and ensuring their peaceful use. The IAEA passed the following resolution in 1985: "any armed attack on...nuclear facilities devoted to peace purposes constitutes a violation of the principles of the United Nations charter, International law, and the Statute of the Agency." This resolution partly arose out of the 1981 Israeli bombing of the Iraqi Osirak reactor, a reactor inspected and designated as peaceful by the IAEA. In November 1990, the IAEA inspected the Iraqi reactors and designated them as peaceful. Only two months later, they were bombed and destroyed.[26]

Another source of nuclear contamination is the artillery shells used by the U.S. military. In a report on the death of U.S. soldiers killed by their own army, it was stated that "[i]n many cases, investigators were able to distinguish casualties caused by American fire because American ground forces used anti-tank rounds made of depleted uranium and Iraqi troops did not. The rounds left radioactive traces of uranium that could be detected with Geiger counters."[27]

Oil spills

Life depends on water, and the Gulf is among the most productive water bodies in the world. Phytoplankton in deeper waters and coral, algae, sea grasses and mangroves in the shallower waters make life possible. Fish and shrimps depend on the smaller marine life. Green and hawksbill turtles (endangered), dugongs or sea cows (vulnerable), dolphins and many birds depend on the coastal lands for nesting and shelter.[28] The Gulf is a semi-enclosed sea. It is shallow, averaging about 35 metres deep but less than 10 metres deep along the coast. It is salty and sedimented, with large temperature changes, making it a demanding environment. Its slow, three to five year, current exchange with the Indian Ocean, through the Strait of Hormuz, prevents pollutants from escaping.[29]

Oil has been spilling into the Gulf for thirty years, peaking during the Iran-Iraq war.[30] The spills arising from the current war are the latest to devastate these waters. Spills are reported to have come from: the Kuwaiti Sea Island Terminal, al-Wafrah, Shuaiba and Mina Abdullah storage sites, the Saudi al-Khafji facility, the Iraqi al-Qadishiah and Mina al-Ahmadi tankers, and the Iraqi Mina al-Bakr terminal. The spills, all starting in the last 12 days of January, were caused by Iraq opening terminal and tanker valves and by U.S.-led bombing of tankers and terminals.[31]

Estimates of the size of the spills have varied profoundly, from almost 500 million gallons (11 million barrels)[32] to around 20 million gallons (0.5 million barrels) one month later. The Saudi Meteorology and Environmental Protection Agency is quoted as estimating the spills at 3 million barrels.[33] The world's largest spill was the Ixotec well spill into the Gulf of Mexico in 1979: 140 million gallons. Even the lowest estimate makes the Persian Gulf spills twice the size of the Exxon Valdez, one of the more infamous.

Some reports may exaggerate: a large spill emphasizes the enemy's badness. Or reports may underestimate: to diminish popular anxiety and concern. Because Kuwaiti oil is "light," some 40 per cent evaporates quickly and much of the rest sinks, as tarry balls, leaving a thin slick and beach residues visible for aerial surveillance, mostly military and secret.[34] Aerial photography may not show whether the spill is 0.1 or 0.3 millimetres thick. Interest wanes, the mileage of the "big spill" diminishes, and a spill not much bigger than Exxon soon sounds moderate and manageable.

Birds are the most visible victims. They take in oil from plant foods and onto their eggshells and feathers. Thousands of cormorants, grebes, rare flamingos, and herons have died of starvation, poisoning or suffocation, and the vast majority of them never made it to shore to be counted. The World Society for the Protection of Birds reports that the spill threatens hundreds of thousands of mallards, curlews, sandplovers and other migratory birds that rest in the Gulf mudflats and marshes on their way north from Africa.[35] Fifty-two species already have become extinct.[36]

The western Gulf shrimping grounds, fish traps, and coral reefs are covered with oil. In such conditions, the marine life suffers and breeds poorly. The shrimp and fish, already overstressed by human use, are declining in number and the coral is hard hit.[37] The World Society for the Protection of Animals fears a similar fate for the turtles. Some 3,500 female sea turtles go to Karan and Jana Islands to lay their eggs by early April, but it would be difficult for their young to survive the tarry beaches.[38]

The cleanup from the spills is very modest. Weeks after only a few hundred people were involved. The allied governments and the U.N. sent in personnel and equipment, but mostly to survey the damage. In contrast, 100,000 people worked on the Exxon Valdez cleanup at a cost of (U.S.) $1 billion. Even so the beaches of Prince William Sound remain fouled.[39]

It may take $5 billion to clean up the spills, yet Saudi Arabia has provided only $2 million for this, less than the price of the United Nations Environmental Protection survey, undertaken in the region after the war. Oil spill cleanup has not been a priority as the cost of cleaning up is high and politically unrewarding. Tar balls from 10-year-old spills still cover about three-quarters of Saudi Gulf beaches.[40]

Controversy over the long-term impact rages. The survival of the Gulf following the Iran-Iraq war makes some people optimistic. Nevertheless, many scientists fear great destruction of life and habitat. The oil can form suffocating mats and bubbles that could open at a later time. The late February conference of the Regional Organization for the Protection of the Marine Environment (ROPME) found cadmium, molybdenum, nickel, lead and zinc in the spilled oil, which could poison marine life and cause widespread reproductive failure of plankton, algae, sea grass, mangrove, shrimp, crab and fish as the oil falls to the sea bottom. Killing of sea plants and coral, in turn, could contribute to erosion of the Gulf islands, resulting in loss of animals such as turtles and terns, who breed there.

DAVID CHIU

Hundreds of burning Kuwaiti oil wells spread a dense smoke plume over several countries.

Under the shadows of burning oil

When all is well, the air is invisible. It is the source of gases used by both plant and animal life. The air in the Gulf has become dark and poisonous.[41] By late February, the Pentagon had announced that fleeing Iraqis set fire to most of Kuwait's oil producing wells. Some 500 fires were reported. By August 13, according to the Kuwaiti oil minister, 439 wells still were burning out of control, though he raised the estimate of the number originally on fire to 732.[42]

It was reported in May that Kuwaiti oil officials estimated six million barrels of oil, roughly one million tons, were burning daily. The fires created dense clouds of tarry smoke. On this basis an estimated 100,000 tons of soot and 50,000 tons of sulfur dioxide will be produced daily, according to Frederick Warner, a climatologist at Essex University, England.[43]

Smoke acts as a blanket, hiding the sun's rays from the earth and sea. When the northeast winds died down in mid-March, the Kuwaiti air was so dark at noon that cars used headlights and people read outside by flashlight. The damaged wells also have been creating "oil lakes," one metre deep and several kilometres across, and volatile gases possibly building beneath the surface.

With the smoke, meteorological models predict temperature drops of 10 degrees Celsius in a region of several hundred kilometres around Kuwait. Temperatures in Kuwait have dropped 15 degrees. In a 1,000 kilometre radius, temperatures are projected to drop one to two degrees Celsius below normal.[44]

The soot particles are complex, containing sulfur, radium, carbon and compounds such as carbon dioxide and sulfur dioxide, the chief constituent of acid rain. This smoke travels on the wind, and greasy black acid rain has fallen on soil and groundwater in Iran and Turkey, and has been reported well over 1,000 kilometres away, as distant as the Soviet Union and Pakistan. Acid rain, according to a model produced by Joyce Penner at the U.S. Lawrence Livermore National Laboratory, will affect regions some 2,000 kilometres from Kuwait, and as far as China perhaps. At the World Meteorological Organization meetings in April, Soviet scientists reported unprecedented levels of acid rain in

DAVID CHIU

High noon in Kuwait City. A dense, heavy cloud of smoke from burning oil wells hangs over the city.

southern Russia. Satellite pictures also show smoke and darkened snow in Pakistan and northern India, which could lead to rapid melting, floods, and ruined crops.[45]

Carbon dioxide emissions may be boosted up to five per cent according to the scientific advisor to King Hussein of Jordan, Dr. Toukan. This, he said, "makes a mockery" of the efforts of international conferences to reduce carbon dioxide emissions by just a small percentage in response to global warming.[46] These air pollutants, of course, irritate lung and plant tissues. In Kuwait it is said to be like breathing car exhaust or 12 packs of cigarettes per day. At an August conference at Harvard's School of Public Health and Center for Middle East Studies, evidence was presented that polyaromatic carbons, known to cause cancer over extended periods, appear in Kuwait at far higher than normal levels.[47]

While the effects on the climate in a radius of 1,000 kilometres are dramatic and undeniable, and will affect food supplies and population migration, there is controversy about the possible impact on global climate. "We have never seen a pollution event on this scale," said Richard D. Small, fire researcher at Pacific-Sierra Research Corporation in Los Angeles.[48] An important factor in determining global impact is the height to which the soot rises. In March British meteorologists concluded that the soot generally was rising no higher than five kilometres. But U.S. scientists have found particle concentrations 100 times normal levels at heights of six to 11 kilometres, the upper troposphere. If these concentrations increase, or "leak" to the stratosphere where they could stay for years, it would have a global effect.[49]

Paul Crutzen of the Max Planck Institute for Chemistry in Germany, who conceived the nuclear winter theory a decade ago, estimated initially that if one per cent of the smoke reaches the stratosphere, at the end of the year enough would have accumulated to cool the entire Northern hemisphere up to two degrees Celsius. "That's enough to worry about."[50]

While several scientists deny the smoke is having an effect on the monsoon cycle, others think it might have helped trigger the typhoon that struck Bangladesh May 1 causing 100,000 deaths. One typhoon expert said the flooding in Bangladesh was two feet higher than ever recorded, and the widespread rains afterward were unusual.

"It's premature to rule out global effects," commented Darrel Baumgartner of the U.S. National Center for Atmospheric Research. And models that project a greater burning of oil than presently is estimated do confirm a global climate impact.[51]

Environmental cause and effect

While we witness the horrors of this environmental disaster, keep in mind that the oil burning daily in the Gulf is an estimated 10 per cent of the oil which is burnt globally each day in our automobiles, factories and homes, contributing heavily to acid rain, global warming and the greenhouse effect. The Gulf war is significant not only because of its environmental effects but also because it reveals so clearly how the struggle for political dominance rests on the struggle for resource control.

The world economy depends on oil. The Middle East has about two-thirds of the world's known oil reserves and supplies about a quarter of the world's consumption. Of the trillions of barrels moving around the world, most moves from the Middle East to the "West": Europe, Japan and North America, where oil meets about 40 per cent of all energy demands. Oil from the Gulf is vital to Europe and Japan, whereas it amounts to only a quarter of U.S. oil imports and only five per cent of total U.S. energy consumption. Gulf oil may not be vital to the U.S.'s own consumption, but control of it is vital if the U.S. is to retain global influence.[52]

Over the decades, Western countries have tried to ensure control over the oil supply by supporting one Gulf state and then another, through aid and arms deals. The Western governments are prepared to fight to ensure their control over the Gulf. Zbigniew Brzezinski, National Security Advisor to President Carter, argued that the war's purpose was to "ensure that the Gulf is the secure and stable source for the industrialized West of reasonably priced oil. . . To put it more crudely, the flow of oil is ultimately an American imperative."[53]

The U.S. government, in particular, continues to avoid energy conservation measures such as efficiency standards for electric lights, tax credits for use-generated energy, and tax rebates for energy efficiency. Cars, buses and trucks account for two-thirds of U.S. oil use, yet the government, in response to strong oil and auto lobbies, avoids higher gasoline taxes, fuel-efficiency standards for vehicles, and major subsidy of mass transit. Instead, governments have subsidized oil, nuclear and massive hydro-electric energy development, assisting firms to drill for oil in Alaska and flood the watersheds of James Bay – so oil and electricity may move to U.S. markets.[54] The U.S. Department of Energy 1990 budget reveals the priorities: of a $15 billion total, about $10 billion was for nuclear weapons, $1 billion each for nuclear and oil technologies, and only $113 million was spent on renewable energy technology, only 0.7 per cent of the total energy budget.[55]

These governments continue to claim that funding for renewables and energy conservation are bad ideas because they interfere with market forces. Clearly, energy subsidies exist already and are a function of politics, not abstract forces of supply and demand. The environmental implications of these policies are: the burning of fossil fuels, the fission of atoms, and the deforestation of lands, with the results of global warming and radioactive contamination. Simply put, our economy, floating on cheap oil and mega-project electricity, discourages investment in alternate energy sources.[56]

For those concerned for the earth, the Gulf war revealed the human addiction to oil, governments' resistance to alternative energy, the common acceptance of bombing and killing as a suitable method to resolve differences, and the willingness to risk the integrity of land, sea and air. This was a war fought by the West to safeguard its access to a resource – oil – whose use has undermined the climate through global warming and, with its attendant droughts and mass starvation, also threatens the survival of plants, animals and human beings.

Disarmament and environment

In 1987 the United States boycotted a U.N. conference on disarmament and development, claiming there was no direct link. It is clear that governments still refuse to accept the findings of the Palme and Brundtland Commissions that a militarized society is undemocratic, impoverished, and environmentally irresponsible.[57] It uses labour, natural resources and capital for weapons and destructive activities exempt from civilian controls. Its military activities destroy the environment, directly through bombing and contamination, and indirectly as displaced peoples settle in new regions. Then, as the land is damaged, resources diminished, and people impoverished, unrest increases and those in power turn to military action, at home or abroad, to remain in control.[58]

Yet militarism is the world's priority: North or South, East or West. The world spends over one trillion dollars a year on arms. For about three-quarters of that amount, it could rebuild topsoil, replant forests, increase energy efficiency, and develop renewable energy sources.[59] But will it?

Perhaps this war has demonstrated a little more how the parts of a stable society – just, peaceful, ecological – fit together.

Those concerned for justice may see that a democratic society and economy exist only in relation to a healthy environment. Many still assume some armed struggles, arms sales, and nuclear or fossil-fuel technology can be justified, ignoring the cost to the air, land, and sea. But we risked climate breakdown and widespread extinction during this war. Perhaps both the left and the right will face the risk of their own extinction and accept that, with today's technology, neither earth nor society can survive militarism and environmental irresponsibility. Those working for peace may see that militarism goes hand in hand with an unhealthy environment and an unhealthy economy: an environment blasted, burnt, smothered and poisoned by weapons testing, transport and use; an economy bound to toxic activities such as the oil-burning automobile.

Those working to permit the earth to remain healthy may see that environmental degradation is not due to individual ignorance or evil, but rather to structural violence: socially fostered dominance. As a society, we justify dominating others, even if the result is war, poverty and environmental destruction. Militarism is supported by this economy, sucking money, labour and resources from people. But militarism, in turn, supports this economy, providing jobs and defending the state when it requests. Most people will defend this economy and the state that supervises it in order to defend their jobs and their "way of life."

We are so used to this that it is hard to imagine an alternative. But, more and more, we see that the world cannot remain healthy unless we convert the economy: stop rewarding militarism and start rewarding environmental responsibility.

Notes

[1] "The Ecology of War and Peace," a report by the Internation Union for the Conservation of Nature and Natural Resources, *Natural History*, November 1990, has a special look at scorched earth policies.

[2] Mayer, Sue and Paul Johnston, "Chemical Weapons and their Effects on the Environment," Greenpeace Report, February 1991. This examines chemical weapons, their history and effects on life-forms, especially in Middle East habitats, and has a strong recent bibliography.

[3] Smith, Gar, "Ecological Impacts of a Gulf War," *Earth Island Journal*, Winter 1991, has insights into Iraq's agriculture.

[4] Mayer, *op. cit.*

[5] See Cloudsley-Thompson, pp.27-29 in Miller, John M. (ed), "The Hidden Casualties: The Environmental Consequences of the Gulf Conflict," Vol.1, Arms Research Centre, San Francisco 1991. This has an excellent set of interviews with experts.

[6] Martin, p.20 in Miller, *ibid.*

[7] "Springtime of despair looms for Persian Gulf," UPI March 18, 1991, Greenbase, provides a summary of looming environmental problems.

[8] Pickaver, Alan, "Danger of Biological Weapons Highly Underestimated," February 14, 1991, Greenpeace Greenbase.

[9] Bryden, John, *Deadly Allies* (McClelland and Stewart Inc., 1989), describes biochemical weapons development by the U.S./European allies around World War Two.

[10] Chown, Diana, "Those Toxic Chemicals in Alberta," *Peace Magazine*, June 1990, pp.12, 31, describes the nerve gas work at Suffield, Alberta.

[11] Hippler, Jochen, "Iraq's Military Power: The German Connection," *Middle East Report*, January-February 1991, documents German industrial export for Iraqi weapons.

[12] *The Globe and Mail*, February 12, 1991.

[13] Wright, Susan, "The buildup that was," *The Bulletin of Atomic Scientists*, January-February 1989, pp.52-56, describes the build-up of U.S. biochemical weapons.

[14] Hippler, *op.cit.*

[15] Klare, Michael T., "Fueling the Fire: How We Armed the Middle East," *The Bulletin of Atomic Scientists*, January-February 1991, is a carefully cited summary of how the U.S. and the U.S.S.R. used arms sales in a war of influence.

[16] Waas, Murray, "What We Gave Saddam for Christmas," *Village Voice*, December 18, 1990, discusses how the U.S. and its allies armed Iraq.

[17] Walsh, Jackie, "Nuclear Dimensions," Greenpeace SITREP 16, February 16, 1991.

[18] Mayer, *op.cit.*

[19] Walsh, *op.cit.*

[20] See Landis in Miller, *op.cit.*, pp.15-17.

[21] "Iraqi Chemical Warfare Capabilities," Center for Defense Information Fact Sheet 23, August 1990.

[22] David Chiu, a member of a World Health Organization investigation team inspecting health facilities in Kuwait in June, found such a poster in one of the bunkers. (personal communication)

[23] Walsh, *op.cit.*

[24] Willis, John, "Farewell Atoms for Peace," unpublished Greenpeace commentary, February 7, 1991, Greenbase, discusses the bombing of the Iraqi reactors, and the credibility of the IAEA, Non-Proliferation Treaty, and "civilian reactors."

[25] Walsh, *op.cit.*

[26] Willis, *op.cit.*

[27] *The New York Times*, August 10, 1991.

[28] Price, Andrew R.G., "Possible Environmental Threats from the Current Gulf

War," Report to Greenpeace International, February 2, 1991; an excellent review of Gulf flora, fauna and habitat.

[29] *Ibid.*

[30] "A Mess in the Gulf," *The Middle East*, December 1989, summarizes the impact of oil spilling during the Iran-Iraq war. Also see Miller, *op.cit.*, pp.22-26.

[31] Walsh, Jackie, "The War on the Environment," Greenpeace SITREP 15, February 1, 1991.

[32] Simmonds, Mark and Kieran Mulvaney, "Environmental Impacts of the Oil Spills in the Persian Gulf," Greenpeace Report, February 1991.

[33] Renner, Michael G., "Military Victory, Ecological Defeat," *World Watch*, July-August 1991.

[34] Stolls, Amy (ed), "Gulf Cleanup Complicated by Lack of Funds as Oil Wells Continue to Burn," OSIR, Cutter Information Corp., Arlington, Ma., March 10, 1991, Greenbase.

[35] Walsh, Jackie, "Oil Spills and Oil Fires," Greenpeace SITREP 35, March 4, 1991, summarizes clean-up efforts and costs.

[36] "Persian Gulf Oil Spill Has Led to Extinction of 52 Species of Birds," DPA March 18, 1991, Greenbase.

[37] "Gulf Oil Spill Hits Key Coral Habitats Say Conservationists," Reuters, March 18, 1991, Greenbase.

[38] Simmonds, *op.cit.*; Walsh, *op.cit.*

[39] Walsh, *op.cit.*

[40] Price, A.R.G., Wrathall, T.J. and Bernard, S.M., "Occurrence of tar and other pollution in the Saudi Arabian shores of the Gulf," *Maritime Pollution Bulletin*, 18, 1987, pp. 650-651.

[41] "Kuwait Suffers Worst Day of Burning Oil Pollution," Reuters, March 18, 1991, Greenbase.

[42] *The New York Times*, August 14, 1991.

[43] Horgan, John, "Up in Flames," *Scientific American*, May 1991.

[44] Horgan, John, "Burning Questions," *Scientific American*, July 1991.

[45] *Ibid.*

[46] Horgan, John, "Up in Flames," *op.cit.*

[47] *The New York Times*, August 14, 1991.

[48] Horgan, *op.cit.*

[49] Horgan, John, "Burning Questions," *op.cit.*

[50] Horgan, John, "Up in Flames," *op.cit.*

[51] Horgan, John, "Burning Questions," *op.cit.*

[52] Tokar, Brian, "Energy Blues and Oil," *Z Magazine*, January 1991, pp.22-27, is an excellent overview of the economics and politics of oil, nuclear and renewable energy.

[53] *International Herald Tribune*, August 17, 1991.

[54] Tokar, *op.cit.*

[55] *Ibid.*

[56] *Ibid.*

[57] Dale, Stephen, "The U.N.: Linking Disarmament and Development," *Press for Conversion*, January 1991, p.32.

58 M'Gonigle, Michael and Suzanne Rose, "Recovering the Root: Militarism and the Ecological Society," in Perry, Tom Sr. (ed), *Peace in the 1990s*, 1991.

59 Rosenblum, Simon, "Militarism and Environmental Security," *Ploughshares Monitor*, September 1990, pp.14-15.

Part 2: REDISCOVERING THE MIDDLE EAST

The People of Iraq

The people, the people and their labour: this is the departure point
and the arriving point in the essay of Marwan Hassan and the
photos of Jamelie Hassan.

They lived and studied in Iraq during 1978 and 1979. News
reports for them were infused with memories of sight and sound
and taste, and most of all, memories of specific, living, people.

In the essay and photos that follow, Jamelie Hassan and Marwan
Hassan offer to us who are outsiders, who have no Iraqi faces, no
Iraqi song birds, no Iraqi marshes in our memories, their own
recollections and understandings of these peoples, their lands and
their histories.

It is upon those that our military, in concert with others,
inflicted the catastrophes of destruction, disease and death. It is
these same enduring peoples, their lands, with their understanding
of our "addition" to their history, whom we face today, and with
whom we will have to make our accounting tomorrow.

al-Iraq:
Etymology Quite Certain

Marwan Hassan

Photographs by Jamelie Hassan

WE HAD TRAVELLED TO QURNA — A TOWN AT THE JUNCTURE OF THE
*Tigris and Euphrates rivers – the mythic setting of the garden of Eden. Here
the sunsets were startling, the sky turquoise, purple and scarlet over the date
palms. The setting sun was reflecting off the three river surfaces and created
the effect of three suns in the horizon descending down, down into this ancient
earth. Throughout the Mesopotamian basin there are hundreds of small culti-
vator villages made of mud bricks with irrigation fields. The peasants still hug
close to the earth, working the soil with a calm endurance.*

*We stayed in a stuffy cinder block hotel on the main street in Qurna. In the
morning we got a ride in a collectivo bus that would take us into the Marshes.
Here the Marsh Arabs have lived for thousands of years cultivating rice. Until
recently they built their homes, their tribal communal long houses, their boats,
their mats, indeed almost all things, out of reeds or clay.*

*In Chubaish, a major village some way into the marshes, we stopped again.
For the children of these marshes not only Baghdad but Qurna itself was a long
way off, a new presence. Oil had been discovered in the south. The Marshes
were changing.*

Women fishing in the marshes of the Tigris and Euphrates rivers in southern Iraq. All the photos accompanying this essay were taken by Jamelie Hassan in 1979.

The most unusual culture of the Marsh Arabs, evolved within this delicate ecology, is just one of many cultures and peoples being levelled and destroyed by the massive U.S.A.-led bombardment authorized by the United Nations Security Council Resolution 678 "to take all necessary measures."

In Baghdad, in the springtime, more than a half dozen different song birds with speckled or ruby throats can be heard trilling in the many public gardens. This great riverine basin is one of the main migratory paths in Asia for hundreds of species of birds and insects. The site of the ancient agrarian civilizations of Ur, Babylon and Assyria, its soil is both harsh and generous. With careful irrigation the earth here is fecund, quick to respond to the human labour that shows her respect. But if neglected, insulted or poorly turned, soil salinity sets in, impoverishing the land. In an ambitious program, the Iraqi government began to wash the soil to remove the salt that has accumulated over decades and centuries.

Now come the bombers laying waste the earth as in Vietnam. "Ten thousand sorties" crows some reporter sounding gleeful at the magnitude of the destruction. Since January 16, 1991, an average of 18,000 tons of bombs per day. Will a crop ever grow here again?

What people, what soil, what nation, what state is the U.S.A.-led coalition laying waste? And for what reasons?

None of these questions can be answered without a sense of the multiple and diverse layers of historic Iraq. None can be investigated from the dominant centre where military and political decisions are made. Each must be pursued, nomadically, from the margins – evading, slipping free, eluding the generalizations and edicts of the authorities and specialists who profess to decode all things Iraqi for the uninitiated.

Remember: The bombing is surgical. The bombs on target. No collateral damage. Pin point accuracy. Eighty per cent effective...

Technoporn.

Iraq is not one people, one culture, one civilization. It is layered over time, history, space, geography and archaeology. It is more than the

Chubaish, a marsh village in southern Iraq.

sum total of Arab or Kurdish, Shia or Sunni, Assyrian or Babylonian cultures. And the emergence of the Iraqi state does not follow along a linear trajectory from Ottoman Turkey to post-Ottoman, from British colonial Iraq to modern Iraq.

Remember: *Baghdad – alf layla wa layla, kan wa ma kan min zaman fi baghdad dar as-salam* – "a thousand nights and a night, there was and there wasn't, once upon a time in Baghdad, the city of peace..."

Baghdad, that figment of Western, orientalist imagination, is a real, live, sweltering city of millions of workers and peasants, bureaucrats and scholars, factories and homes. Outside it lies Medinat at-thawra, a working class city of more than a million people, created after 1959 for peasants from the south of Iraq. The U.S. high command would have us believe that this is a nation of concrete, of military installations, and not a single human. When I heard that B-52 bombers and Tomahawk cruise missiles were striking the outskirts of Baghdad, I did not think of military installations but of this congested working class city of cinder block and mud homes with many children. Where would the children run to?

I wandered through the paper souk, looking for a fountain pen. Booksellers and paper merchants were talking, reading books, sleeping. Near the entrance I stopped and had a yoghurt, I went out into the dusk and walked along the old embankment of the Tigris River. The sky turned a deep green from the sunlight reflected off the crowns of the mighty date palms. The palms explained to me the ancient meaning of the sun.

Yes, the invasion of Kuwait is illegal. Unacceptable. The majority of Arabs and Arab Canadians do not support the action. If they express solidarity with Iraq, it is not with the regime but with the Iraqi people; the mainstream press distorts this solidarity, ignoring all historical facts. We must recall that those very same states (England, France and the U.S.A.) stood by while Israel invaded and demolished Lebanon not once but twice, in 1978 and 1982; they sought only to dilute the United Nations Security Council resolutions and then subjected the General Assembly to a campaign of hatred and ridicule.

For the Palestinians and Lebanese under brutal, Israeli occupation,

A tailor's niche, Shar'a Rashid.

for Iraqis whose nuclear reactor was destroyed by Israel without any Euro-American moral outrage, the standards imposed by Euro-American interests reduce international morality and justice to an obscure, medieval discipline.

This conflict however breaks through the old, eurocentric paradigms. *The Arab mind* or *the Muslim mind* – where are these metaphysical entities? The Palestinian or Iraqi as terrorist? Who are these children with stones and school notebooks? Sixty per cent of the population in Arab countries is under twenty. So just who is dying?

We hear the outcry that no moral norms or civil society exist within the region. One wonders what the police bombing of Philadelphia African Americans conjures up for Arabs with respect to *the American mind,* or the siege of Oka with respect to *the Canadian mind.* If Saddam Hussein is the new, diabolic, global dictator, classification: subhuman, then one wonders what Bush, Mitterand, Mulroney and the other cohorts represent for laying waste Baghdad and Basra? Thus the slide into platitudes, to justify the destruction.

I awoke at sunrise, lay in bed half restless, half stiff, finally I got up. I went over to the baker's across the street and waited in line for fifteen minutes, and watched the baker load the oven. I was not bored at all while watching this fellow work quickly in front of the hot open oven, sweat running down him, his hair damp on his forehead. He went about his labour in a steady, quick, precise manner, not wasting a gesture. . . loading the oven as his young apprentice handed him trays of loaves that he sprinkled with flour, and he placed each loaf diagonally on a sixteen foot long spatula-like board, he then made a small diagonal incision on the top of each loaf with a thin piece of wood; then he basted the loaves. And he pushed the baker's pole into the oven, tilted it and the loaves adhered to the hot floor of the oven. . . this step he repeated until the oven was full in a semi-circle with about ten to fifteen rows, then he proceeded to withdraw the first loaves. The customers waited in a queue, often took the number of desired hot loaves themselves; they made their own change – during all this hardly anyone spoke, neither an unfriendly nor impatient atmosphere pervaded, but rather one of steady calm unison, as everyone's eyes were fixed expectantly on the sweating human being. . .

The long road to shaping new polities in the Middle East has been barricaded by repeated blockages in each state experiment: in Nasserist Egypt and Communist Iraq, in Libya, in Algeria and in Lebanon. One consequence is the emergence of more and more forceful and authoritarian political entities. The Ba'th Party – which began by idealizing a cultural renaissance wedded, in theory, to democratizing socialist and statist models of nationalist politics under its secular founders, Michel Aflaq and Salah ad-din al-Bitar, one Christian and the other a Muslim – was transformed into an authoritarian party with a strong military echelon. Ba'thism became a durable force, which was to give continuity in two different versions in Syria and Iraq.

In the face of a ruthless U.S.A. foreign policy which treated each democratizing endeavour in an Arab country or Turkey or Iran, as a threat to U.S.A. economic interests, it was not surprising that a party such as the Ba'th, and an individual as ruthless as Saddam Hussein, would emerge to challenge the U.S.A. hegemony, while covertly co-operating with the CIA. Double dealing, secret accords, lies and the hyper-security state apparatus became necessities for securing and retaining power by the Ba'th leadership. These forces resulted in the militarization of the state and the abuse of human rights.

Having said this, the modern phase of development between 1969-1979 was not without accomplishments as a result of the collective labour of Iraqis. During the period of British hegemony, 1919 to 1958, most development had been directly connected to either the military or the exploitation of oil. Diseases such as bilharzia, cholera, smallpox, dysentery, malaria, polio, trachoma and other ophthalmic diseases were either epidemic or endemic. After 1969, village clinics were established in many towns and most diseases were brought under control or eliminated. Education, formerly elitist, private and often militaristic under the British, became egalitarian and free to the PhD level for both women and men. Military training continued but under Ba'th control. Literacy classes were established. Those workers who were illiterate were given free time off work to attend classes. Minimum wages were implemented. Housing was built and rent controls introduced.

These changes were paid for by nationalizing the oil industry and redistributing capital back into small scale factories which produced local consumer goods: milk, hygienic items, paper etc. Two new classes emerged: a national capitalist and a modern middle class, both of which challenged the old landholding and tribal elites and the traditional merchant and religious classes. As Hanna Batatu has carefully documented in his book, *The Old Social Classes and the Revolutionary Movements of Iraq*, this wrenching modernization process – introducing technology and science into an agrarian society, and the nationalization of oil – furnished the capital for national development. But it did not bring about democratization.

The regime's authoritarian nature and its repressive state apparatus were not politically accepted. But the economic transformation and social improvements affected enough people, particularly among the new, urban middle classes, to keep the administrative infrastructure functioning. All these innovations of party and state were being outstripped by the global economy.

At the martyrs tomb in Samarra, after we had climbed the minaret, we went to the mosque. The peasant women tied coloured ribbons and paper prayers to the gold and silver bars and chanted Koranic verses.

Karbala mosque, Baghdad.

This Janus-faced regime has a semi-secular mask. No one in the streets of Baghdad, down on Saddoun Street or in the souks behind Rashid street in the old quarter, would imagine Saddam Hussein or the Ba'thists as devout Muslims. Indeed, some of their most bitter clashes have been with the Islamic movements, ranging from the Muslim Brotherhood to the Iranian clerical revolutionaries. Five or six per cent of the population is Christian; they have played a leading role in the economic and educational development of the culture, and have a lot at stake in maintaining the fragile secularism.

While Iraq transformed itself economically, it was also transformed in other spheres. A neo-patriarchy emerged among the new elites, the result of multiple collisions between the traditional religious and merchant classes and values, and the new processes of modernism and westernization. The contradictions between modernity and the old patriarchy gave rise to this distorted force, which sought to contain the frustrations of traditional culture and the animosities which arose: between colonialism and neo-imperialism; between the authoritarian state and the cultural revival; between the struggle of old classes still wedded to old ethos and the new classes attracted to inchoate new values; between the division of sexes and the emerging secularist impulses.

Carlos, my closest friend, and I were in the foreign student dormitory of the University of Baghdad, where students from Japan, Vietnam, China and many other countries lived. I was having tea with Carlos and a Chinese student from Kanzu province who was studying Arabic. The Chinese student asked me about North America. I found it difficult to describe.

Arabs, people from other developing countries, and indeed thousands of Europeans, in particular English, Germans and Russians, became Iraqi citizens through marriage, or as a result of working in the country. This is in contrast with Saudi Arabia, Kuwait and other Gulf states, where foreign workers are generally denied citizenship, and locked out of the social and political structures of the state. This is particularly significant for the tens of thousands of Palestinian and Lebanese migrants made homeless by Israeli invasions and occupation of

Palestine and Lebanon. Iraq built a more complex social infrastructure and redistributed the wealth to a greater number of people – although not widely enough, not quickly enough.

The emergence of an industrialized, autonomous Iraq, distorted by and connected to an authoritarian party though it was, disturbed the elites in the despotic Gulf states and in Spartan Israel.

Nevertheless the U.S.A., Britain, France and the U.S.S.R. found it convenient to fuel Iraq with weapons to contain Iran, through eight horrible years of war. Arabs, Kurds and Iranians suffered grievously through those years. A general perception emerged among some in the region that the Emir of Kuwait, the ibn Saud family, and the U.S.A. altogether were bleeding Iraq dry to halt and contain Iranian power and expansion. For the new militancy of Iran could not be countered by these old oligarchies in Saudi Arabia and Kuwait without destroying their own fossilized political and economic foundations. This occurred while the Iran-Iraq war enriched the European, American and Japanese economies while it bankrupted both the combatants, leaving the majority of people in the region from Lebanon to the West Bank to the Syrians to the migrant workers throughout the Gulf in harsh circumstances.

And then, between 1988 and 1990, Kuwait helped drive down the oil prices, syphoned off oil from an Iraqi-Kuwaiti disputed zone, and over-produced in violation of OPEC agreements, all to the economic detriment of Iraq.

Meanwhile the questions of Palestine and Lebanon remained unresolved, sustaining the general instability of the region. It became clear that neither the U.S.A. nor the Europeans desired a meaningful peace, and that Israel would not come to the negotiating table with the PLO as Palestinian representatives. Palestinian openness to a political solution, after three long years of the intifada and the PLO opening at the Algiers conference of the PNC, accepting the two-state solution, all U.N. resolutions and recognizing the state of Israel, is lost in the pursuit of other aims by a rejectionist U.S.A. and Israel.

I was with my Central African roommates, Everiste and Carlos. They were unhappy in Baghdad, they wanted to return to Africa, but Bokassa was in

*power in the Central African Republic, and they were worried and anxious
about their families. Carlos, dissatisfied with Baghdad, would eventually
leave and go to a polytechnical institute in France. He would work long hours
in a restaurant in Nice to pay for his education. And then return to Central
Africa after the fall of Bokassa.*

Workers and peasants of the Middle East, who created the petroleum
industry and all its possibilities, saw the oil spill upon the earth, an
historic opportunity seeping away while Kuwait and Saudi Arabia rein-
vested their surplus capital overseas rather than back into the
region... while Israel bombed Iraq's nuclear facility... while Israel and
Syria demolished Lebanon... while the U.S.A. landed troops in Lebanon and bombed the Bekaa town of Ba'albek and later Libya... while
Egypt went bankrupt after the rapprochement... while Algeria fell into
a new servile relationship with France... while the CIA cynically used
the Kurds, goaded them on, giving them enough covert assistance to be
weak combatants but not enough to achieve their nationalist goals and
then left them nakedly vulnerable to Ba'th, Turkish and Iranian
repression... while the Iran-contra intrigues took place... while Israel
bombed the PLO headquarters in Tunisia...

Where was the U.N. Security Council to censure these events and
take unanimous concerted action to guarantee international law?
Where was the West's humane concern? But in those days the U.S.A.
dismissed the U.N. as a harlot of the Third World.

In the region, cynicism set in. The people close to the ground, the
tillers, the workers in the oil industry, the cleaners in the street, the
women doing double duty in the fields and village homes lived in desperate circumstances from which their leaders could not deliver them.

On the ground, the peasant cultivators in Mesopotamia, the
Palestinians in the West Bank and Gaza under Israeli occupation, the
Lebanese displaced by the war, the migrant Egyptian, Sudanese and
Yemeni labourers in the Gulf, and the poor North African immigrant
workers in France realized that history and water would leave them
behind, that change and bread would not come from Europe and
America, or redound to their benefit. It would not come from their own
elites. But it might come if they challenged Europe and America
through popular uprisings.

The evening had folded in upon itself and was quite beautiful, I sat shirtless . . . no flies bugging me . . . the chirping of crickets in the short grasses by the plaster wall reminded me of my last night in south-western Ontario before I had left for Iraq, when two different insects – a cricket and some sort of beetle – were playing a duet in the middle of the night. The cricket with its steady constant chirping provided the rhythm, the beetle, a violin-like solo, fashioned a strange counterpoint into the dawn. This is one sound that is universal, the chirping of the cricket . . . I'd heard it in Colorado, Mexico, British Columbia, Ontario, now Iraq. It was repetitive without being monotonous . . . now it momentarily halted . . . I heard a car going down the road . . .

A constant hunger mixed with ennui was palpable in the air, it was difficult to imagine what was in the minds of some people here . . .

Saddam Hussein did not invade Kuwait for the sake of the Palestinians, any more than his invasion of Iran was for the liberation of the Iranian Arabs in the south. These military actions were tactics to evade the new populism growing from below, and which could not be bought off. The capital – both economic and political – was running out.

But it would be naive to think that a comprehensive, negotiated peace settlement for the entire region is a false notion just because Saddam Hussein insists on linkage. Such a peace, not this neo-imperialist Euro-American adventure, is the real vehicle for stability for all the countries in the region.

Two Finnish women friends were drinking date arak on the patio. They were laughing. One wrote a rollicking, humorous poem about men. They each spoke several languages fluently and wrote poetry. One liked the desert. They sometimes did translations for Finnish companies while studying.

By invading Kuwait, Saddam Hussein furnished the U.S.A. with the pretext for military intrusion in the region. However the U.S.A.'s deliberate misuse of the United Nations will only bring further instability. On the ground – down in the street where Bush and Mitterand, Shamir and Mulroney don't venture – where the Arabs, Iraqi and Palestinian, Egyptian and Lebanese, scrape and scramble for a crust, things are happening. And not just among Arabs, not just among Muslims.

Samir Amin wrote: "Throughout all history, capitalism has polarized at the global level. It has not lessened the gap between West and South, or North and South. On the contrary, this gap has deepened over time. I believe that this polarization at the global level is going to be worse in the future than it has been in the past. That is, the North-South gap will continue to deepen and to increase in severity...."

In developing countries throughout Asia, Africa and Latin America, the people are anxiously watching this war. They do not support Saddam Hussein who really is a small figure at the back of the stage. The vilification of Saddam is not new. They've heard it all before: the British doing it to Nasser, the Americans doing it to Ghaddafi, Israelis doing it to Arafat... Such jingoism dismisses the Arabs from history. For the Arabs this is not a crisis based on a challenge from pan-Arabism, or pan-Islamist movements, nor does it represent a retreat from history, or collective identification with Saddam Hussein. Their challenge is an insistence on fuller participation, in every way, to transform their own societies into developing, autonomous and democratizing societies. After the passing of the Ba'th, these aspirations will persist. And it is this which is lost in the bombing reports and the glorification of the celestial armada assembled by the Euro-American coalition.

From the heavens the U.S.A. may achieve a humiliating military victory over the Iraqi people, remove Saddam Hussein from power, even occupy the country. But it is unlikely that any of the present regimes of the region will be able to sustain hegemony in collaboration with this aggression. A newer and far worse crisis will erupt, demanding an even higher level of intervention. After all, this U.S.A. hegemony is the old one retailored, and its goal is not to clothe the people either in the coat of democracy or in the trousers of autonomous development. No one can seriously believe for an instant that any of the nations – France or Italy, U.S.S.R. or U.S.A., England or Canada (given their inventory of crimes in the region) – seriously care one ounce about the Kurds or any other Iraqis.

For those who want to know what's going on, go down to the streets and into the fields, sit in the stone houses, mud huts and reed homes, talk to the women and children, rather than the patriarchs on Capitol Hill or Parliament Hill, in Riyadh or Tel Aviv. Find out what the real

Brass workers in the Baghdad souk.

cost of *khubz, summun*. . .bread. . .amounts to, not in U.S. bucks, not in British pounds, not in French francs, but in human sweat.

The objective of this destructive engagement is not the liberation of Kuwait, nor the removal of Saddam Hussein from power, nor the assertion of a new order governed by some moral imperative and a revitalized United Nations. Suddenly Bush and Baker take the United Nations for an evening waltz at the Waldorf Astoria: the U.S.A. has more cynically exploited the United Nations than Saddam Hussein has misused the Palestinian cause. No, the objective is more tragic. It is the destruction of the Iraqi people and their potential. After all the moral outrage by Western leaders to justify the bombing of Iraq, the fact is that those bombs are killing people not simply taking out military installations – despite all the assurances of General Powell and Secretary Cheney.

We smoked cigarettes together in the alcove of the rose garden by the pool. A close Iraqi friend cautioned me not to pass harsh judgments against her culture. That it was a society in change, in struggle. Momentarily this Iraqi was enigmatic, but it was my impatient and judgmental self that made her so. And my failure to not quite grasp the substance of Iraqi culture.

The Arabs and the Kurds are the primary victims in all of this. But unnoticed, unrecorded is the development that the Europeans, while receiving Christmas gifts and Easter eggs from Uncle Sam, are now indentured in a renewed vassalage to an arrogant U.S.A.; they are consigned to a second class role in the persisting brutal relations with the Arab peoples, to insure a secure supply of oil from the U.S.A. transnational petroleum corporations. For the Arab heads of state, history will consign them to the garbage heap. The Arab peoples will not forget the level of brutality that has been meted out to them in the name of a perverse and disjointed interpretation and application of international law. The consequences we cannot even begin to know or anticipate; we can only be assured of one thing: a new and more disturbing *khamsin*, on the horizon. The contradictions run deep, the tillers of the soil are persistent.

Remember: al-Iraq, etymology quite certain from the Arabic 'araq meaning: "perspiration" – quite literally, "sweat." Or again in the more inflected forms of the verb: "to strike roots," or "to be deeply rooted," or again in the noun 'irq: "root" or "stem" or "vein" or "descent." Sooner or later it all gets back to mother earth.

Samir Amin noted in his book *Eurocentrism* : "A more humane future – one that is universalist and respectful of all – is not an ineluctable necessity, destined to impose itself; it is only an objectively necessary possibility, for which one must strive. . . ."

To reduce the present tragedy to either the troubled Arabs or mindless Muslims or even the authoritarian personality of one man is to dismiss history. It is to climb on the backs of the wretched of the earth, the dead Iraqis; it is to believe that as victor, one has arrived at a transcendental plane of pure righteousness; it is to reveal the self-justifications, the deluded morality, and ultimately the mass psychosis that only a war has the power to induce.

We were walking down a dusty road to the Gates of Babylon. Beautiful date groves were near the river, we stopped beneath them. A peasant was working nearby tending the palms, he asked if we wanted some dates. He tied up his jellaba – gown – between his legs and quickly climbed up the date tree and cut down a cluster of dates and offered them to us. We ate them squatting on the ridge of the irrigation ditch, in the heat, dust and sun.

[*An earlier version of this essay appeared in*
Canadian Forum, March 1991.]

Drawing Boundaries, Dividing Cultures

Emile Nucho

Can anyone claim to be utterly without interest in the Arab
people – even if it takes some spectacularly newsworthy event to
arouse that interest?...And who can claim that the Arabs never
figure in his conversation – for most of us are quite ready to form
opinions and pass judgments without having all the facts in
hand.[1]

THE GULF CRISIS, LIKE NO OTHER CRISIS BEFORE IT, SHOWED MANY
Canadians how very little they knew about the Middle East, its constituent countries, its Arab population, their culture, religions, in short
who they are.[2] To make matters worse, the media certainly did not provide the necessary historical tableau needed to put events in perspective. This tableau, like a great abstract painting, has both complexity
and discernible patterns.

The Middle East has been one of the civilizational heartlands of the
world, sharing for 50 or 60 centuries an uninterrupted history.[3] It also
has been, particularly its Syrian core, a crossroads of migrating people
and trade, and has seen an almost continuous mixing of cultures and
armies from Asia, Africa and Europe. It is probably most familiar to

126

readers as the birthplace of three of the world's major religious movements.

Ancient civilizations

Ancient civilization first appeared in Mesopotamia (today's Iraq), where the Euphrates and Tigris rivers meet, and later in the Nile river valley and delta (Egypt). Born of primitive agricultural settlements, these civilizations early developed into strong centralized states.

Egypt's history has been unique: the impression of an integral 5,200 year history, with its absorptive abilities, gave its people a sense of national distinctiveness which rarely has been lost, either by them or their neighbours, to this day.[4]

The same could not be said of Mesopotamia, with its succession of rival empires and a geography much more open to the migration of people within and through it. These ancient, semitic empires left such indelible effects on the people of the region that many groups still trace their myths of suffering and hope to that era. And through the semitic Phoenicians, these same empires/kingdoms transmitted to the Greeks such things as the plough, the wheel, the division of the year into 12 months, the week into seven days, and many still existing systems of weights and measures.[5]

The advance and retreat of conquering states, with the attendant rebellions of fragmented local populations, often seeking help from other, rival external forces, continued through the Persian, Greek, Roman, and Christian Byzantine empires. (This pattern has remained generally unchanged to this day.) For centuries the Middle East was a strategic trading and cultural crossroads of the world. But during the Byzantine era, intra-Christian sectarian rivalries and wars with Persia exhausted the economies of the area and the energies of the people. This was a prelude to the Arab-Muslim conquests of the 7th century.

The Arab-Muslim era

In less than 100 years following the affirmation of Islam in Makka (Mecca) and Madina, the Arabs fanned out of the Arabian peninsula, north and east into Syria and Persia, then westwards to North Africa and Spain, where they established and consolidated great empires with relative speed and ease.

Although most Arabs consider that Arab history began with the Islamic period, pre-Islamic Arabs were important for 29 centuries in the Arabian peninsula and beyond. They migrated to Syria, Mesopotamia, Egypt and Africa, establishing settlements, kingdoms and trading routes, transferring goods, services and cultures. Most were animists or pagans, but many were Christian or Jewish.[6]

Generally speaking, the Arabs are semites who originated in the Arabian peninsula. As they spread, they mixed with and Arabized local populations. The cohesiveness of the Arabs rests upon a common sense of history, a common written language, common customs and culture and, to a very large extent, shared religion.[7] While there is also a great diversity within the overall sense of oneness, and though today Arabs live in various recently formed nation-states, there remains among them a supra-national ideal of Arab unity.

The 7th century Arab conquests, while military in nature, did not destroy the local people and cultures. The Christian and Jewish populations of northern Arabia, Syria, Palestine, Egypt and Mesopotamia were given the respect due "Peoples of the Book" (Bible). While there is no question that there were persecutions of local minorities from time to time, by rulers and/or mobs during the next centuries, Christian and Jewish minorities participated quite fully and thrived under the Islamic regimes.

The 7th to the 11th centuries were a "Golden Age" of learning and progress for the Arabs, whether Muslim, Christian, or Jewish. The relatively prevalent western folk perception of Muslim hordes riding out of the desert, a sword in one hand and the Qur'an in the other, giving all non-Muslim peoples they conquered the choice of one or the other, is long discredited, though regrettably still bandied about. The tolerance and the stability which the Arabs, by and large, maintained in the region through two successive empires, the Umayya centred in Damascus (661-750) and the Abbassi centred in Baghdad (750-1258), allowed for the flowering of a new Arab-led culture, based on combination and adaptation.

The Arabic language quickly became the bond which connected the empire's several regions. It was not only the language of the ruling elites, but the religious language of the Qur'an as well. It became the language of learning and the arts, and for a time even was used as the language of science in parts of Europe. Arabic was to survive all the vicissitudes which befell the Arabs, partly because of its connection with Islam, and partly because of its richness and adaptability. Arab culture also had a profound influence on Europe, ranging from the very mundane (how to make sugar) to the philosophical, by way of the medical (surgery), mathematical (the zero and algebra), the artistic (lute and flamenco), and the culinary.

What then went wrong after the 11th century?

The very size of the empires created serious centrifugal forces and fragmentation, particularly at the outer edges of the domains. From the east, Mongol incursions into the Abbassi empire culminated in a full-fledged invasion, the sacking of Baghdad (1258), the devastation of northern Syria, and an end to the empire. The horror of this continues to be remembered as a seminal, historic event. The memory was rekindled in the psyche of modern-day Arabs with the American bombing of Baghdad.

One parallel is uncanny. The Mongol attacks systematically destroyed the intricate agricultural irrigation system, much of which was constructed of underground ceramic piping, which sustained the rural economy of Iraq. This plunged the area into a severe economic decline. In time the irrigation system was slowly and painstakingly reconstructed, which helped in the relative agricultural recovery of Iraq over the next seven centuries. The new system remained in continuous use until it was again destroyed, this time by technologically advanced hordes of American B-52s carpet bombing the Iraqi countryside.

The decline of Arab-Muslim power also was accelerated by events on the Mediterranean coast, with the arrival from Europe of the Crusaders, in Arab history known as the *Franj*.[8] This was to be the Islamic Middle East's first confrontation with European invaders, who came to capture Jerusalem and booty, and remained in the area for two centuries.

Beginning in 1097, European campaigns established a string of kingdoms and principalities along a coastal strip from Turkey in the north to Palestine in the south. Their presence in the region, and the almost continuous Muslim efforts to evict them, and the turmoil and devastation caused by the Mongols were enough to disrupt permanently and reorient trading routes and patterns.

Thus to a large extent, the decline of the Arab world resulted from a diminution of trade between the Arab heartland and Byzantium/Europe, on one side, and Persia and India on the other. By the end of this period, the Arab-Muslim east no longer was the main repository of science, of philosophy and the arts. Arabs completely lost control of their destiny. Islam, not coincidentally, became stagnant and unimaginative. Attempts to vitalize it were viewed with suspicion by clerics and rulers alike, in a spirit of tantamount isolation from the outside world. Aspects of orthodoxy which encouraged submission to the ruler and which emphasized "order" were enhanced, while aspects of Islam which focused on justice and an equitable society were played down.[9] Ironically, the final ejection of the Europeans left behind an exhausted and weakened region, opening its population to conquest by a new and vigorous power that would rule it for the next four hundred years.

The Ottoman Turkish era

The Turks, like the Mongols and Tartars before them, came from central Asia, and settled in areas occupied today by Afghanistan, northern Iran, Soviet Central Asia, and Anatolia, the heartland of modern Turkey, during which period they had converted to Islam. Initially, Arab rulers of Baghdad recruited them in ever-increasing numbers as mercenaries, but the slaves gradually became the masters, and by 1051 the Seljuk Turks were in control of Baghdad and what was left of its empire. The Ottoman Turks succeeded the Seljuks and by 1493 they had captured the capital of the Christian Byzantine empire, Constantinople (Istanbul). By 1516 the Ottomans were in control of most of the Arab regions.

> Ottoman political theory, ... as understood by the average [governor] held that the conquered peoples, especially if non-Muslim (or non-Sunni) were flocks ... As human cattle the

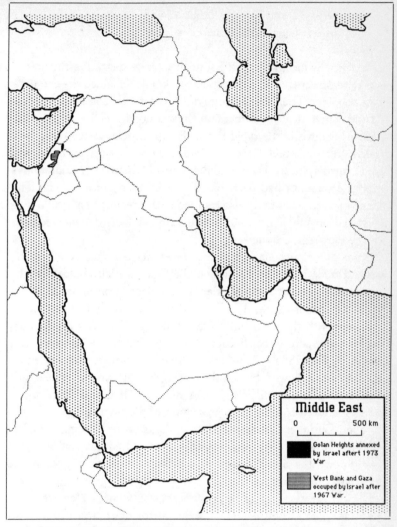

B.C. TEACHERS' FEDERATION: *UNDERSTANDING THE MIDDLE EAST CRISIS*
The Middle East. Dotted line represents current borders.

conquered were to be milked, fleeced and allowed to live their own lives so long as they gave no trouble.[10]

This essentially meant that the political, social and ethnic structures of the Arab east were not seriously affected. Arabic remained the language of the people.[11] The four centuries of Ottoman rule combined oppression and benign neglect, with a resulting economic decline of the Arab regions. Meanwhile the rapid rise in European technology, and their parallel and successful search for alternate sea routes to India and China, further eroded the foundations upon which the Middle East's regional economies had been based: the India-to-Europe trade. The decline of this transit trade also resulted in the decline of a local industry specializing in luxury and agricultural products destined for the wealthy European consumer.

Syrian merchants made a desperate effort to revive some of the overland trade routes to Persia and the Gulf. Initially helped by the Venetians, the effort restored Aleppo to a place of prominence in the overland trade for a time. The French King Francis I quickly signed an agreement with the Ottoman Sultan, Suleyman I, laying the foundation for wider and deeper European incursions into the eastern Mediterranean. This 1535 "Capitulation" treaty concerned with trade monopolies was followed by another in 1740 with more far-reaching implications. It put all French and non-French Christian pilgrims, traders and visitors, under the protection of the French flag. The way was open for direct interference in the affairs of the Ottoman empire. The French established trading settlements and educational missions up and down the Syrian coast, soon claiming to protect all Catholic Christians of the east.

The British were not to be outdone by the French. However, as a Protestant power, they had no natural constituency in the Middle East. But with Napoleon's invasion of Egypt and Palestine in 1799, a squadron of the British Navy helped the besieged Ottoman troops halt the French advance and force their ultimate withdrawal from Egypt. In the same year, that British squadron whisked to safety a soon-to-become-powerful ruler of Mount Lebanon just before he was to be arrested by the local Ottoman governor. This act established them as friends of the Druze of Lebanon, and with their role in ousting Napoleon, the British gained full entry into the politics of the Middle East.

European domination

The modern history of the Middle East can be said to begin with Napoleon's invasion of Egypt. The French Emperor's reason was mainly strategic: to cut off British access to India and the East and establish French hegemony. But, like the British later, French ambitions also were fuelled by a certain romantic view of the East, some residual "crusading" spirit, a new post-revolutionary rationalist sense of having a special mission to spread the new spirit of equality, fraternity and liberty to other, less fortunate people (*mission civilisatrice*), an early manifestation of the British "white man's burden." In fact, Napoleon brought along a veritable army of archeologists, scientists, doctors, linguists and dreamers who became the founders of modern "Orientalism," the outside "experts" on the Middle East and its peoples.[12]

The swift Napoleonic invasion prompted a process of critical self-examination, among the religious and later among the more secular intellectual Muslims. Arabs rapidly divided into different schools of thought as they tried to come to grips with the new reality.

Several intelligent and ambitious rulers in Egypt and North Africa, seeing the Ottoman empire was no match for European military technology, resolved to learn and to utilize European methods. Muhammad Ali of Egypt imported French instructors to establish a European-style military academy. He also sent small groups of Egyptian youth to Europe to be educated. At about the same time, Protestant and Catholic missionaries were arriving in Beirut, in ever greater numbers, to establish schools there and in some of the hinterland towns. These missionaries inevitably planted the seeds of dissent among members of the nascent urban bourgeoisie.

While the urban Muslim populations of the Syro-Palestinian littoral were not immune to these influences, local Christian communities were the most affected. By the mid-19th century an important number of intellectuals in Beirut, Damascus and particularly Cairo began an intellectual renaissance known as the "Arab Awakening."[13] It was inevitable, under the circumstances, that the ideas of nationalism, central to several European 19th century revolutions, began to circulate in the large cities of the Middle East. The conviction that Ottoman control could be weakened or overthrown developed, even though not all sectors of the population entertained such notions.

The opening of the Suez Canal in 1869 was a momentous event, spurring the transformation of the Egyptian economy and politics. More importantly, it became the instrument of future European, particularly British, intervention in Egyptian and Middle East affairs. Indeed, in 1882 the British invaded Egypt to crush their first serious challenge. Led by an officer educated in the new military academy established by Muhammad Ali, the revolt threatened the rule of Britain's local allies, the landed and merchant class, and British control over the vital Suez Canal, the new path to India and Asia.

Whether in Egypt, Syria, or Palestine, the old local establishment was being challenged by a new urban middle class. The former were composed of notables whose power derived from landed, feudal relations, from inherited socio-religious lineage, or from wealth gleaned from mercantilism or imperial favour-mongering. The younger, more educated challengers viewed them as impediments to their new nationalist and reformist aspirations.

World War One

1914 changed the face of the Middle East. Germany was allied with Turkey, against France and Britain. Three persistent problems – Palestine, Lebanon and the Gulf – are legacies of that war. Thus, it would be no exaggeration to say that the Persian Gulf crisis of 1990-1991 is a direct descendant of the events shaped by World War One.

The British entered the war firmly in control of Egypt. The French were seeking imperial parity with Britain, and both wanted to grab territory from the Ottomans, a persistent, long-standing obsession which was shared by the Austrians, Russians and Germans. Indeed, the Germans recently had received several important commercial concessions from the Turks which, among other things, would have given them rail access to the Gulf.

Coinciding with war in Europe, there was an Arab revolt in western Arabia. Initiated by the Sharif Husayn, ruler of Makka and Madina, and led by his son, Faysal, the revolt reflected Arab frustrations with Ottoman misrule. The goal, supported by a variety of Arab nationalists in the great urban centres, was to overthrow the Ottomans and establish an independent Arab Kingdom with Damascus as its capital. Conservative religious groups, critical of Ottoman behavior, also supported it.

The British government decided to encourage and arm the revolt, hoping to harness it to their own planned military drive from Egypt northward, thereby gaining control of Syria.[14] Negotiations to that end were initiated (the Husayn-McMahon correspondence), and the emissary was T.E. Lawrence, alias Lawrence of Arabia. In return for Arab help, the British gave assurances that if and when the Ottomans were defeated, Britain would assist the Arab nationalists to achieve their aim, an independent kingdom, understood to encompass Syria, Palestine, and Iraq.[15] Faysal, who knew of the special interest that Britain had in Palestine, made the mistake of agreeing to leave its status vague and open for future consideration.[16] The alliance was concluded.

The British interest in Palestine had to do with a secret declaration made by the British Foreign Secretary, Lord Balfour, to a group of Jewish Zionists, promising them a homeland for Jews in Palestine. Britain envisaged the Zionists would help protect a safe route to India and a secure route to the new oil sources in Persia, as well as provide a brake on French ambitions in the area.[17] In addition, the British shared a European cultural alienation from Islam, a desire to revive Christian dominance over the Holy Land, anti-Jewish sentiments compatible with the Zionist theme of getting Jews to leave their place of birth for Palestine, and hopes that the Zionists would weaken Russian Jewish support for the revolution there and halt Russia's withdrawal from World War One as a British ally.

In the meantime, Britain and France secretly agreed to divide the Ottoman Empire and share the spoils. In effect, the imperial powers were going to divide land which they did not control (not even by conquest yet) among themselves and a third party, the Zionists, who wished to establish a settler state. There never was any question of consulting with the resident population. The plan was a sure recipe for trouble.

With fine pronouncements of "self-determination" in the new post-World War One order, the idea of colonial expansion was discredited as such. Instead, the League of Nations was created, ostensibly to provide a forum for peaceful resolution of conflicts and to oversee emancipation from empires. Under that guise, Britain and France obtained "mandates" from the League of Nations to reorganize the Middle East, with a view to "assisting" and "preparing" the native populations for self-rule and emergence as democratic, independent states, at some undetermined future date.

And so, they dismembered the Ottoman empire, but only to establish their own control over its former Arab provinces. In 1920, the French invaded Syria, abolished the new Arab state and ousted its king, Faysal. They then divided Syria into two parts, Syria and Lebanon, and even attempted to divide the rest of Syria into three states based on religion. This failed because of nationalist revolts in 1921-22 and 1925-26.

The displaced, hapless Faysal turned to his old allies, the British, who now were in control of Iraq, and long had been in control of Kuwait and parts of the coast of Najd (eastern Saudi Arabia today). Britain instructed its senior representative in Iraq, Sir Percy Cox, to cut out borders and create the Kingdom of Iraq for Faysal to rule, much to the anger of the local population. The British then carved out of Syria the Emirate of Trans-Jordan (since 1946 a Kingdom), and established Faysal's brother Abdallah (grandfather of Jordan's King Hussein) as ruler.

The Kuwait-Iraq border: A case study

The creation of Iraq and Kuwait in their modern guise was a classic colonial performance. Until just before the turn of this century, the small fishing village of Kuwait was administratively part of the Ottoman-ruled southern Iraqi province of Basra. Its local ruler and Ottoman vassal was the head of the Al-Sabah clan. This Sheikh also had de facto control over coastal estates stretching north to the mouth of the Euphrates River (Shatt al-Arab), and an area stretching 258 kilometres south and almost as many west. However Bubiyan Island, which modern Iraq claims and repeatedly has offered to purchase, was ruled directly by the governor of Basra. It lies at the mouth of the Shatt al-Arab and without it, Iraq's access to the sea is reduced to a scant 10 kilometres of navigable waters. Later, in 1921, when the British created Iraq, excluding Bubiyan Island, they were well aware of this fact. As was the case with other petty rulers, the Ottomans left the Sheikh of Kuwait alone as long as he paid up and gave no trouble.

In 1899, in an effort to out-manoeuver the Russians and the Germans in their quests for direct access to the Indian Ocean, the British signed a secret pact with the Sheikh of Kuwait. It prevented him from entering into international agreements without their prior approval. Later, the Sheikh also agreed to call on British assistance in the event of any "aggression" against his territory. And in 1913 the British and the Ottomans signed an agreement confirming the de facto boundaries of Kuwait outlined above, though the Sheikh was a party neither to the negotiations nor the agreement.

No sooner had these arbitrary borders been established than disputes ensued. The first was between Iraq and Najd which was ruled by the head of the Al Saud clan, ibn Saud (later founder of the Kingdom of Saudi Arabia). After six days of futile negotiations, the British High Commissioner, Sir Percy Cox, simply drew a red line on the map. This resulted in Iraq receiving a large piece of land which had been claimed by ibn Saud. Following a tearful protest by ibn Saud, and an equally tearful reaction from Sir Percy, the British High Commissioner compensated ibn Saud with two-thirds of the territory previously allocated to the Sheikh of Kuwait.[18] At a stroke, British colonial policies created resentments and grudges three different ways.

Iraq, like all other artificially created countries of the Middle East, was left with troublesome and strange geographic facts. In Iraq's case the most damaging was the lack of an easy maritime passage to the Gulf, a vital necessity for its trade. Kuwait was allocated entire areas of the mouth of the Euphrates River, including Bubiyan Island, which it did not need. Given Britain's view of the Iraqis as "troublesome," because of their constant demands for independence, the British left them in a potentially crippling situation.

There were a series of revolts in Syria, Iraq and Palestine. The most brutally suppressed was in Iraq where in 1920, on orders from Winston Churchill, the British airforce for the first time in history used large-scale aerial bombardment against civilians. "I am strongly in favour of using poisoned gas against uncivilised tribes," wrote Winston Churchill. "We cannot acquiesce in the non-utilisation of any weapons which are available to procure a speedy termination of the disorder which prevails on the frontier."[19]

By 1925 most of the map of the Middle East as we know it today had been drawn by bureaucrats in France or Britain, and the dreams of a generation of idealistic nationalists to establish an independent Arab state were shattered.

The history of the Middle East during the last 65 years has been the history of a people trying to adjust their dreams of unity to the reality of the divisions imposed upon them, and to achieve their independence from European and American control of the region and its resources. From this matrix come the client kings and dictators, the Israeli Sparta, the gross inequalities of wealth, popular rebellions, bloody conflicts and the suppression of democratic life.

Notes

[1] Rodinson, Maxime, *The Arabs* (Chicago, University of Chicago Press, 1981), p. ix.
[2] Middle East is one of several terms used to describe this region. "Near East," also referred to as the "Levant" and the "Fertile Crescent," were coined to suit particular European geopolitical perceptions. Today "Middle East" is used to describe an area including Syria, Jordan, Lebanon, Iraq, Palestine/Israel, Turkey, Cyprus and Egypt. Iran, Sudan and Libya often are included by journalists. Some writers erroneously include Pakistan, Afghanistan and Arab countries of North Africa – Tunisia, Algeria, and Morocco.
[3] Hitti, Philip, *The History of Syria* (New York, The MacMillan Company, 1951), p. 5.
[4] Rodinson refers to a "...thousand-year-old Egyptian nationalism," *op.cit.*, p.99.
[5] Hitti, *op.cit.*, chapter XI.
[6] For an excellent and detailed account of this period, see Hitti, *ibid.*, chapter XXIX.
[7] There are important minorities of Christian Arabs particularly in Egypt, Syria, Lebanon, Palestine and Iraq. As well, there still are groups of Arab Jews in these countries, and in Morocco and Israel. Nor are all Muslims

Arab: of an estimated 550,000,000 Muslims in the world only about 150,000,000 are Arabs. There are 145,000,000 Muslims in Indonesia alone.

[8] An excellent history of the crusades, from a point of view seldom encountered by westerners by many Arab school-children, is Amin Maalouf's *The Crusades Through Arab Eyes* (New York, Schocken Books, 1987).

[9] It would be a fair generalization to say that, if Christianity is a religion based on the principle of love, then Islam is one based on the principles of a just and equitable society. The achievement of these ideals is another matter.

[10] Hitti, *op.cit.*, p.667.

[11] The language of culture in Ottoman circles was Persian until the 19th century. The language of administration was Turkish, and those who aspired to positions in the state bureaucracy and in certain professions had to learn Turkish.

[12] For a critical study of the effects of "orientalism" on western scholarship of the Middle East, see Edward Said's *Orientalism*, Vintage Books, 1979.

[13] For an account of this period, see George Antonious, *The Arab Awakening*, London, 1938.

[14] At the same time, Britain would land troops in Kuwait, which they already controlled, and drive to Baghdad to establish control of the oil fields.

[15] George Antonious, *op.cit.*

[16] The reader will notice that while Palestine and Lebanon were regions with their own names, due to extraordinary circumstances, and developed their own importance and special status, particularly in the view of Europeans, they nevertheless always were considered to be parts of the greater entity known as Syria.

[17] The whole British fleet recently had been converted from coal-fuel to oil, under the leadership of Winston Churchill, who urged the British government to acquire a controlling share of the Anglo-Persian Oil Company, later renamed British Petroleum, or BP.

[18] Dickson, H.R.P., *Kuwait and Her Neighbours* (Unwin, 1956).

[19] For the history of these events see David E. Omissi's *Air Power and Colonial Control: The Royal Air Force 1919-1939* (Manchester, Manchester University Press, 1990).

Israel Without Boundaries

The United Nations, in a General Assembly resolution of November 29, 1947, had specified boundaries when it approved the creation of two states, one Jewish, one Arab, and a "Special International Regime for the City of Jerusalem." (See Map 2) U.N. Resolution 181 (II) also provided that the two states were to be proclaimed simultaneously, two months after the British Mandate forces withdrew, and no later than October 1, 1948.

The Jewish political forces decided to pre-empt the U.N. resolution by unilaterally proclaiming their state in advance, immediately upon the formal end of the British Mandate, May 14, 1948.

Two days before their unilateral Declaration of Independence, the Jewish provisional government debated whether or not they should specify any boundaries for their new state.

They decided, on the urging of Israel's first prime minister, David Ben-Gurion, neither to specify boundaries nor to mention the U.N. partition plan which had drawn boundaries for the Jewish and the Arab states-to-be.[1]

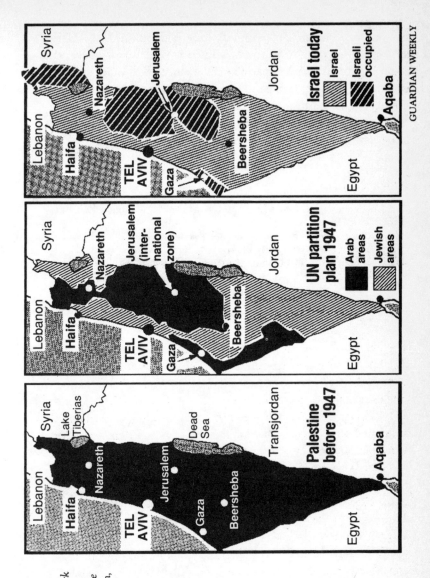

Maps show Palestine (black area) before 1947, after the U.N. partition, and now.

From its unilateral declaration of independence on May 14, 1948 until now, the state of Israel has refused to declare any boundaries, to set any limits on its expansion. Ever since 1948 Israel has expanded – by war, occupation and annexation – the territory originally allotted to it by the U.N. (See Map 3)

Consistent with early Zionist discussion, Israel still considers its frontiers mobile, expanding according to the "opportunities."[2]

Notes

[1] Flapan, Simha, *The Birth of Israel: Myths and Realities* (Toronto, Random House, 1987), pp.34-36.

[2] See Shabtai Teveth's *Ben-Gurion and the Palestinian Arabs: From Peace to War* (New York, Oxford University Press, 1985) for Ben-Gurion's desired boundaries in 1918, incorporating present-day Jordan to within 20 miles of Damascus, pp.33-36.

Devastation of Iraq

Dave Rogers

Black smoke meets the morning sun,
Devil's work has just been done,
Tomahawk and Cruise attack,
Devastation of Iraq.

"Our Boys" with the laser eye,
Surgeons of the midnight sky,
Smash the bones, implode the flesh,
To safeguard freedom for the West.

Newsmen speak on auto-cue,
To orchestrate the common view,
Word and image sanitised,
Carpet bomb my ears and eyes.

Bush and Major put the case,
Killers with a caring face,

Kinnock bleats and wrings his hands,
Then votes for the murder plan.

The Bishops kneel, the Bishops pray,
The Bishops rise, then turn away,
Bless the carnage, bless the gore,
Sanctify the Holy War.

Warlords wage the just Crusade,
Mammon's might must be obeyed,
Blood for oil and war for peace,
Subjugate the Middle East.

A billion eyes gaze on the screen,
Hooked into the war morphine,
Frozen on the edge of time,
Doing nothing, final crime?

Black smoke meets the morning sun,
Devil's work has just been done,
Tomahawk and Cruise attack,
Devastation, devastation,
Devastation of Iraq.

Innocence

How difficult it is for citizens to know the cunning of governments. Intermittent "scandals" expose a hardened habit of secrecy, ruthlessness and unblushing deceit. Then the scandal is quickly buried, before the citizenry grasps its full dimensions and ponders drastic changes. Particularly is this so in international affairs.

Of all the cunning governments involved in this war, and they all were cunning, only one was portrayed as innocent: the Israeli. It is a curiosity that, in a pamphlet produced by the U.S. Central Command and distributed to all its forces in Saudi Arabia, the first in a list of "sensitive subjects" that "should be avoided or handled carefully" by soldiers are: "Articles and stories showing U.S.-Israeli ties and friendship." This ranked above "Material deemed immoral..."[1]

In North American political culture the foreign policy of Israel has been presented more unrealistically than the foreign policy of any other country. Israel's close alliance with South Africa, its support of Noriega in his last days and its training of drug cartel militias in Colombia, its arms merchandizing to the most repressive regimes in Latin America, Asia and Africa: none of these realities are presented as mainstream fare.[2] Hence many, otherwise opposed to this war, accepted the depiction of Israel as the passive and persecuted victim of an entirely unprovoked Iraqi aggression. But Israel's disconnectedness, its "passivity," was pure propaganda, not policy. Israel was anything but innocent and uninvolved.

As Jane Hunter documents in the following essay, during the 1980s the Israeli state debated some surprising twists in its policies towards Iraq. At the end of the debates, Israel committed itself to destroy Iraq, separate from and well before the invasion of Kuwait. Once Iraq had invaded Kuwait, Israel pushed hard for war when U.S. popular, and elite, opinion still was divided.

Pursuing the tangled skeins of the worlds of diplomacy, intelligence, and lobbying, Jane Hunter reconstructs an account of Israel's very active role in the war against Iraq.

Notes

[1] *Harper's Magazine*, November 1990, p.18.

[2] *Israeli Foreign Affairs*, published monthly by Jane Hunter is an excellent source of documented information on Israel's foreign policy and practice, and since beginning publication in 1987 has reported on these topics. Another excellent reference is by an Israeli author, Benjamin Beit-Hallahmi, *The Israeli Connection: Who Israel Arms and Why* (New York, Pantheon Books, 1987).

Israel and Iraq:
The Fateful Choice

Jane Hunter

"WE COULD HAVE OFFERED IRAQ COOPERATION AND THE USE OF THE HAIFA PORT. Instead, we backed Iran, which is today undoubtedly the most anti-Israel country in the world." Almost 11 years after Iraq marched into Iran and half a year after it invaded Kuwait, this notion, proposed by Israeli Major General (retired) Dr. Matti Peled, seemed preposterous.[1] Iraq and Israel were sworn enemies. Peled, a former leftist member of Israel's parliament, the Knesset, counted himself in the small minority of the Israeli peace movement that, while unhappy with Baghdad's move into Kuwait, nevertheless opposed the U.S.-led war against Iraq.

And yet, there was a time when the rapprochement between Israel and Iraq that Peled visualized was possible. And there was another time when the possibility of an "Iraqi option" was the subject of public consideration in Israel. In retrospect, the choice was a stark one – the difference between peace and war.

Feelers

In 1985, the fifth grinding year of the war between Iran and Iraq, Israel's leading newspaper *Ha'aretz* reported that Prime Minister

Shimon Peres "has been considering the possibility of changing Israel's policy vis-à-vis the Iran-Iraq war." Peres, said the paper, was considering turning away from Israel's longtime ally and client, Iran, and toward Iraq: "The new direction is in keeping with the prime minister's comprehensive conception of an Arab bloc which is in the process of consolidation, including Egypt, Jordan, Saudi Arabia and Iraq."

Ha'aretz noted that Peres had spoken positively about a recent visit to Iraq by President Hosni Mubarak of Egypt and King Hussein of Jordan.[2] But because the paper also cited a widely disparaged British report that Israel had ceased shipping arms to Iran,[3] the *Ha'aretz* report was not given great credence. Indeed, many analysts believed this report was simply a feint to deflect increasingly harsh criticism of Israel's supply line to the Islamic Republic. The report followed an earlier assertion by Peres to the *New York Times* (a prime channel for Israeli communication with U.S. "opinion leaders") that "we are not going to sell any arms to Iran."[4]

Had it been known at the time that Peres's Labour Party stood to profit handsomely from a deal involving an Israeli promise not to attack an Iraqi oil pipeline that the Bechtel construction company wanted to lay across Jordan, Peres's statement would have provoked more sideways looks. Later, when that particular scandal broke, it became known that E. Robert Wallach, a flunky attached to then U.S. attorney general Edwin Meese, and Bruce Rappaport, a Swiss-based Israeli "businessman," had planned to funnel part of a U.S.-financed insurance payment (the "non-attack" bond, as it were) to the Labour Party.[5]

Almost a year went by, and then in early 1986 the government of Saddam Hussein stretched out a hand to Israel. Sometime in January or February an Iraqi military delegation made a secret visit to Egypt, the only Arab government that maintains diplomatic relations with Israel. The Iraqis asked Egyptian officials to put them in touch with Israel. But Israel, according to a report which cited intelligence sources in London, refused to deal through a third party. So Iraq's then deputy foreign minister Tahir al-Qaysi travelled to New York to meet with Israel's ambassador to the United Nations at the time, Binyamin Netanyahu.[6] (Another version has Iraqi and Israeli military intelligence officers meeting under Egyptian auspices in Europe.)[7] Al-Qaysi reportedly asked for weapons and for intelligence that Israel would have gleaned through its sale of arms to Iran.[8]

Israel had been a key supplier of weapons to the Iranian government of Ayatollah Khomeini since the war began, despite that government's routine denunciations of the "Zionist enemy." Curious as this relationship with the militant Islamic Republic seemed, it was rooted in Israel's adoption, soon after its founding, of a "peripheral" strategy of befriending non-Arab and non-Muslim peoples and governments. Pursuing this strategy over the following decades, Israel befriended Iran, Turkey, Ethiopia (ruled by the Christian Amhara minority), Lebanese Christians, Christians and followers of traditional religions in the southern Sudan, and the Iraqi Kurds, often finding an advantage in assisting them in their wars and schisms.

The Islamic nature of Iran in the wake of the Shah's overthrow did not deter Israel. It shipped weapons to the new government over the protests of the Carter administration, which was trying to negotiate the release of the Tehran embassy hostages[9], and it continued to ship weapons through at least 1987. According to one report, when the Shah fell Israel held $800 million of Iran's funds. It sent the Khomeini regime $500 million worth of weapons, and used the $300 million balance as leverage on Iran, which at Israel's request, attempted to destroy Iraq's nuclear reactor. Iran only managed to damage some nearby laboratories, according to the report, leaving it for Israel to undertake the attack in 1981.[10]

Meeting face-to-face with the Iraqis in 1986, Israel reportedly demanded diplomatic recognition. When Iraq only agreed to take that step once the Gulf war with Iran ended, Israel posed two "interim" conditions: that Iraq help with the "peace process" and that it sever links with Palestinian groups. Iraq promised to consider how it could take these steps and both sides reportedly took the proposals home to mull them over. Publicly, both sides denied emphatically that any such deal was in the works.[11] Israel's government radio jumped in to say that the Reagan administration "is said to have been actively, though quietly, encouraging an arms deal between Iraq and Israel," and that Iraq had expressed interest in Israel's pilotless (drone) aircraft.[12] The irony of this report would not be fully appreciated until some months later when it became known that, at Israel's urging, the Reagan administration had been selling arms to Iran!

Iraq's aims

What – beyond the obvious desire of wanting to cut Iran's arms supply – had prompted Iraq to make contact with Israel? Was Iraq simply trying to cultivate the U.S., especially Israel's supporters in Congress? They had always been ready to echo Israel's charges against Baghdad, the more so after Washington re-established diplomatic ties with Iraq in 1984.

People still talk about the "new look" diplomacy implemented by Iraq's ambassador to Washington at the time, Nizar Hamdoon, especially his outreach to Israel's friends in Congress who were publicly treated as anathema by Arab governments. Hamdoon was skilful, and he may, at times, have gotten out ahead of Baghdad. Hamdoon also was daring. He gave an interview to the newsletter affiliated with Israel's congressional lobby, AIPAC, in which he stated that Iraq was "no longer a confrontation state" and that it did not want another Arab-Israeli war.[13] He spoke at Brandeis, telling the audience at the Jewish-supported university in Massachusetts that the Palestine problem was for the Israelis and Palestinians – not Iraq – to solve.[14]

If it was not the active diplomacy of Nizar Hamdoon that prompted the Iraqi initiative, there is the possibility that Iraq knew, early in 1986, that the Reagan administration had secretly agreed the previous August to Israel's proposal to sell weapons to Iran. The aim of the secret U.S.-Israeli sales was supposedly to obtain the release of hostages held in Lebanon, but Israel's success in enlisting the administration in its pro-Iranian policy was a threatening contradiction to the administration's pro-Iraqi "tilt."

Iraq may well have received some intelligence on the secret dealings – they would soon become known as the Iran-contra affair – from the Soviet Union, one of its main arms suppliers. In the months following the Iraqi-Israeli contact there were several Soviet media reports that suggested Moscow was aware of the Iran-contra relationship. For example on June 3, 1986, Tass quoted a Kuwaiti paper saying that the U.S. had agreed to sell Iran "a batch of weapons" and that under an agreement to revive U.S. listening posts aimed at the U.S.S.R., "a group of U.S. specialists and Israeli experts with U.S. passports arrived in Iran and started work on reactivating and modernizing these stations." The report was wrong about the listening posts (at least so far as is known), but it was compellingly accurate about the U.S.-Israeli visit to Iran: Oliver North, his Israeli counterpart Amiram Nir, and other Reagan administration conspirators had secretly visited Iran a week earlier. And of course, it was right about the arms.[15]

If Iraq knew about the secret Reagan policy at the time, its approach to Israel would make even more sense. Official U.S. policy was becoming ever more partial to Iraq,[16] and Iraq, naturally, would have done everything possible to safeguard its position.

The propitious moment passed quickly, almost without notice. The Iraqi initiative toward Israel faded away, and it would be almost two years before any light was shed on the thinking of the Israeli establishment that let it pass. Finally, in the autumn of 1987, a series of events forced the issue of Israel's Gulf policy into the open. Most notable among these was the Iran-contra affair, which was exposed to the U.S. public in December 1986 and investigated (after a fashion) throughout much of the following year.

Sheltered from the scandal's worst revelations by its friends on the special congressional committee investigating the affair,[17] and unabashed by the negative public reaction to its dealings with the Islamic Republic, Israel simply continued throughout 1987 to sell arms to Iran.[18] In September there were reports that representatives of Israel's defence and foreign ministries met in Europe with Ahmed Khomeini, the Ayatollah's son, to discuss an arms deal that included permission to emigrate for Iran's 25,000 Jews.[19]

Meanwhile a chastened Reagan administration began protecting shipping in the Persian Gulf – a policy that was avowedly neutral but manifestly supportive of Iraq. The administration was also anxious to put the Iran-contra affair behind it. Israel's arms sales were an unwelcome reminder of the scandal, not to mention a challenge to U.S. policy. Perhaps most galling were reports that Israel had helped Iran obtain the Chinese Silkworm anti-ship missiles that threatened the U.S. ship "reflagging" exercise in the Gulf.[20]

It was not only the Reagan administration that genuinely opposed

Israel's succour of Iran. So did Egypt. According to Israeli military radio: "People familiar with the Egyptian scene this week warned about irreparable damage to Israeli-Egyptian relations in the wake of these reports [of arms sales]. Several weeks ago, an Egyptian diplomat told his Israeli counterpart that Israel has made a serious mistake in supporting Iran rather than Iraq and the Arab world's struggle against Shiite extremism."[21]

Egypt's view was particularly important at that moment. Iraq, eager for support in its war, had just renewed diplomatic relations with Egypt. Some Israelis regarded the move as a breakthrough – proof that countries which followed Egypt's lead in making peace with Israel need not be condemned to permanent ostracism.

Israel's pro-Iraqi boomlet

All these factors combined to unleash a pro-Iraqi boomlet in Israel. Gad Yacobi, the Israeli economics minister returned from a visit to the U.S. bearing an Iraqi message passed through Frank Jabir, a Lebanese-American, that if Israel changed its attitude toward Iran "there will be something to talk about."[22]

The sometimes-sensationalist, sometimes-accurate daily *Hadashot* went so far as to report, quoting senior political sources, that "Israel is changing its orientation in the [Iran-Iraq] Gulf War from an official line of neutrality to political support for Iraq." One of those sources told the paper:

> We should develop a pro-Iraqi political orientation, which may bear political fruit in the long run. In recent months senior Iraqi officials have indicated a willingness to examine the possibility of changing the policy toward Israel if the latter supports Iraq in the Gulf war.[23]

This echoed the tone earlier attributed to Shimon Peres. Peres, then sharing the reins of government with Likud's Yitzhak Shamir, and taking his turn as foreign minister, was again – after initiating the Iran-contra affair with two of his favourite arms dealers – publicly criticizing Iran and warning of the danger of Islamic extremism.[24] Peres also contended that Arab states now considered Iran – rather than Israel – as "the major danger," a "reactionary force that will drive the Arab world back into the dark ages." Speaking in London in November 1987, Peres commended Iraq for militarily confronting Iran and praised a recent decision taken by the Arab League in Amman to politically oppose Iran.[25]

The more phlegmatic *Jerusalem Post* deprecated the apparent policy flip-flop, charging it off to muscle-flexing by the "pro-Iraqi" lobby in the foreign ministry. The lobby's leader, ministry director-general Avraham Tamir and his "political patron" Ezer Weizman, at the time minister-without-portfolio, "have been arguing for at least two years that Iraq has recently sent out some low-key signals to Israel and that it is high time that Israel responded," explained the *Post*. Tamir did not advocate arming Iraq, said the paper, only "sending out political signals that would smooth Baghdad's way into the moderate orbit."

Later the same week Tamir told the *Post* that it would be "absurd" for Israel to ignore the outcome of the recent Arab League meeting in Amman, in which Egypt, Jordan, Saudi Arabia and Iraq had come to an understanding on the peace process.[26] Even the subject of Israeli arms sales to Iraq came up, initially as a way of countering the growing strength of Iranian-funded groups in Lebanon. Israel was becoming so concerned about the "threat from the north," reported *Jane's Defence Weekly*, that "some Israeli officials have suggested that Israel should supply arms to Iraq."[27]

Iraq dismissed that idea immediately: "There is no likelihood of Iraq buying from Israel; you can discount the reports you have read in the press," the military attaché's office at Iraq's London embassy told an Israeli paper.[28] Iraq, analysts pointed out, did not have the difficulty Iran did in obtaining arms, so any sale would benefit Israel – not only in terms of profits but also to score points with the Soviet Union, Iraq's major arms supplier.[29]

It is worth noting that ministry director Tamir and some of the other figures identified with the "pro-Iraqi" bloc – particularly Yossi Beilin, a Labour "dove" close to Peres – have also been identified as supporters of a negotiated withdrawal from occupied Palestine. Ranged against Tamir's lobby was a group led by then defence minister Yitzhak Rabin.[30] Rabin, long Shimon Peres's rival for leadership of the Labour Party, contributed mightily to the launching of the debate on Israel's Gulf policy when he was quoted saying that Iran was "Israel's best friend" and "we do not intend to change our position toward Tehran."[31] The defence ministry hastened to claim that Rabin's statement "had not been said at all." What the ministry called "an accurate account" of Rabin's remarks (to the Association of Foreign Journalists) had the defence minister saying:

> Iran today is Israel's bitter enemy from the viewpoint of its general outlook...Nevertheless, when I served as an ambassador in Washington, when I was a prime minister and a minister, when I visited the United States, everybody in the administration and media there told me that to resolve a conflict we should talk with the enemy.

Rabin went on to say that it would be wrong to underrate Iran's enmity to Israel, which he did not think would change as long as Khomeini was in power. Then, he continued: "At the same time, allow me to say that during 28 out of Israel's 39 years of existence, Iran was a friend of this country...." And he concluded: "[W]hy can't this situation exist again, when this idea of insane, Islamic Shi'ite fundamentalism passes away?"[32]

However, according to the *Jerusalem Post*, Rabin and his cohorts in the pro-Iranian camp – prominent among them Ariel Sharon, then trade and industry minister, and some high-ranking military officers – argued that Israel's peripheral policy had worked for years, weakening its enemies, and that Israel should safeguard its historic friendship with Iran by sending friendly signals to Khomeini's possible successors. Among pro-Iranian circles in the Labour Party, there was also out and out nostalgia for the relationship that existed in the time of the Shah.[33]

Prime Minister Yitzhak Shamir appeared to split the difference. Perched next to Ronald Reagan for a White House photo session on November 20, two days after the congressional Iran-contra committee released its final report, Shamir denounced both Iran and Iraq as "extreme enemies of our country." He also approximated an endorsement of the U.S. ship-flagging operation in the Gulf, saying it would strengthen U.S. credibility in the region.[34]

Years later, Labour member of Knesset (MK) Binyamin Ben-Eliezer would ascribe a more active role in the policy struggle to Shamir. Had Shamir not sabotaged Shimon Peres's secret "London Accord" with King Hussein of Jordan, argued Ben-Eliezer, the Israeli-Jordanian agreement could have drawn Iraq into a comprehensive U.S.-sponsored regional peace arrangement. Instead, continued Ben-Eliezer, Shamir was responsible for pushing the Jordanian king into his war-time alliance with Iraq, an alliance that offered protection against the rampant claims of Shamir's coalition allies that "Jordan is Palestine."[35] The 1987 pro-Iraqi boomlet soon fizzled. By the end of the year the Israeli debate had gone silent. A news report said that "many leading Israeli political thinkers and politicians still believe Israel's long-term strategic interests lie in keeping the gulf war going through the quiet support of Iran."[36] Nevertheless, the opportunity for a rapprochement with Iraq did not vanish. It was to be seen in Saddam Hussein's positioning of his government with the "moderate" Arab states when he strongly backed the PLO's 1988 offer to negotiate a two-state solution with Israel, according to Haifa University Professor Amatzia Baram, Israel's most prominent expert on Saddam Hussein.[37]

On the Israeli side, there continued to be some interest in the benefits of peace with Iraq. In 1991 Avraham Tamir acknowledged that in 1988 he met a number of times in the U.S. and Europe with Iraqi officials, three of whom he named: Ambassador Nizar Hamdoon, Vice-President Saadoun Hammadi, Foreign Minister Tariq Azziz. Tamir identified a fourth only as a relative of Saddam Hussein. The talks were substantive. At the first meeting, with Ambassador Hamdoon in New York, Tamir said Hamdoon told him that Iraq wanted a peaceful settlement of the Arab-Israeli conflict and was willing to talk about arms control if an agreement included Iran, as well as Israel. Hammadi told Tamir that Iraq was willing to support Arab-Israeli peace talks without demanding that Israel first withdraw from the occupied territories or recognize the PLO.[38]

Also around this time, conciliatory signals flashed between the two countries. In a speech broadcast in May 1988 on the Iraqi radio, Saddam Hussein remarked: "I think the Zionists and the Israelis have come to regret their role in continuing this [Iran-Iraq] war." And a month later Defence Minister Yitzhak Rabin said, also in a broadcast statement, "I've changed my mind; the continuation of the Iran-Iraq war no longer serves Israel's interests because of the arms race it generates."[39]

At the end of 1989, a senior Israeli foreign ministry official told journalists that a key Israeli objective in the years ahead would be the achievement of a "strategic understanding" with Iraq. "Israel has no territorial conflict with Iraq, and our problems with them are solvable," he asserted. If such an understanding is reached, he added, "our entire strategic situation will change." The heretical official did not allow the journalists to identify him.[40]

As late as May 1990, when tension was reaching a fever pitch in the Middle East (see below) and some of Israel's friends in the U.S. Congress sought to impose sanctions against Iraq, Senators Robert Dole (Republican, Kansas) and Howard Metzenbaum (Democrat, Ohio), who had recently met with Saddam Hussein, argued vehemently against the move. Metzenbaum, usually identified as a stalwart friend of Israel, contended that there were the "slightest indicators" that Saddam Hussein was willing to move forward on the peace process and that sanctions would alienate him.[41] Even after the war Iraq's defence minister passed a message through former U.S. attorney general Elliot Richardson, saying that Baghdad wanted peaceful relations with all the countries in the Middle East – including Israel.[42] By early 1988, however, Israel was resolutely headed down another track, although, arguably, one with the same purpose that would have been achieved by peace: the elimination of Iraq as a meaningful challenge.

Israel's crusade to hobble iraq

At a heated post-mortem in the Israeli Knesset, days after the end of the war against Iraq, Labour MK Michael Bar-Zohar faulted the government's failure to make Iraq an appropriate priority for its intelligence agencies: "Appropriate priority means a decision by the upper political echelon to carry out an intensive intelligence effort, to recruit and dispatch spies, take strong action against foreign scientists and experts [working for Iraq] and send up a spy satellite."[43]

Bar-Zohar's criticism aside, Israeli intelligence had indeed consistently worked to thwart Iraq's efforts to develop weapons, including taking "strong action" against foreign experts. As Foreign Minister David Levy had told the Knesset some weeks earlier: "Even before the facts about foreign technological aid to Iraq became public, we did not sit idly by. We acted to frustrate the transfer. Some things cannot be spelled out in public."[44]

Israel's spectacularly public destruction of Iraq's nuclear reactor at Osirak[45] was an expression of what the *Los Angeles Times* recently called a doctrine of "assertive disarmament."[46] Nuclear physicist and former head of the Stockholm International Peace Research Institute, Frank Barnaby, believes that "[o]ne, if not *the* main aim of Israel's foreign policy is to prevent the emergence of any other nuclear-weapon power in the Middle East."[47] Israel sent messages conveying that sentiment by a series of actions undertaken in the late 1980s against Iraq's efforts to build delivery systems that would negate the pre-eminence of Israel's airforce.

Most alarming to Israel was the acquisition by Iraq and other Middle Eastern countries of surface-to-surface missiles. In 1988, then defence minister Yitzhak Rabin called these "the name of the game."[48] Israel's prime target was the Condor, a sophisticated missile that Argentina, Iraq and Egypt began jointly developing in 1984.[49] At one point there were reports that Israel was trying to persuade the Reagan administration to drop charges against Egyptians that had been caught smuggling sophisticated missile technology for the Condor in exchange for an Egyptian pledge to drop work on surface-to-surface missiles. It was also reported that the U.S. investigation that resulted in those arrests was sparked by a tip from Israeli intelligence.

At the same time as this Israeli "diplomatic" activity was underway, there were reports that Mossad, the Israeli secret service, had detonated car bombs in Cairo and in France to warn Egypt to stop work on the project.[50] According to the *Independent* of London, the car bomb in Cairo exploded outside the home of European technicians working on the missile (which Egypt called the Badr-2000), some of whom "got the message" and left Egypt.[51]

The grand finale came on March 22, 1990, when Gerald Bull, the Canadian-born designer of the 155 mm howitzer that formed the core of Iraq's artillery, was assassinated outside his Brussels apartment. The howitzer was old history: CIA and Israeli operatives had helped South

Africa put it into production in the 1970s and, during the Iran-Iraq war, South Africa sold it to Iraq. But Bull had been developing a new "supergun" for Iraq that was putatively able to lob munitions into Israel. In April the U.K. impounded Iraq-bound steel pipe sections said to be intended for Bull's supergun. Israeli intelligence officials later claimed responsibility for Bull's murder.[52]

Meanwhile, Israel's friends in the U.S. worked to raise the alarm level over the acquisition of missiles and other advanced weapons technology by Arab governments. It is quite likely that the European governments which participated in the U.S.-initiated 1987 Missile Technology Control Regime (MTCR) never moved to curtail technology transfers to Iraq because the MTCR's agenda already was so manifestly biased in Israel's favor. Attention was focused on the Condor,[53] but not on Israel's operational, nuclear-capable Jericho missile, which Israel was happily sharing with South Africa.[54]

U.S. legislation followed a similar, biased route. In 1989 Senator John McCain (Republican, Arizona) conceded that a bill he was sponsoring "differentiate[d]" Israel (along with France and Britain) from Arab nations.[55] When asked in 1989 why his bill to contain missile technology made no provision for Israel's sharing of its Jericho missile technology with South Africa, Representative Howard Berman (Democrat, California), said his bill would not penalize past deals.[56] In 1991 Israel (along with a number of non-missile-technology producing European states, Turkey, Australia and Japan) was explicitly excluded from the U.S. provisions seeking to enforce the MTCR.[57]

Whether there were direct orders from Israel or its congressional lobby to accomplish these legislative feats is not known. But the underpinning for this targeting of Arab missiles was to be found, among other places, in numerous warnings by Israeli officials, echoed by pro-Israeli members of Congress. A 1988 "study" on the threat to Israel of missiles being acquired by Arab countries was compiled by an influential group of Israel's U.S. supporters. They called for the U.S. to urge other countries to stop selling arms to these countries and backed Israel's development of the Arrow anti-tactical ballistic missile which Israel is building with U.S. funding, under the Star Wars program. The group, whose broader mandate was to assemble recommendations on Middle East policy for the administration that was to take office in January 1989, included former vice-president Walter Mondale and (then) former undersecretary of state Lawrence Eagleburger. The group had worked under the auspices of the unabashedly pro-Israel Washington Institute for Near East Policy.[58]

The fact that these dangerous Arab missiles – and the nuclear, chemical and biological warheads they were designed to carry – were being developed at least in part to counter the menace of Israel's nuclear weapons, was a logical construct that was completely absent from the U.S. political dialogue. Moreover, twice – once at the 100-nation conference on chemical weapons in Paris in early 1989 and once in April 1990 – the U.S. government explicitly rejected disarmament proposals linking elimination of Arab chemical weapons to elimination of Israeli nuclear weapons.[59]

The road to war

It is particularly striking, in the period leading up to the U.S.-Iraqi war over Kuwait, that an altogether different war seemed to be developing – one between Israel and Iraq over Iraq's acquisition of sophisticated weapons and its defence of its right to possess them in the face of Israel's infinitely more sophisticated arsenal. Perhaps when historians examine this period they will determine that it was really the same war after all. But for now it is worth contemplating the notion that the war against Iraq was a sudden detour from a collision course between Iraq and Israel.

The wheels started rolling some time in 1989, soon after the end of the Iran-Iraq war. In March of that year it was Israeli sources that provided the information for a *Washington Post* story that Iraq had embarked on a crash program to build nuclear warheads and a missile system (most likely the Condor) to deliver them. U.S. military analysts confirmed the Israeli claim. Israeli officials, the *Post* was told, were "following the [nuclear] project with mounting anxiety and debating a course of action."[60] All that year Israel's friends in Congress continued their assault on Iraq's weapons programs. The administration – and corn belt representatives who were anxious not to lose lucrative grain exports to Iraq – continued to dodge the flak. But Iraq hardly could have been oblivious to the direction things were taking: a succession of Israeli missile launchings, including a satellite launch in September 1988, Jericho missile tests over the Mediterranean in May 1987 and September 1989 and a joint missile test with South Africa in July 1989.

In December 1989, Iraq test-launched a crude missile, saying the test was part of a space program. When Washington expressed concern, the ruling Ba'th party paper *Al-Thawra* accused the Bush administration of "turning a blind eye to the nuclear arms held by the Zionist entity while raising the alarm when Iraq launches a rocket in the service of peaceful scientific purposes." *Al-Thawra* accused Washington of "prepar[ing] the ground for a Zionist attack on Iraqi scientific facilities."[61]

The following March, after British authorities arrested three people for trying to smuggle devices for triggering nuclear weapons to Iraq and announced that additional investigations into illegal exports to Iraq were under way, the Iraqi News Agency charged that: "The current British campaign is trying to provide the groundwork for an Israeli aggression on Iraq."[62] On April 3, 1990 Israel launched a satellite, called Ofek-2. Yuval Ne'eman, the head of Israel's Space Agency, insisted that the launch was not in response to Saddam Hussein's military program. But there was likely no more truth to that than to Ne'eman's contention that Ofek-2 was "not a spy satellite and has no military significance."[63] Ofek reportedly carried a sophisticated camera capable of monitoring military activity in Arab countries.[64] There is near unanimity among analysts that Israel's satellite program is entirely military in nature. In 1991 Defence Minister Moshe Arens told the Knesset that "No one should be surprised if one of these days...we launch a spy satellite."[65]

The following week the U.S. dismissed Iraq's offer to destroy its chemical weapons if Israel agreed to give up its nuclear and chemical arms: "We have made clear that we oppose linking the elimination of chemical weapons systems to other issues or weapons systems," said the State Department spokesman.[66]

Saddam Hussein parried with an announcement that he had given his commanders the freedom to respond with chemical weapons to an Israeli nuclear attack, without awaiting orders from him. Robert Dole, the Senate minority leader who visited Iraq that week, said that

Saddam was seriously worried that Israel would launch a pre-emptive strike against Iraq.[67] In May, Iraq began civil defence drills in its major cities to prepare citizens for a nuclear or chemical attack by Israel.[68] Saddam's rhetoric became more militant: "The Arab nation," he told one audience in early May, was determined "to acquire sophisticated technology for its national security and defence." And, he continued, "how can we calm things down with Israel... how can we tranquilize matters before we obtain our rights in full – the rights of the Palestinian people... The enemies fired their arrows, organized their plans and created a Western campaign against Iraq. If we have to calm matters down without our counter-attack... it means that they have defeated us."[69]

Then came the Arab League summit in Baghdad, thought by some to have been the turning point in Iraq's relations with the West. Saddam, some noted, revived the spectre of Egyptian leader Gamal Abdel Nasser. And once again he inveighed against Israel: "If Israel attacks, we will hit back strongly, and if it uses weapons of total destruction against our nation, we will use weapons of total destruction against it."[70]

By the summer of 1990, the prospect of an Israeli pre-emptive strike against Iraq was common currency.[71] "It's getting goosey out there," a U.S. arms salesman said in June. "The Arabs think Israel needs a war, and they're getting hostile as hell."[72]

In late July 1990, Yuval Ne'eman, the Israeli science and energy minister, said that Israel had "an excellent response" to Saddam Hussein's threats to burn half of Israel with chemical weapons (as a response to an Israeli nuclear attack) "and that is to threaten Hussein with the same merchandise."[73] Iraq rose in high dudgeon and, in a message to the United Nations secretary general, "warned the international community of the dangers of Western and U.S. dualism in their Middle East policy which concentrates on making the Zionist entity the hegemonic power in the region."[74]

This was not solely an Iraqi view, as evidenced by this broadcast on Egypt's government radio:

> Israel has never before declared that it possesses nonconventional weapons. It has always evaded comment on all reports about its possession of nuclear, chemical, and biological weapons ...

This means that Israel had these chemical weapons even before Iraq's declaration that it possesses such weapons. This also means that the Israeli uproar following the Iraqi statements were aimed at defaming Iraq in the eyes of [the] world. . .and at depicting the Baghdad government as a terrorist government. The aim of the Israeli campaign against Iraq was to take the Iraqi statements out of context and portray the issue as if it were merely a matter of a terrorist threat to Israel. Israel has attempted to give this artificial campaign against Iraq a political hue to claim to the world that the Arabs do not want peace and that international pressure on the Shamir government to hold a dialogue with the Palestinians was prompted by inaccurate calculations and misleading Arab information.

What is astonishing is that this Israeli declaration was made at the very moment when the U.S. Senate, by a majority of 80 to 16, passed a resolution calling for the imposition of economic sanctions on Iraq, including the abolition of the U.S. government's guarantees for Iraqi loans, amounting to $1.1 billion for the purchase of subsidized American products. The U.S. resolution against Iraq was adopted because of what the senators described as the danger of Iraq's possession of chemical weapons. It seems as if Israel wants to push the Arabs into a battle with the United States at this particular time, especially after the U.S. administration had suspended the American-Palestinian dialogue.[75]

Only days before, from July 20 to 24, Defence Minister Moshe Arens had made an urgent visit to Washington to argue for U.S. action against Iraq's military arsenal. "Before the war broke out I met my American counterpart Dick Cheney in the company of the Mossad (secret service) chief and General Amnon Shahak, the head of Israeli military intelligence, and our talks centered on the Iraqi question," Arens was quoted as saying.[76]

The U.S. administration swung from its 1989 enthusiastic embrace of Iraq as an arms-marketeer's dream and, perhaps, as the Middle Eastern strategic ally that Iran had been in the days of the Shah, to making Iraq the object of a massive bombing campaign in January 1991. Unquestionably this was the realization of Israel's most fervent dreams. So it becomes relevant – indeed, unavoidable – to ask: how big a role did Israel play in the prelude to the war?

The number and the weight of all the influences that led President George Bush to decide to send troops to Saudi Arabia after Iraq's invasion of Kuwait might never be assayed with absolute precision. An assortment of factors fired George Bush's lust for war: to consolidate the *raison d'etre* of the U.S. as a military power, to establish a special relationship with the Gulf monarchies that would offer military facilities and influence on the price of oil, to demonstrate that the only superpower to survive the Cold War would respond harshly (insanely harshly) to an uppity Third World leader.

Israel had no overriding influence on those factors. But it is compellingly clear that, had Israel accepted a peace settlement in the 1970s or the 1980s, instead of seeking to accumulate more weapons of mass destruction and engage in aggression, there might never have been this last war. Moreover, Israel's policy contributed to a cycle that allowed the war to be marketed by the administration as the "timely extermination of a Hitler with weapons." It is unlikely that, without this selling point, the Bush administration could have pulled the U.S. public and its foreign allies on to the fast-track to war. Finally, once troops began pouring into the region, it is quite clear that Israel and its U.S. supporters played a considerable role in building the political climate for an early attack on Iraq.

Israel's U.S. backers lobby discreetly

While much of the world waited in horror of war once the U.S. troops were dispatched to Saudi Arabia, the months between August 1990 and January 1991 were, for Israel, a time of anguished uncertainty. Israel worried that the U.S. forces might leave the Gulf without destroying Iraq's military infrastructure. Its fears sometimes overcame its commitment to obey Washington by keeping a low profile, lest Washington's Arab allies shrink back.

Israeli newspapers quoted an official saying anonymously that if the U.S. and its allies didn't destroy Iraq, "the Israeli army would destroy

Saddam." Such sentiments intensified as it appeared that Iraq might agree to pull out of Kuwait – as part of an agreement (worse yet, from the Israeli point of view) that included a Middle East peace conference, referred to off-the-record as a "nightmare scenario."[77] "We say there is danger if [the U.S.] does not finish with it," Foreign Minister David Levy told a U.S. congressional delegation in January.[78]

In contrast to Israel's openly expressed objectives, its normally vocal U.S. supporters were eerily silent. That, however, did not indicate a lack of concern. Said Leonard Fein, a liberal Jewish analyst, "There is near universal consensus [in the Jewish community] that Iraq's war-making capability has to be destroyed."[79] Ann Lewis, a director of the Committee for Peace and Security in the Gulf (CPS), said that until just before the critical mid-January war vote in the U.S. Congress (see below), "the Jewish community stayed silent as an organized community, not wishing to give the impression in any way that their interest and concern for the survival of the state of Israel would dictate what United States policy should be."[80]

Everyone with a sliver of political sensibility knew, of course, that the matter was of tremendous concern to Israel's U.S. supporters. How could they not know, when Saddam Hussein was conditioning Iraq's pullout from Kuwait to an Israeli pullout from occupied Palestine? That so few in the U.S. sought to spare the murder of thousands of Iraqis by joining Saddam – and France, until shortly before the war – in this eminently just demand is worth reflection. But nobody wanted to talk about it. A *Washington Post* report on foreign policy debates within the Democratic Party noted that "sentiments on Israel are clearly related to attitudes toward Bush's Iraq policy."

> Israel and its supporters would like to see Saddam weakened or destroyed, and many of the strongest Democratic supporters of Bush's policy on the gulf, such as Solarz, are longtime backers of Israel. Similarly, critics of Israel – among conservatives as well as liberals – are also among the leading critics of Bush's gulf policy. "That's embarrassing," said William Schneider, a political analyst at the American Enterprise Institute, "because there seems to be a hidden concern – either pro- or anti-Israel."[81]

While the major Jewish organizations hung back, Ann Lewis's CPS played an important role in advancing Israel's agenda: an early and dev-astating war against Iraq. CPS was a curious organization. Launched in September 1990, it did not go public until December,[82] when the focus of the then-ascendant anti-war forces shifted to Congress where a vote authorizing President Bush to attack Iraq was planned. Stephen Solarz,[83] a Democratic member of Congress from Brooklyn, organized the group in partnership with Prince Bandar bin Sultan Al-Saud, the Saudi Arabian ambassador to Washington. While Bandar, who is regarded as an ace operative in the shadowy realm of U.S.-Saudi covert operations, conducted his pro-war agitation independently, as a repre-sentative of the Saudi monarchy, he used his connection with CPS to befriend a number of leaders of pro-Israeli organizations, even hosting a group on an unprecedented visit to Saudi Arabia. The pro-Israeli leaders "waxed eloquent on Bandar's role and on the prospects for peace between Israel and the gulf states." But Bandar's main goal was to stop his new friends from lobbying against congressional approval of post-war arms sales to Saudi Arabia.

After Bandar was enlisted, Richard Perle, Ronald Reagan's far-right assistant secretary of defence and Israel's unflinching friend, was brought on board.[84] Solarz and Perle "split the fundraising duties" and Perle acknowledged that much of the money raised for CPS (and, pre-sumably, for the overwrought full-page nation-wide newspaper ads it ran) was donated by defence contractors. Perle also got money from the right-wing Bradley Foundation in Milwaukee.[85] Ann Lewis, a former aide to Jesse Jackson who was very defensive about her connection with CPS, said the organization had decided not to disclose the identities of its donors.[86] CPS, which had official non-profit status, moved into the office of a marketing company run by a friend of Perle's.[87]

Solarz, Perle and Lewis became incessant fixtures on radio and tele-vision programs, their hawkishness offsetting the many quasi-dovish former defence, intelligence and diplomatic officials. They took pains to portray CPS as an organization primarily concerned with U.S. – not Israeli – policy.[88]

It is impossible to know how effective the CPS ads and media appearances were in ratcheting-up the bellicosity of the U.S. public.

Certainly their warnings of Iraq's military potential deterred some people from lobbying their elected representatives against the war.

As it turned out, pro-Israeli Democrats, led by Solarz, played a major, but by no means a crucial role in the January 13 vote of 250-183 in the House of Representatives that authorized President Bush to wage the war he was bound to launch anyway. Significantly, a number of representatives whose pro-Israeli voting pattern had never deviated before, voted against what was widely viewed as a dangerous and criminal (under international law) war. They, as some of their pro-Israeli counterparts in an earlier, closer Senate vote, made it clear they were responding to strong anti-war sentiment in their districts, an important phenomenon that pro-Palestinian activists would do well to remember. On the eve of the vote, it became known that the American Israel Public Affairs Committee (AIPAC), Israel's congressional lobby, while keeping "an unusually low profile during the congressional vote," did quietly lobby undecided legislators.[89] Abraham Foxman, the national director of the Anti-Defamation League of B'nai B'rith, allowed that Jewish organizations had conducted "lobbying in the unclassic sense. We let our views be known without an all-out offensive."[90]

On the road again

In the same breath that he congratulated the U.S.-led allies on their victory when the bombing stopped, Prime Minister Shamir announced that Israel would seek the removal of all of Iraq's unconventional weapons and missile launchers.[91] Senior Israeli officials said a message they were sending Secretary of State James Baker outlining their demands for a post-war settlement included a requirement that Iraq recognize Israel and publicly state it would not attack it in the future.[92]

The military component of Israel's desires was enshrined in the U.N. Security Council Resolution 687, which established an unprecedented hands-on procedure for dismantling Iraq's unconventional weapons. Israel's own status as the sole nuclear weapons power in the Middle East was given an unprecedented endorsement in May, when President Bush's grand plan for arms control in the Middle East made clear that

Israel would not be required to dismantle its nuclear weapons – a proposal Israel greeted with calls to limit the flow of conventional weapons to Arab governments.[93] But even as the five major weapons-selling countries met in Paris to discuss how they could exercise "greater responsibility" in their arms sales to the Middle East,[94] the process of disarming Iraq was breaking down. And something else – the original premise of its anti-Iraqi stance – was making Israel uneasy.

In June 1991, an Israeli weekly noted "Iran's $120-billion five-year plan designed to make Tehran a regional superpower and a member of the nuclear club."[95] The director-general of Israel's defence ministry, David Ivri, warned that "Iranian weapons procurement threatens to kindle conflicts throughout the Middle East, and since Iran thinks of Israel as an enemy, Israel should take the threat seriously."[96] Western "military sources" told the *Jerusalem Post* that, "in the future conflict scenarios Israel was preparing in the wake of the war, it was paying particular attention to Iran."[97]

Iran would seem to multiply by two the observation made in 1989 by the *Economist*: "Israel's safety depends more on winning a stable Middle East peace than on wiping out the Iraqi dictator's nuclear plants every few years."[98]

Notes

The abbreviations used for publications and broadcast services in the footnotes are the following:

AFP: Agence France-Presse *AP*: American Press Service *BG*: Boston Globe *D*: Davar *E*: Economist *FBIS*: U.S. government's Foreign Broadcast Information Service *HA*: Ha'aretz *IDF*: Israeli Defense Force *IFA*: Israeli Foreign Affairs *INA*: Iraqi News Agency *JDS*: Jerusalem Domestic Service *JDW*: Jane's Defence Weekly *JTA*: Jewish Telegraphic Agency *KH*: Kol Ha'ir (Jerusalem) *LAT*: Los Angeles Times *NCJB*: Northern California Jewish Bulletin *NO*: New Outlook *NWR*: U.S. News and World Report *SFC*: San Francisco Chronicle *UCT*: Universal Coordinated Time *UPI*: United Press International *WJW*: Washington Jewish Week *WP*: Washington Post *WSJ*: Wall Street Journal *WT*: Washington Times *YA*: Yediot Aharonot

[1] *NO*, February-March 1991.
[2] *HA*, March 29, 1985, *FBIS-MEA*, April 1, 1985, p.I-3.
[3] *JDW*, March 30, 1985. The report said that Prime Minister Peres had ordered

a halt to arms shipments to Iran both because of the possibility of a rapprochement-*cum*-arms deal with Iraq and for fear that arms sent to Iran would be passed on to pro-Iranian groups in Lebanon which were taking their toll on Israel's proxy forces there. (Although the date of this article is later than the HA article, as a weekly, it would have been published prior to the Israeli daily.)

4 NYT, February 5, 1985.

5 JP, July 19, 1988.

6 HA, March 7, 1986; FBIS-MEA, March 7, 1986, pp.I-5-6.

7 BG, October 14, 1990. This is a very propagandistic article by Laurie Mylroie (see footnote 85).

8 HA, *op. cit.*

9 NYT, article and op-ed, April 15, 1991 and *Frontline* documentary, "The Election Held Hostage," aired by U.S. Public Broadcasting System the same week contained new revelations about the "October surprise" – the 1980 Reagan campaign's alleged deal with Iran to keep the hostages until after the elections.

10 *Foreign Report* (the publication of the E cited by HA), December 5, 1986.

11 HA, March 7, 1986; FBIS-MEA March 7, 1986, pp. I-5-6. On the same pages FBIS publishes a transcript of a Jerusalem radio report in Arabic (1625 UCT, March 6, 1986) citing the well-connected intelligence unit of the E's small circulation *Foreign Report*, on the Iraqi-Israeli meeting. It is worth remembering that these events occurred while the Labour Party leader Shimon Peres was prime minister in a government in which he shared that post with Likud leader Yitzhak Shamir. Connected with Peres, the term "peace process" connotes, as it does for most non-Israelis, the notion of land for peace with Palestinians and neighbouring Arab countries (although Labour does not call for a Palestinian state). Shamir and his associates use the term to refer to Arab governments agreeing to negotiate with Israel on its own win-lose terms.

12 JDS, 1100 UCT, March 21, 1986; FBIS-MEA, March 25, 1986 p. I-1.

13 *Near East Report* (n.d.) quoted by JP November 20, 1987.

14 KH, February 8, 1991, cited by JTA, NCJB, February 8, 1991.

15 *Tass*, 1816 UCT, June 3, 1986; FBIS-USSR, June 4, 1986, p.D-4. Tass quotes the Kuwaiti paper *Al-Watan*, which, of course, could have been the original source of the information. However, this type of foreign attribution was a common way of disseminating Soviet-gleaned intelligence. Moreover, the article fits nicely with a commentary by a Col. A. Ivanov in *Krasmaya Zvezda* the preceding week (May 25, 1986, translated in the June 3 FBIS-USSR, p. A-1 – FBIS, incidentally is widely known to be a product of the CIA, although its daily reports are issued by the U.S. Department of Commerce). The colonel accuses the Reagan administration of "stating its 'neutrality' vis-à-vis the Iran-Iraq conflict" but "not stopping its efforts to deepen the contradictions between Iran and Iraq and between Iran and the other Arab states" by (among other things) "manipulating deliveries of weapons and military hardware to the warring sides."

16 A 1984 U.S. Senate staff study first identified the "tilt," pointing to $1 billion in commodity credits and a $570 million commitment by the Export-

Import Bank to finance an oil pipeline through Jordan, according to the *NYT* (August 28, 1984).

[17] As it was defined by the special joint congressional committee that investigated it, the Iran-contra affair encompassed the arms-for-hostages deals with Iran and the Reagan administration's secret assistance to the anti-Sandinista contras after Congress had cut off aid for that covert program. The connection between the two was made when it was discovered that some of the profits from the arms sales were diverted to the contras. Israel's role in the affair was shielded by all but a few members of the panel, and by the decision of the panelists to limit the investigation to events that occurred from 1984 on. There was no investigation into the "October surprise": an alleged agreement between the 1980 Reagan presidential campaign and the Islamic Republic in which the U.S. embassy hostages were to be held until after the election, and in exchange Israel would deliver weapons to Iran.

[18] *IFA*, June 1987, December 1987, August 1989.

[19] *Observer* (London), September 13, 1987.

[20] These were first reported by *Le Journal de Dimanche* (Paris)(n.d.), cited in *YA* (Tel Aviv), July 27, 1987; *FBIS-MEA*, July 28, 1987, p. L-2. It was subsequently reported that Israel's leading arms dealer, Shaul Eisenberg, had facilitated the China-Iran missile deal. See also *AFP* (which cites *Newsweek*) in *JP*, July 5, 1988.

[21] *IDF Radio*, 0600 UCT, November 13, 1987, *FBIS-NES*, November 13, 1987.

[22] *D*, November 12, 1987; *FBIS-NES*, November 13, 1987, p.44.

[23] *HA*, November 13, 1987; *FBIS-NES*, November 13, 1987, p.44.

[24] *IDF Radio*, 0600 UCT, November 13, 1987; *FBIS-NES*, November 13, 1987.

[25] *JP*, November 25, 1987.

[26] *JP*, November 20, 1987.

[27] *JDW*, November 11, 1987, quoted by *JP*, November 12, 1987.

[28] *JP*, November 17, 1987.

[29] *JP*, November 17, 1987.

[30] *JP*, November 17, 1987.

[31] *IDF Radio*, 0600 UCT, October 29, 1987; *FBIS-NES*, October 29, 1987, p.29.

[32] *IDF Radio*, 1030 UCT, October 29, 1987; *FBIS-NES*, October 30, 1987, p.18.

[33] *JP*, November 20, 1987.

[34] *SFC*, November 21, 1987.

[35] *KH* (Jerusalem), February 8, 1991, cited by *JTA*, *NCJB*, February 8, 1991.

[36] *WSJ*, December 17, 1987.

[37] *WJW*, January 31, 1991.

[38] *YA*, February 22, 1991, cited by *AP*, *Forward*, February 22, 1991.

[39] *BG*, October 14, 1990.

[40] *JP*, November 23, 1989.

[41] *UPI*, May 17, 1991. Legislators from farm states were also reluctant to adopt sanctions which would deny Iraq the credits it used to purchase food crops.

[42] *NYT*, July 13, 1991.

[43] *JP*, March 7, 1991. A month earlier in the Knesset, Labour MK Shevah Weiss had urged Foreign Minister David Levy to "harness" the intelligence services to compile a list of individuals involved in helping arm Iraq. "Their names should be published, not only in order to blacken their reputation, but also to put them in physical danger from those seeking vengeance," declared Weiss. cf. *JP*, February 7, 1991. For a more analytical view of the controversy over intelligence priorities see *Guardian*, February 22, 1991.

[44] *JP*, February 7, 1991.

[45] While Israel rejoiced in the attack and still continues to unabashedly celebrate it (*JP*, May 17, 1991 on the 10th anniversary of the raid) the operation was roundly – if not entirely sincerely – condemned at the time in Washington. But the war against Iraq brought *post facto* kudos from Israel's friends in the U.S. capitol and even grudging approval from critics. "I'm certainly not prepared to be critical of the action with 20-20 hindsight," said Secretary of State James Baker. "We ourselves had done a great deal of bombing of similar facilities." However, Baker noted, "We did it with full approval of the international community...and in a manner called for by a resolution, in fact, of the U.N. Security Council." (*Newsday*, quoted in *JP*, July 18, 1991.) Nothing like a little legality.

[46] *LAT* "World Report" section, March 5, 1991.

[47] Frank Barnaby, *The Invisible Bomb* (London, I.B. Tauris & Co. Ltd., 1989), p.66.

[48] *WP*, June 29, 1988.

[49] *WP*, September 19, 1988. Argentina, the prime mover of this missile – which would have greatly surpassed the accuracy and destructive ability of the Scuds Iraq used during the war – recently succumbed to U.S. pressure and dismantled the Condor program.

[50] *JP*, August 21, 1988; WAKH (Manama) 0950 UCT, September 5, 1988; FBIS-NES, September 6, 1988, p.10; EFE, *El Dia*, (Mexico City) August 21, 1988.

[51] *Independent*, September 24 1988, quoted by David Horovitz, "Mossad reported determined to halt Cairo missile project," *JP*, September 25, 1988.

[52] *WP*, February 10, 1991. This is an article by David Halevy and William Scott Malone, who say the admission came during interviews they conducted. For more on the background, see *IFA*, May 1990, September 1990 and February 1991.

[53] *WP*, September 19, 1988.

[54] This was extensively reported by NBC *Nightly News* in a series of reports during the week of October 25, 1989. U.S. administration officials responded to the reports by confirming the transfer of the Jericho (and many other weapons systems). See also *IFA*, July, August, November and December 1989, February, March, June and December 1990 and No. 5 1991; *WP*, February 24, 1991: in a letter, Carol Pollard, sister of convicted spy Jonathan Jay Pollard, cites government information given to the sentencing judge that included mention of the sharing of the Jericho with South Africa.

[55] *JP*, December 17, 1989.

[56] *WP*, November 1, 1989.

[57] [U.S. Senate bill] S.1507, Report No. 102-113, July 19, 1991.

[58] UPI, September 19, 1988. *WJW*, July 7, 1988 identifies the institute as Israeli-connected.

[59] *NYT*, January 9, 1989; AP, April 13, 1990.

[60] *WP*, March 31, 1989.

[61] *Newsgrid*, an electronic database accessed through CompuServe, December 20, 1989.

[62] Quoted by AP, March 29, 1991.

[63] AP, April 3, 1991.

[64] *WP*, April 4, 1990.

[65] *Newsgrid*, March 6, 1991.

[66] AP, April 13, 1990.

[67] AP, April 17, 1990.

[68] AP, JP, May 17, 1990.

[69] UPI, May 8, 1990.

[70] *Reuters*, May 29, 1990.

[71] Such an attack headed the list of possible scenarios in a June 14, 1990 *LAT* article on rising tension in the Middle East; *WT*, July 13, 1990 reports it was a featured scenario at a seminar, "Strategy 90," sponsored by the International Strategic Studies Association.

[72] *LAT*, June 14, 1990.

[73] AP, *NYT*, July 28, 1990.

[74] INA, 1700 UCT, July 31, 1990; *FBIS-NES*, August 1, 1990, p.21.

[75] Cairo Domestic Service, 1730 UCT, July 28, 1990; *FBIS-NES*, July 31, 1990, p.9.

[76] *Newsgrid*, March 6, 1991; *JP*, March 7, 1991; *WJW*, January 31, 1991.

[77] AP, January 6, 1991.

[78] UPI, January 9, 1991.

[79] NCJB, January 4, 1991.

[80] *LAT*, January 19, 1991.

[81] *WP*, January 3, 1991.

[82] John Judis, "On the Home Front: The Gulf War's Strangest Bedfellows; Will the AIPAC/Bandar/Defense Industry Alliance Survive the Peace?" *WP*, June 23, 1991. This is an abridged version of a piece by Judis in the May-June issue of *Tikkun*.

[83] While Solarz is regarded as the archetypal "Israel firster," according to Michael Tomasky, author of a lengthy profile of Solarz (*Village Voice*, June 18, 1991), Israel's lobbyists regard him as an unmanageable Solarz "firster." Solarz, however, has never done anything that could be remotely considered harmful to Israel.

[84] Judis, *op. cit.*

[85] Tomasky, *op. cit.* On the back cover of the instant book she co-authored with Judith Miller, *Saddam Hussein and the Crisis in the Gulf* (New York, Times Books [a division of Random House], 1990), Laurie Mylroie is identified as "Bradley Foundation Fellow at Harvard University's Center for Middle Eastern Studies." According to Egyptian President Hosni Mubarak, Harvard Professor Laurie Mylroie was an intermediary between Iraq and an

Israeli minister, Moshe Shahal. On French television Shahal referred to "messages" she carried between the two. Mylroie emphatically denied a New York journalist's query about "the apparently widespread belief around Harvard that you have at least informal relations with Mossad." In 1986 and 1987, when pro-Iraqi sentiment in Israel was at its peak, Mylroie wrote and spoke in favor of greater U.S. support for Iraq. (*Left Business Observer* [New York], February 28, 1991) After Iraq invaded Kuwait, Mylroie co-authored the super-heated *Saddam Hussein and the Crisis in the Gulf*. In the lead-up to the war she at least twice advocated lines that were clearly to Israel's advantage. After the war she became a leading advocate of further intervention: "We should start talking to the Iraqi opposition and help liberate Baghdad." (*Forward* [New York], July 11, 1991).

[86] Judis, *op. cit.*
[87] Tomasky, *op. cit.*
[88] Judis, *op. cit.*
[89] LAT, January 19, 1991.
[90] JP, January 14, 1991.
[91] *Kyodo*, February 28, 1991.
[92] WP, March 1, 1991.
[93] WP, May 31, 1991.
[94] AP, July 9, 1991.
[95] JP, June 13, 1991.
[96] IDF Radio, 1400 UCT, June 5, 1991; FBIS-NES, June 6, 1991, pp. 24-25.
[97] JP, June 7, 1991.
[98] E, April 8, 1989, quoted in *Proliferation Watch*, a newsletter published by the U.S. Senate Committee on Governmental Affairs, January-February 1991.

Collateral Damage
Carel Moiseiwitsch

Messages and Messengers

The saying goes: don't blame the messenger for the message. In the war against Iraq it also might have been said: because of the messenger, don't tear up and throw away the message.

The message was: withdrawal from Kuwait is linked to the application of United Nations resolutions on the question of Palestine and Palestinian rights.

One of the messengers was Saddam Hussein. On August 12, ten days after his invasion of Kuwait, he proposed "that all cases of occupation, and those cases that have been portrayed as occupation, in the region, be resolved simultaneously and on the same principles..." The message was discarded with the reply: "There can be no linkage."

Another messenger brought a similar message. But he was not the enemy, he was part of the U.S.-led coalition, a partner in war preparations. French President François Mitterand spoke before the United Nations on September 24 and proposed a four-phase, connected approach, including an international peace conference that would address, among other matters, the Palestinian right to their homeland. "I find it impossible not to say this loud and clear: the law must apply equally to all, both in regard to its principles and to its consequences." Again the now stock reply, "there can be no linkage," and the war plans went forward.

After the bombing ended, in negotiations for the exchange of Western hostages held in Lebanon for Lebanese hostages held by Israel, the organization Islamic Holy War sent a message on August 12 to the U.N. Secretary General. It reiterated the now familiar refrain: "Why were the United Nations resolutions implemented immediately after their adoption during the Gulf crisis while none of the resolutions adopted in regard to the just Palestinian cause have yet been put into effect decades after their adoption?"

Thomas Hurka is a Canadian professor of philosophy and columnist for the conservative *Globe and Mail* newspaper. He is far – far indeed – from the world-view of Islamic Holy War. And yet an open letter he wrote to Canadian Prime Minister Brian Mulroney, before the U.S.-led bombing began, shares this one element.

> "Iraq must not benefit from its aggression against Kuwait." This is a reasonable principle to apply in the Persian Gulf, but it mustn't be interpreted too narrowly. If Iraq had legitimate grievances against Kuwait and gets them redressed in a peace settlement, it is no better off than it would be had it used proper procedures in an ideal world. So how, in a morally relevant sense, has it benefited from aggression? (It has caused harm to Kuwait and should pay reparations. But its original grievances are a separate issue.) It's the same with an international conference on the Palestinian question. If this conference should have happened a long time ago, how does it benefit Iraq if we hold it now? Is our bottom line for negotiation that we will keep doing the wrong things we've done in the past?

In the real world of politics, Iraq undoubtedly would have benefited if the U.S. abandoned its long resistance to applying U.N. resolutions on the question of Palestine. Iraq would have gained political credit for helping correct a profoundly felt injustice to the Arab people. The U.S. and Israel would have paid a political penalty for their long defiance of the international consensus on this matter, a consensus that recognizes the Palestinians' right to an independent homeland.

But in the real world of politics, Kuwait was not the issue for the U.S. or Israel, except in propaganda terms. The self-evident diplomatic solution, involving linkage of the Iraqi and Israeli occupations, only would have diverted the U.S. and Israel from their war objectives of destroying Iraq, politically, economically, socially and hence militarily. International consensus and elementary justice were not a strong enough incentive for this peaceful diversion.

The world's single military superpower was prepared to organize its own Middle East conference only after it had made war against Iraq, but not to avoid it. An international conference to avoid war also would have been a conference based on the United Nations resolutions on the Middle East, and on the widely shared international consensus on the question of Palestine, a consensus shared by Washington's two main economic rivals, Europe and Japan. In a conference to avoid war the U.S. would have found itself diplomatically isolated with its ally Israel, whereas its economic rivals would be important participants.

By contrast, the conference after the U.S. waged its war is a conference where: the U.N. and the European roles have been explicitly marginalized, where the international consensus on Palestine has been unabashedly discarded, and where the U.S. is the sole decisive power orchestrating arrangements.

Nonetheless, the Palestinian question remains irrepressible, unavoidable, and hence central to peace in the region, as Marion Qawas explains in the following article. That really is why so many different messengers keep returning with the same message.

Palestine and Palestinians

Marion Qawas

GENUINE PEACE IN THE MIDDLE EAST WILL NEVER BE ACHIEVED WITHOUT A JUST settlement of the Palestinian issue. The uprooting of the Palestinian people from their homeland is intertwined with the history of colonialist plunder in the region, with the resistance of the Arab people to that intervention, with contemporary U.S. designs of hegemony on the region, and therefore, with any solutions for peace in the area.

Historical background

Zionism developed as a political movement in the late 19th and early 20th centuries in Europe. Theodore Herzl, credited as its founder, attempted to curry the favour of first one European power and then another, in order to find a backer for his idea of an exclusive Jewish state in Palestine. He eventually found such a collaborator in Britain, a leading colonial power of that period.

British colonialists supported the Zionist aims, strictly in service of their own interests. Lord Arthur Balfour and then Prime Minister Lloyd George were interested in maintaining British control of the Suez

Canal, and saw the creation of a Zionist state in the midst of the Arab countries as the ultimate in "divide and rule." Zionist leaders at the time were well aware of the motives of the British government and openly endorsed them. Chaim Weizmann, then president of the British Zionist Federation, stated: "a Jewish Palestine would be a safeguard to England, in particular in respect to the Suez Canal."[1]

The Balfour Declaration of November 2, 1917, which promised the Zionists a "Jewish national home" in Palestine, coupled with the British Mandate over Palestine after the First World War, gave the Zionist movement its chance to gain a foothold in the area. The British authorities implemented the Balfour policy, despite the fact that they had promised the Arabs independence for their part in World War One, and despite the fact that in 1917, the Jewish community in Palestine was a mere eight per cent of the population. British support from 1917 to the early 1930s facilitated Zionist immigration from Europe to Palestine. The Jewish population tripled, from 56,000 to 174,616, during those years. As Yasser Arafat, chairman of the Palestine Liberation Organization, said in his address to the United Nations General Assembly in 1974:

> If the immigration of Jews to Palestine had had as its objective the goal of enabling them to live side by side with us, enjoying the same rights and assuming the same duties, we would have opened our doors to them, as far as our homeland's capacity for absorption permitted... But that the goal of this immigration should be to usurp our homeland, disperse our people, and turn us into second-class citizens – this is what no one can conceivably demand that we acquiesce in or submit to.[2]

As the aims of the Zionist immigration became clearer to the Palestinian population, the level of resistance increased accordingly. It was this resistance, combined with the international situation in the 1930s, that brought about changes in the British policies. Some limits were placed on Jewish immigration to Palestine, and strains developed in British-Zionist relations. However, with its declining power in the aftermath of World War Two, the British washed their hands of their Mandate over Palestine.

A new set of circumstances came into play. The shock waves of Hitler's mass genocide against the Jews in Europe, along with the Zionist movement's courting of their new sponsor, the United States, resulted in the U.N. Partition Plan of 1947. With this plan, the U.N. proposed a Jewish state on over half of the land area of Palestine, although Jews constituted only one-third of the population and owned only six per cent of the land. The plan was eventually passed, amid significant arm-twisting by Western powers, especially the United States. Experts on international law have expressed doubts if the United Nations ever had the legal right to divide Palestine, especially without the approval of, or even consultation with, the indigenous Palestinians.[3] The U.N. Resolution, 181 (II), also called for a Palestinian state in the remaining original Mandate territory.

In 1948, in the first of several wars involving the new Israeli state, Zionists occupied even more land than the U.N. had granted them, ending up with 80 per cent of Palestine. A campaign of terror and killings preceded and accompanied the war. The most infamous just before the unilateral declaration of an Israeli state was at Deir Yassin on April 9, 1948, in which 254 Palestinian civilians were massacred by Menahem Begin's Irgun. Begin went on to become prime minister of Israel in the late 1970s. Recent Israeli scholarship shows that a calculated plan was implemented by the Ben-Gurion led Israeli government to drive the Palestinians from their homes.[4] In the area taken over by Israel in 1948, 385 Palestinian villages and towns were completely razed to the ground and erased from the map. The first wave of refugees had been born.

The expansionist nature of the Zionist state, along with its desire to expel most of the indigenous population, are two of the characteristics that distinguish it from other settler-colonialist entities. According to the writings of Zionism's founder, Herzl, the boundaries of the state will expand as the Jewish population grows – "The more immigrants, the more land." A similar sentiment was stated by Rabbi Fischmann, member of the Jewish Agency, in his testimony before the U.N. Special Committee on Palestine in 1947: "The Promised Land extends from the River of Egypt to the Euphrates; it includes parts of Syria and Lebanon."

The noted Egyptian scholar, A.M. Elmessiri, points out other dimensions to this expansionism. "Israeli expansionism has its hard economic aspects and yields many benefits..." These benefits include water resources, economic markets, as well as land for future settlements. Scientific specialists have stated that Israel's refusal to give up the West Bank has more to do with control of the water resources than anything else.

Subsequent wars in 1956 and 1967 and the invasion of Lebanon in 1982 have reinforced the expansionist and militarist aspects of Israeli policy. Israel has annexed the Golan Heights and East Jerusalem, occupied and still occupies by military force, the West Bank and Gaza, and occupies by proxy its "buffer zone" in south Lebanon. The actions of the Israeli government during its 1982 invasion of Lebanon and its "iron fist" policies in the occupied West Bank and Gaza, a phrase consciously chosen by Israeli cabinet minister and former prime minister Yitzhak Rabin, have demonstrated that Israeli policy is both brutal and aggressive. Twenty thousand Lebanese and Palestinian civilians were killed in Lebanon in 1982, as Israeli jets dropped cluster bombs and vacuum bombs on apartment buildings. Over one thousand Palestinians have been killed in the West Bank and Gaza during the first three years of the intifada at the hands of Israeli troops.

Israel could not sustain such policies if it were not for massive infusions, billions of dollars, of U.S. economic and military aid. Israel currently receives over $3 billion a year from the U.S., a significant portion of that in grants.[5] It has also requested an additional $13 billion, $3 billion in grants to reimburse for losses from the Gulf war, and $10 billion in grants and loan guarantees for the resettlement of Soviet immigrants. If all of this aid is approved, it would amount to $3,770 assistance for each and every Israeli, or $18,850 for a family of five. The U.S. has given more money to Israel than to any other country in the world, and by 1984, the U.S. had given Israel double the aid it had given the entire continent of Africa.

The military aid given to Israel has allowed it to become a major military power, and in 1984, the Institute for Strategic Studies in the U.S. said Israel had the fourth most powerful military establishment in the world. It is technologically by far the most developed military force in the Middle East, and is the only state in the region to have confirmed nuclear warheads. The Israeli state often puts forth the notion that it is a small, defenceless country, surrounded by a "horde of hostile Arabs." This is an idea that still lingers in Western public opinion. Even a glance at recent history, however, indicates the opposite. The Israeli march into Lebanon, the destruction of much of Beirut, and the ruthless suppression of the intifada in the occupied territories, all would lead us to believe that it is the Arab people who have the right to be fearful of a militarist Israel.

Palestinian and Arab resistance

It should not be surprising, then, to discover that there has been sustained Palestinian resistance to both the Zionist ideology, which denies the very existence of the Palestinian people, and to Israeli state policies, which attempt to reduce the Palestinians to refugees and to suppress their inevitable opposition to occupation.

In the 1920s, when the Palestinians first became aware of the Zionist objectives, they launched appeals and protests to the British Mandate authorities. They called on the British government to respect Arab rights in Palestine, but to no avail. Demonstrations and acts of other civil disobedience culminated in the 1936 general strike, which halted the economic life of the country. This six-month general strike was followed by an all-out armed uprising that lasted until 1939, and was eventually crushed by the British.

After the creation of Israel in 1948, the Palestinian people were, for the first few years, preoccupied with the task of simply trying to stay alive in the miserable conditions of the refugee camps. They then appealed to world opinion and to the United Nations to solve their plight. The U.N., since 1948, has passed numerous resolutions calling on Israel to allow the refugees to return or to offer them compensation, but none were ever implemented.[6] The Palestinians looked to the Arab regimes to take up their cause and to help them regain their national rights, but this also proved futile. The Arab regimes were either incapable of assisting the Palestinian struggle in any significant way, or had their own motives for not wanting to offer that assistance.

Finally, the Palestinian people came to the conclusion, as have so many other oppressed peoples, that they could rely only on themselves for their liberation. They launched their armed resistance in 1965 and took up the task of building an effective national movement with the Palestine Liberation Organization (PLO). In many Western countries, the PLO is often portrayed only as a military organization. This is far from the truth.

In fact, the PLO and its parliamentary body, the Palestine National Council, represent Palestinians everywhere, under occupation and in the diaspora. The PLO encompasses every facet of Palestinian society, from unions to artist guilds to medical associations to women's groups. This is why most Palestinians, even if they don't agree with all of the policies of the Palestinian leadership, will say they support the PLO. They consider the PLO to be part of themselves, and to speak for them.

This explains why both Israel and the U.S. are adamant in trying to destroy and discredit the PLO, or at least modify and weaken its positions. Israel has enacted a law that forbids any Israeli from contacts with the PLO. Jewish Israelis who have defied this law to promote peace by meeting with PLO representatives, including Yasser Arafat, have been imprisoned. The Israeli government knows that the PLO, as long as it insists on its independent decision-making, represents a kernel of national hope for the Palestinian people.

Cultural heritage is a vital link to hold together the dispersed Palestinian nation, currently estimated at over five million. Of these, 1.7 million live under direct military occupation, 700,000 are third-class citizens inside the pre-1967 boundaries of Israel (17 per cent of the total population), and the rest constitute the Palestinian diaspora.[7] The preservation of culture and language, of a sense of national geography – hometowns and birthplaces – keeps a certain cohesion among dispersed Palestinians. The Palestinian people also consider education as part of national survival. An educated population not only is more able to withstand the economic ebbs and flows of unstable conditions, but also is more capable of challenging a sophisticated occupier. Israeli authorities in the West Bank and Gaza are equally aware of the significance of education for the Palestinians, and have kept most Palestinian institutions of higher learning forcibly closed since the onset of the intifada.

The current flashpoint of Palestinian resistance is the intifada or "uprising" in the occupied West Bank and Gaza. The intifada represents the most developed form of Palestinian self-reliance in this century. It is not just an insurrection, a movement of civil disobedience; it is an effort in transforming a society, in creating new social relationships, in building new and more equitable structures in the occupied territories. It is agricultural co-operatives and home education; it is Palestinian women taking up a more complete role in their community; it is Palestinian youth saying – we are staying here and we want a better future for our generation.

The Palestinian struggle is, in its essence, a struggle for legitimate national rights. However, due to its unique circumstances, it cannot achieve those national rights without also making far-reaching social changes. The Palestinian struggle will not be successful without the full participation of all its social groupings, in creative and democratic ways that are still evolving. As such, it represents not only a challenge to the political status quo in the region, but also a challenge to the more traditional elements of the social status quo in the Arab world. Since its inception, the Palestinian struggle has threatened the more reactionary Arab regimes, both in their pro-Western bias and in their feudal social policies. The so-called ripple effect of the intifada, wherein the populations of other Arab countries would follow the example of launching social and political change, causes very serious anxiety to those arbitrary regimes.

The Arab context

Why does the Palestinian struggle seem to be so popular with the Arab people? Why is there such hostility towards Israel and the U.S. in the Arab world?

The Palestinian struggle represents the focal point of Arab aspirations to rid themselves of domination by outside forces. Two themes run through the efforts for Arab independence – Arab unity, the kind of unity that existed before colonial powers carved up the area to serve their own interests, and a burning desire to be free of subjugation by Western powers. As such, the struggle of the Palestinian people to regain their homeland has symbolized the yearnings of most Arabs of this generation. They see it as the most consistent hope for foiling the ambitions of successive U.S. administrations, contrary to what is perceived as the servile behaviour of many of the Arab regimes.

The response of the Arab regimes to Israel's policies has two faces: one for domestic consumption, and one for actual implementation. Due to the enormous popularity of the Palestinian struggle in the Arab world, Arab leaders cannot publicly show disinterest in, or disregard for, Palestinian rights and aspirations. However, the reactionary Arab regimes also have their economic and military well-being tied into U.S. interests. Thus, we have the curious sight of regimes like Saudi Arabia declaring publicly the virtues of liberating Jerusalem, while at the same time, pumping billions of dollars into the United States economy, which in turn helps fund and maintain the Israeli state. This dichotomy between Arab popular sentiment and the actual policies of most Arab regimes poses a difficult challenge for the Palestinian movement. On the one hand, most Palestinians are aware that the public posturing by Arab regimes is just empty words; on the other hand, the Palestinian struggle, existing without a secure land base of its own, must extract what it can from those empty words in the way of resources and bases of operation. Nonetheless, Palestinians are aware that an inevitable showdown is coming with these regimes. The break in relations between the PLO and the Gulf countries may well be the beginning of that showdown.

This was the backdrop to the crisis in the Gulf, and to Iraqi President Saddam Hussein's proposal linking Iraq's withdrawal from Kuwait with Israeli withdrawal from the occupied West Bank and Gaza. Whatever the motivations behind his proposal, it touched a nerve of Arab popular sentiment, both in its call for justice for the Palestinians, and in its "calling the bluff" on stated U.S. intentions in the region. It made eminent sense to the average Arab that U.N. resolutions on Palestine, having gathered dust on the shelves for over 40 years, should be implemented at least at the same time as six-month-old resolutions on Iraq's moves against Kuwait. Arabs could see no reason why the daily Israeli brutality against Palestinians was less significant than Iraqi actions in Kuwait. The U.S., and other Western powers, must realize that as long as the Palestinian issue remains unresolved, it will be a part of any hostilities in the area. The Arab people have a keen sense of the double standard employed in the region, especially by the U.S., and the Palestinian tragedy is a daily reminder to them that the U.S. is not interested in their liberation.

Options for the Palestinians

The Gulf crisis has had profound effects on the Palestinian people, both economically and politically. The Palestinian community in Kuwait was estimated at 350,000 prior to Iraq's invasion. It was the largest Palestinian community outside of historic Palestine and Jordan, was thriving and prosperous, and helped build the Kuwaiti infrastructure in many significant sectors. Due to stringent Kuwaiti citizenship laws, however, none of these Palestinians were ever allowed to become full Kuwaiti citizens, not even those born there. The Palestinians in Kuwait also contributed large amounts of money to families and institutions in the West Bank and Gaza.

All of this, of course, is now ended, probably permanently. Many of the Palestinians who fled Kuwait, left with only the clothes on their backs and what they could carry in their cars. They now are trying to resettle elsewhere. The Palestinians who remained in Kuwait also are facing harsh conditions. Bands of armed Kuwaitis and private militias declared open season on any available Palestinian. Immediately after the Iraqi evacuation, Palestinians were being arbitrarily rounded up, beaten, imprisoned, and even executed. Their neighbourhoods were under virtual siege, with armed checkpoints at all entrances.

The political stand of the Palestinian people vis-à-vis the Gulf war has been largely misunderstood in the West, partly due to deliberate distortion by the U.S. and Israel. These interests felt that if they could show the Palestinian struggle as having aligned itself with the vilified Saddam Hussein, then increasing Western sympathy for the Palestinian plight could be nipped in the bud. In fact, this strategy succeeded to some extent, at least in the short term. The official stand of the PLO from the beginning was that it did not agree with Iraq's invasion of Kuwait, and it would do all in its power to try and mediate an Arab solution to the crisis. Palestinian diplomacy was extremely active in the first weeks following the invasion, as PLO officials flew from one Arab capital to another. A comprehensive peace initiative was formulated by the PLO, but it never was allowed on the table, not even for discussion, at the August 10, 1990 Arab Summit in Cairo.

Once the U.S. administration intervened militarily in the area, however, the PLO saw the first duty of all Arabs was to condemn such outside interference. Nevertheless, the PLO consistently continued with its attempts to bring the problem to a peaceful resolution, and Yasser Arafat, along with leaders from Yemen and Jordan, was credited with the release of all Westerners trapped in Iraq and Kuwait.

Palestinians started their intifada in December 1987. They have made untold sacrifices, both personally and, as a nation, politically. The Palestine National Council made a historic compromise in 1988, recognizing the right of Israel to exist, calling for acceptance of all U.N. resolutions, and declaring a Palestinian state. They did this in the hope of launching a new era in Middle East peace, of gaining some semblance of national life for this Palestinian generation and the generations to follow. The initiation of the U.S.-PLO dialogue seemed to justify that hope. But, given the halting way the dialogue proceeded, and its arbitrary suspension by Washington, Palestinians concluded that the U.S. simply did not want to deal in good faith. This made them more than ready at the popular level both to oppose and confront U.S. hegemony in the region.

Palestinians and most Arabs feel that the time is long overdue for a shake-up in the status quo in the Arab world, especially amongst the Gulf regimes. Wealth from the oil resources, now shamelessly squandered, is looked upon as wealth that belongs to all Arab people, and not just a few emirs and princes. Development of industry, technology and education has been neglected, even in the Gulf countries themselves, let alone in the Arab world at large. Financial support of the Palestinian cause has been miserly, a pittance when compared with the assets of the oil-producing countries.

There is no doubt that the Palestinians in the occupied territories suffered increased hardships as a result of the Gulf war. From the first day of the U.S.-led bombing raids on Iraq, the entire West Bank and

Gaza were under the strictest of curfews. This total curfew meant the Palestinians were prisoners in their own homes, unable to leave for any reason. They were even denied access to proper medical care, and more Palestinians died during the curfew period for lack of proper medical attention than Israelis died from Scud missiles. Intermittent breaks of a few hours were allowed in some areas, but then only women were permitted out to purchase necessities. There were stepped-up arrest campaigns by the Israeli authorities who used the war atmosphere as a cover to arrest leading Palestinian intellectuals, like Sari Nusseibeh. Whole growing seasons for citrus fruit in Gaza, and other crops in the West Bank, were lost. Workers were not able to go to their jobs, hence no paycheques, and no money for food. International aid organizations have issued urgent appeals because of the lack of adequate nutrition for mothers and babies.

Combined with these hardships was the fear that the Israeli authorities had an unwritten agenda, that of "transfer." "Transfer" is the euphemism used to describe the policy of expulsion from the West Bank, Gaza and Jerusalem that many right-wing Israeli political parties have been demanding for some time. Israeli Prime Minister Shamir, a few weeks after Iraq's invasion of Kuwait appointed Rehavam Ze'evi of the Moledet Party as minister-without-portfolio. Ze'evi and his Moledet Party are well known for their vociferous support of the expulsion of Palestinians. In the Nov. 12, 1990 issue of *Newsweek*, Ze'evi was quoted saying: "The only solution for the Palestinian people is separation from the Jews." He recommends either forcing Arab countries to take 1.5 million Palestinians as part of peace negotiations, or using his "negative magnet" theory, which would force Palestinians to leave by making their living conditions so unbearable – no work, no industry, no universities – they would have no other choice. Ze'evi stated that his appointment confirmed that the majority in the Israeli cabinet had adopted his position on expulsion.

The issue of the massive immigration of Soviet citizens, many not even Jews, highlights Palestinian fears of another unspoken aim of the current Israeli government. Palestinians feel that their response to the original Zionist immigration in the 1920s was too little, too late, and they don't want to make the same mistake this time. Shamir and other members of his cabinet have made statements indicating they plan to settle some of the Soviet immigrants in the occupied territories. These new immigrants already are being used to force Palestinian day labourers in Israel out of their jobs. Although Israeli officials have made some weak commitments to equally weak U.S. administration demands that the new immigrants not be resettled in the West Bank and Gaza, reports show that such activity is occurring. On March 11, 1991, the Israeli Housing Ministry, under Ariel Sharon, unveiled a plan to build 10,000 residential units in the occupied territories to absorb the new immigrants. Then at a press conference on March 22, Sharon upped the figure to 13,000 units. Palestinian leaders in the area are insistent that this issue must be kept front and centre, or else more of Israel's "faits accomplis" will once again create a new reality.

What does the future hold for the Palestinian people? How has the Gulf war affected their struggle? These are issues now hotly debated amongst Palestinians themselves. The moves by the current U.S. administration towards a regional peace conference present a historical challenge to the Palestinian movement, as it strives to act upon the gains of the intifada, maintain a minimum program of national demands, and still respond creatively to the changing international situation.

In the immediate future, it seems apparent that U.S.-Israeli hegemony in the region has been strengthened. The most likely scenario is for them to try, yet once again, to find an alternative to the PLO that will accept a settlement imposed on Israel's terms. Their chances for success are extremely limited as there is no credible Palestinian leadership that is interested in helping the U.S. and Israel undermine the PLO. Palestinians feel that it is hypocritical for the United States to say it respects Palestinian national rights, and then refuse to deal with their chosen representatives. What more fundamental national right is there than the right to govern yourself and choose your own leaders?

However, the Palestinian national movement has survived severe crises before, and actually emerged even stronger. The invasion of Lebanon in 1982 is an example, where Western sources were predicting the imminent collapse of the PLO as a viable player in Middle East politics. Although there were short-term losses and setbacks, 1982 is now seen as having been the labour pains for the birth of the intifada. Palestinians stress that their struggle, although influenced by events in the Arab countries, is not dependent upon them. The Palestinian struggle does not rely on money or weapons for its validity, but rather on its people, its ideals and its democratic structures.

Finally, Palestinians point out that they never expected the Iraqi regime, or any other Arab regime, to liberate Palestine for them. The linkage proposal was important because it put the Palestinian issue where it belongs, at the core of any settlement for the region. The Palestinian struggle is a struggle for national rights, and those national rights cannot be bypassed in any comprehensive settlement for the Middle East. By denying the centrality of the Palestinian question, the U.S. and Israeli governments only prolong instability in the area and sow the seeds for further Middle East crises.

Notes

[1] Weizmann, Chaim, *Trial and Error* (New York, 1949), p.243.

[2] Hussaini, Hatem I. (ed), *Toward Peace in Palestine* (Washington, D.C., 1975), p.9.

[3] *Principles of Public International Law* (Oxford, Clarendon Press, 1966), pp.161-162; Kelsen, H., *The Law of the United Nations* (London, 1951), pp.195 & 287.

[4] Morris, Benny *The Birth of the Palestinian Refugee Problem 1947-1949* (Cambridge, Cambridge University Press, 1987); Flapan, Simha, *The Birth of Israel: Myths and Realities* (Toronto, Random House, 1987); Kidron, Peretz, "Truth Whereby Nations Live" in *Blaming the Victims*, Said, Edward and Christopher Hitchens (eds) (London, Verso, 1987).

[5] *Middle East Report*, No. 164-165, May-Aug, 1990, pp.12-15. Figures for 1989 show $3.7 billion in government aid and $2.5 billion in private aid.

[6] U.N. Resolution 194, Dec. 11, 1948, affirmed the right of return or compensation for Palestinians who had been driven out. U.N. Resolution 3236, Nov. 22, 1974, reaffirmed the right of the Palestinian people to self-determination and independence.

[7] Palestinians living in Israel face institutionalized discrimination in many aspects of daily life. For example, they are not allowed to buy or rent any property from the Jewish National Fund, which controls over 90 per cent of the land in Israel. Their towns and municipalities receive less government money than comparable Jewish towns, and furthermore, Palestinian land still is being expropriated by Israeli authorities in Galilee, in the north of Israel. Also see the article "From the Hebrew Press" by Israel Shahak in Part 3.

Water Resources and the Occupied Territories

Nassib Samir El-Husseini

THE WATER RESOURCE SITUATION ON THE ARAB SIDE OF THE MEDITERRANEAN basis is critical, a matter of survival. Yet relations in the region are so poisoned that any hope for co-operation seems impossible. It is not rhetorical to ask if the "necessary" can force the "impossible."

A few basic facts

- By 1995, Israel, Jordan and the West Bank will have exhausted nearly all of their renewable sources of fresh water if the present consumption pattern is not changed rapidly and radically.
- There are no formal agreements in the whole region to regulate conflicts stemming from water use, except between Egypt and Sudan, and no one knows if that agreement will stand the test of time.
- Specialists say that since 1985 Israel annually has consumed more than 500 cubic metres of water per capita. The annual total consumption was roughly two billion cubic metres by the end of the 1980s, three-quarters for agricultural use. [1]
- Nearly half of Israel's supply consists of water diverted or confiscated from regions outside the pre-1967 Israeli borders.

- The total area of the Jordan River basin is 18,300 square kilometres; but only three per cent of this lies within Israel's pre-1967 borders. The upper Jordan River represents, on average, 40 per cent of Israel's water consumption. The upper Jordan is fed by three rivers, one of which originates in southern Lebanon (the Hasbani) and another originates in the Golan Heights (occupied since 1967 and annexed on December 14, 1981). Therefore, besides their strategic importance, the occupation and annexation of these regions corresponds to a takeover of a main source of water for Israel.
- In the West Bank the annual per capita Palestinian consumption is around 140 cubic metres, less than one-third of an Israeli's; and the total Palestinian consumption is only 5.5 per cent that of all Israelis.[2]

Climate and hydrology

There are two climatic regions in the West Bank, one Mediterranean, one semi-arid. By regional standards, the West Bank is relatively rich in water resources as 68 per cent of its total area receives more than 300 millimetres of annual precipitation. The water reserves of the West Bank are estimated at around 800 million cubic metres, of which two-thirds feed the subterranean aquifers supplying a third of Israel's total consumption. From the beginning of its occupation of the West Bank, Israel placed water resources under the control of the Department for the Allocation and Control of Water. Specifically: on October 30, 1967, under Military Order no. 158, Israel amended Jordanian law no. 31 and took control of water resources. Since then, it has been Israel's prerogative to grant water-use permits, and under the new clause no. 5A, all decisions of this department are final.[3]

Palestinians have completely lost control over their water resources. They must even buy drinking water from the Israeli authorities who draw it from under the Palestinians' own feet, ship it inside Israel's pre-1967 borders, and then export it back to the West Bank residents who receive it out of their taps. Palestinians can only use their own water in driblets to fulfill essential needs, while Jewish settlers, often only a few hundred metres away, enjoy swimming pools for recreation.

The numerous constraints and restrictions imposed by Israel puts West Bank Palestinian agriculture at the mercy of atmospheric precipitation. In fact only five per cent of arable land is irrigated, against 45 per cent in Israel.[4]

According to Antoine Mansour the situation in the Gaza Strip is less catastrophic.[5] Despite the differences pointed out by Mansour, the situation in the Gaza Strip remains critical; and in the aftermath of the Gulf war, the situation is radically different from that which prevailed at the time his book was written. Considering only the demographic dimension in the Gaza Strip, one can easily expect an acute crisis in terms of fresh water supply in the coming decade.

Palestinians assess their needs

The intifada has shed light on many of the region's needs; the recruitment of a certain number of engineers, including hydrologists, is a very pressing one. There now are 12 hydrology specialists working to establish a data bank of West Bank water resources.[6] Israeli studies are not impartial and the figures they present, which are used by Palestinian economists, stem more from propaganda than from accurate and reliable studies.

This group of hydrologists is undertaking specialized studies useful for specific development projects in the region, and is stressing the need to use surface and spring waters as well as to recover rain water. This is a direct consequence of the Israeli authorities' prohibition of new artesian wells for Palestinians. But at present, recovery of rain-water falls outside Israeli prohibitions.

These hydrologists also have initiated many experimental projects, including the construction of a water tank with a capacity of 50 cubic metres in the village of 'Arura, and the increase of the daily production of the village's spring from 45 to 80 cubic metres.[7]

Non-governmental organizations

Because of the dramatic situation created by the Israeli occupation and the ensuing repression, the contribution of non-governmental organizations in the field of water resources cannot be a decisive factor.

Nevertheless, these organizations can help fund projects both for the recovery of rain water and for establishing a data bank of the region's water resources.

The continuing Jewish immigration from the Soviet Union and the ever-rising demographic curve raise one obvious question: is there enough water for everybody? Now that U.S. Secretary of State Baker has resumed his pilgrimage, will he be able to perform a miracle of water in this region where someone once performed a miracle of loaves and fishes? Otherwise peace may well die of thirst.

[*Thanks to Raymond Legault for translating this article from the French.*]

Notes

[1] It is important to stress that, on this matter, specialists do not agree on precise figures. In this article I have tried to make approximations based on the various studies. Since major differences in estimates are infrequent, these figures are very close to those currently given by the different specialists. The following references are useful: Naff, Thomas and Ruth C. Matson (eds), *Water in the Middle East: Conflict or Cooperations?* (Westview Press Inc., 1984); Dillman, Jeffrey D., "Le pillage de l'eau dans les territoires occupés," *Revue d'Études Palestiniennes*, Fall 1990. Other references in Arabic are listed below.

[2] Awartani, Hisham, "Markaz Dirasate al-Wihda al-'Arabiya," in el-'Abd, Georges (ed), *Al-Iktisad al-Falastini*. Also see the United Nations publication *Politique d'Israel en ce qui concerne les ressources en eau de la Rive Occidentale* (New York 1980). This is also available in English.

[3] For more details on this matter, see Shou'oun Tanmawiyyeh (Development Affairs) #2, *Al-Miyah fi Falastine*, Al-Multaqa al-fikri al-arabi, Jerusalem 1988, pp.21-23.

[4] Awartani, Hisham in el-'Abd, Georges, *op.cit.*, p.153.

[5] Mansour, Antoine, *Palestine: une économie de resistance en Cisjordanie et à Gaza* (Paris, L'Harmattan, 1983). See also Benvenisti, Meron, *The West Bank Data Project* (Washington D.C. and London, American Enterprise Institute for Public Policy Research, 1984).

[6] Part of the information presented here has already been published in *Le Developpement en Palestine* under the direction of Rachad Antonius and Pierre Beaudet of the Centre d'études arabes pour le developpement (Canada), 1990. For more information, the Centre is located at 1265 rue Berri, bureau 210, Montreal, Quebec. Telephone: (514) 843-7872 Fax: (514) 499-0153.

[7] On this topic, see Shou'oun Tanmawiyyeh, *op.cit.*, pp. 26-27, which provides technical advice on construction techniques for the tanks and the costs of such operations (approximately 10 dinars per cubic metre in the case of the pear-shaped model).

Drawn From the Fire

Heather Spears

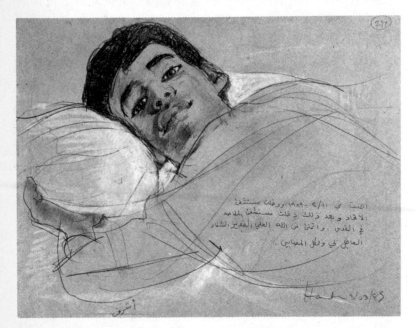

Yasser: "I was shot February 11, 1989. I hope that I will soon recover, I and all the other injured ones."

Akram: "I am Akram Sadik Barbak of the people of Khan Younis in Gaza. I am 43 years old and I have 13 children, all of them still young. On the 26th of November I was sitting in my electrical shop when the Israeli soldiers came, they told me to extinguish a burning car tire, while it was burning. So I told them to be patient till I could bring some water and some sand. So they told me, extinguish it with your hands, and your feet. So I said to them, this is not fair, but they said, you have to, and they insisted. Then they took me to a hidden street and there were eight of them and they started to beat me in a terrible way with their sticks and the butts of their rifles, on every part of my body. Then they hit me against the wall and on the asphalt of the road. My wife knew about it and she came and started pleading with them, it is not fair. So they beat her also and two of my girls and my big brother. They beat me until I was unconscious in all my senses. I can't talk I can't hear I can't move I can't feel I am just an object. I lie on a bed and I feel nothing. I am Akram Sadik Barbak of the people of Khan Younis in Gaza." – written by his brother.

*Fatma Hassan
Abu-Khudair: nurse, shot
in the arm, then three
times in the chest, while
helping the wounded. "In
the name of God. This is
my fate. I was there at
Al-Aqsa, because it is our
duty to defend it."
(October 17, 1990)*

Now the Cameras Have Gone

The Kurds were prominent in the media in the aftermath of the U.S.-led bombing of Iraq. Encouraged to revolt against Saddam Hussein, and then abandoned to his repression, Iraqi Kurds in March and April 1991 fled in millions to the borders of Turkey and Iran. They became, for a short while, the object of popular compassion, and were placed under the control of U.S.-led coalition forces.

But a bare four months later, when the Kurds of Iraq had been returned, with carrot and stick, to the homes they had fled; when the U.S.-led coalition had withdrawn; then Turkey's airforce and army attacked the very same Kurds we had been watching on our TV, and Turkey occupied a Kurdish "zone" inside Iraq. Were the Kurdish victims on our screens again? Did the U.S.-led coalition protest? Hardly. "Humanitarian" concerns were for the spring, not the fall.

The major regional governments whose borders cross and incorporate the land of Kurdistan – Turkey where 10 million or more Kurds live, Iran home to five million, Iraq four million, Syria

0.6 million, the Soviet Union 0.2 million – have feared and
suppressed Kurdish national movements for self-rule, autonomy, or
independence. So have the major colonial and imperial powers,
first Britain after World War One, and the U.S. since World War
Two.

The plight of the Kurds has been played with by Western and
regional governments for their own, not the Kurds' political
advantage. In Turkey, even to speak the Kurdish language publicly
has been a crime, punishable by years of imprisonment. But Turkey
is part of the U.S.-led coalition, while Saddam Hussein is the
current enemy. So it is not the act of persecution, but the actor
who counts, not human rights but strategic interests, as the
Kurdish-Canadian Amir Hassanpour argues in the following article.

The United States, the Kurds and Human Rights

Amir Hassanpour

THE 1991 TRAGIC EXODUS OF MILLIONS OF IRAQI KURDS REVIVED MEMORIES OF 1975. In both instances the U.S. was involved first in inciting the Kurds to revolt against Baghdad, and then in abandoning them to cruel repression. In both cases many observers in the West, and Kurds themselves, called U.S. policy a "betrayal," a "double-cross," "hypocritical." Underlying these labels is the view that U.S. foreign policy is based, at least in part, on the promotion of freedom and democracy. According to this view, the main problem is inconsistency, selective application, or the occasional abandonment of these decent objectives by individuals like Henry Kissinger.

This essay argues, to the contrary, that U.S. foreign policy on the Kurds has been fairly consistent, based on the application of a single standard: U.S. strategic interests. From this vantage point the U.S. has never admitted, verbally or otherwise, the existence of a Kurdish nation with legitimate rights to any degree of self-rule, let alone self-determination. It has never supported the demand for administrative and cultural autonomy within the borders of Iraq, Iran, Turkey or Syria. In fact, the U.S. consistently has contributed, directly and indirectly, to the suppression of the Kurdish people in all these countries.

What happened in 1975?

In March 1970, Kurds and the Iraqi government reached an agreement which promised autonomy, to be implemented after a four year transition period. This agreement followed nine years of intermittent war between various Iraqi governments and the autonomy-seeking Kurds. There was initial progress in implementing the agreement, though relations between the Ba'th regime of Baghdad and the Kurdish leadership remained uneasy, largely due to the Ba'th party's policy that Kurdistan is an integral part of the "Arab homeland," and their desire to impose Ba'thist ideology on all Iraqi peoples, whether Arab, Kurd, Assyrian, Turkman or other.

Ba'th ideology, in Iraq and in Syria, does not allow for the autonomous existence of political parties, media, education, economic enterprise, or any sizable non-Arab population, like the Kurds. Thus from

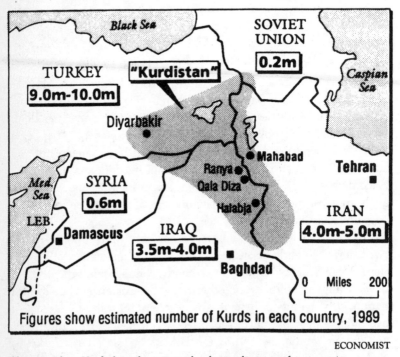

Figures show estimated number of Kurds in each country, 1989

The area where Kurds form the majority has been split among four countries.

the very beginnings of the transition period, the Kurds experienced a policy of "Arabization" and "Ba'thization."[1] The Ba'th party accused the Kurds in Iraq of receiving arms and training from Iran, and of cooperating with the Shah. It certainly was true that Iran, Israel, and the U.S. all helped the Kurds and discouraged a settlement between them and Baghdad. The U.S. sent some $16 million together with arms, through Iran, which also was providing arms, training and logistical support.

During the early 1970s Iran and Iraq also engaged in extensive propaganda against one another. Five clandestine radio stations in Iraq were operated by anti-Shah Iranian groups. And inside Iran, Iraq was supporting autonomist movements: the Kurdish Democratic Party of Iran, Baluchi nationalists, and Arab people in the Iranian province of Khuzistan.

When the transition period ended in March 1974, Iraq announced a unilateral plan for autonomy. Simultaneously it waged an all-round military offensive against the Kurds. The Kurds rejected Baghdad's unilateral plan and, relying on U.S. aid and advice, resisted the Iraqi army. Only one year later, on March 6, 1975, the Shah of Iran and Saddam Hussein reached a secret agreement in Algiers. All U.S. and Iranian aid to the Kurds was abruptly stopped. The Kurds had served their purpose of weakening Iraq and now were abandoned by the U.S. administration, President Ford and Kissinger.

A secret report of Representative Otis Pike's U.S. Congressional Intelligence Committee was leaked to the *Village Voice*, and published February 16, 1976. It stated in part:

> Documents in the Committee's possession clearly show that the President, Dr. Kissinger, and the foreign head of state [Shah of Iran] hoped that our clients [the Kurds] would not prevail. They preferred instead that the insurgents simply continue a level of hostilities sufficient to sap the resources of our ally's neighbouring country [Iraq]. This policy was not imparted to our clients, who were encouraged to continue fighting. Even in the context of covert action, ours was a cynical enterprise.
>
> . . . The insurgents [Kurds] were clearly taken by surprise as well.

Their adversaries [Iraqi government], knowing of the impending aid cut-off, launched an all-out search-and-destroy campaign the day after the agreement was signed. The autonomy movement was over and our former clients scattered before the central government's superior forces.

The cynicism of the U.S. and its ally had not yet completely run its course, however. Despite direct pleas from the insurgent leader [Barzani], and the CIA station chief in the area to the President and Dr. Kissinger, the U.S. refused to extend humanitarian assistance to the thousands of refugees created by the abrupt termination of military aid. As the Committee staff was reminded by a high U.S. official [Dr. Kissinger], "covert action should not be confused with missionary work."[2]

The Shah of Iran withdrew his aid before the ink was dry on the Algiers agreement, without even giving the Kurds "a few day's notice so that they could get their women and children across the border before the time of killing began."[3] More than 200,000 refugees, mostly families of Kurdish *peshmargas* (partisans) who had participated in the revolt, had to flee their towns and villages to the bitterly cold and snow-covered mountains. The Geneva-based International Human Rights Federation called on the U.N. and the Red Cross to intervene to save the Kurds from the "threat of genocide," but this fell on deaf ears.[4]

The Turkish army blocked Kurdish entry into Turkey at gunpoint, while Iran interned them at camps under brutal conditions. In one camp, Iranian soldiers fired on them, killing eight and wounding 27 men and women. The refugees were denied the right to organize, to maintain educational and social services, or conduct cultural activities. International humanitarian organizations, the International Red Cross Committee, and foreign journalists were not given access to the refugees, while Iraqi officials were allowed to visit the camps to apply psychological pressure on the refugees to return to Iraq. Those who did not were forcibly dispersed throughout non-Kurdish areas of Iran.[5]

Although Iraq declared an amnesty, in fact the Kurdish population was subjected to depopulation of regions along the Iraq-Iran and Iraq-Turkey borders, mass deportation to the deserts of southern Iraq, destruction of hundreds of villages, and mass executions. Tens of thousands perished in the reprisals.[6]

Initially, the U.S. refused even to receive Kurdish refugees, though eventually a token 700 were admitted.

> Kurdish leaders were instructed to keep quiet about even this minor gesture... The Kurds who arrived in the United States were granted no special privileges. They were sponsored by international refugee organizations, which gave them personal loans to pay their air fares and expenses. Some were thrown into resettlement camps in San Diego. Later, they were actually asked to pay for their care and maintenance at the camps. A refugee was warned that non-payment of his loan might cause difficulties in his permanent residence. The refugees from other U.S. foreign-policy flops, on the other hand are treated royally by comparison. Over $1.3 billion has been lavished on Cuban refugees since 1961...[7]

Strategic interest

How then can U.S. policy be explained? Joseph Sisco, U.S. Assistant Secretary of State, speaking before a sub-committee on foreign affairs of the U.S. House of Representatives in 1973, outlined "important and significant political, economic, and strategic interests" of the United States in the Gulf region. These included:

> support for indigenous regional collective security efforts to provide stability and to foster orderly development without outside interference. We believe Iranian and Saudi Arabian cooperation, inter alia, is of key importance as a major element of stability in this area. We also welcome the fact that Kuwait, the United Arab Emirates, and North Yemen are each, in their own way, seeking to strengthen their defensive capacities.

Sisco then proceeded with his list of "principal policy objectives":

> Continued access to Gulf oil supplies at reasonable prices and in
> sufficient quantities to meet our growing needs and those of our
> European and Asian friends and allies;
>   Enhancing our commercial and financial interests.[8]

The historical context was one where domination of the region was
being transfered from British to U.S. hands. Britain had dismantled its
military network in the region by 1971 and Western domination was
being restructured under U.S. leadership. In the aftermath of the U.S.
defeat in Vietnam, the Nixon doctrine was to rely on regional powers,
particularly Iran in the Middle East, to protect U.S. interests.
    Deputy Assistant Secretary of Defense, James Noyes, explained in
1973:

> In the spirit of the Nixon doctrine, we are willing to assist the
> Gulf states but we look to them to bear the main responsibility
> for their own defense and to cooperate among themselves to
> insure regional peace and stability. We especially look to the
> leading states of the area, Iran and Saudi Arabia, to cooperate for
> this purpose.[9]

The Shah of Iran, who owed his throne to a CIA-staged coup in
1953, was elevated to the position of U.S. policeman in the Gulf. Iran
was allowed to occupy three strategic Gulf islands in the Strait of
Hormuz. In spite of verbal protests, all the Arab regimes in the region,
except Iraq, accepted the occupation as part of the U.S. "restruc-
turing." Top U.S. officials glorified the Shah who, according to Henry
Kissinger, was "that rarest of leaders, an unconditional ally, and one
whose understanding of the world situation enhanced our own."[10]
    International human rights organizations exposed Iran as the worst
of violators. But the attitude of the U.S. administration to this is captured in the comments much later of an American political officer
stationed in Iran from 1976 to 1979.

> Iran is and has been a violent society – often cruel by U.S.
> standards. Every regime has had its political police...By the

standards of Iran, the abuses against political opponents were relatively rare and mild.[11]

Clearly racist and chauvinist logic, this argument also ignores "U.S. standards" of rampant wife-beating, child abuse, rape, serial killing, police brutality reminiscent of lynching and government massacres of native peoples and of workers. While the oil revenues of Iran were spent on naval and air bases, military networks, and siphoned into Western corporate accounts, "U.S. standards" left Iranians in abject poverty.[12]

The "stability and order" Joseph Sisco spoke of meant maintaining and strengthening the dictatorial powers of Shahs, kings and emirs imposed on the region by Britain and the United States. These are rulers ready to sacrifice the natural and the human resources of 'their' countries, in order to maintain control for themselves and their foreign masters. "Outside interference" referred to interference by anyone other than the U.S., primarily the Soviet Union. There were, however, obstacles to the realization of U.S. objectives. In the 1970s the U.S.-allied kingdoms were threatened by armed revolutionary movements, especially in Oman, Yemen, and Iran. Secondly, there were increasing military, economic, and political ties between Iraq and the U.S.S.R.

Living in dire poverty, under politically oppressive conditions but in the midst of the richest natural and human resources, the people of the Middle East have struggled for emancipation from colonial and neo-colonial rule. In the early 1970s, the Popular Front for the Liberation of Oman and the Arab Gulf (PFLOAG) was conducting a successful revolutionary struggle and had established control over most of the Dhofar province of Oman. According to the U.S. Deputy Assistant Secretary of Defense, James Noyes, the PFLOAG was an "active, radical group which is also seeking to subvert existing regimes in the lower Gulf states."[13] Another significant anti-Western development was the establishment of the People's Republic of South Yemen in 1967, after four years of armed struggle against Britain. The Yemeni leaders declared adherence to Marxism and vowed to expel Britain from the whole of the Arabian peninsula, and to turn their country into a base-area for revolutionary armed struggle which had started in Oman two years earlier.[14] In Iran, urban guerrilla operations to overthrow the Shah and U.S. domination had started in 1971.

The other threat to America's "principal objectives," as outlined by Joseph Sisco, was the increasing influence of the Soviet Union in the region, especially in and through Iraq. The Ba'th first came to power in June 1968, in a coup d'etat. Although Ba'th ideology essentially is anti-communist, in the regional and international context of the time, the Ba'thists gradually established political and economic ties with the Soviet Union. In 1972, Iraq nationalized the European and American-dominated Iraq Petroleum Company, and Soviet Prime Minister Kosygin came to inaugurate production at the Rumaila oil field, the first major Soviet entry into Middle East oil production which was a Western monopoly until then. Kosygin also signed a fifteen-year Iraqi-Soviet Friendship Treaty.

Given U.S. interests as outlined by Sisco, and given the challenges the U.S. faced from revolution in the region and the Iraq alliance with the Soviet Union, it was not the human and democratic rights of the Kurds that concerned them in 1975. Had they been genuinely concerned with Kurdish rights it would have been a challenge to their own client in Iran, and it could have emboldened democratic trends throughout the region, which ultimately would jeopardize Western control of oil resources. The grievances of the Kurds merely provided an opportunity for the U.S. to weaken Iraq which, while in words staunchly anti-Western and anti-Zionist, didn't give practical support to the struggles of the Palestinian and Omani peoples.[15]

What happened in 1991?

President Bush began bombing Iraq on January 17, 1991. A month later, on February 15, he rejected Saddam Hussein's conditions for withdrawal from Kuwait as a "cruel hoax" and called on the "Iraqi military and the Iraqi people to take matters into their own hands and force Saddam Hussein, the dictator, to step aside. . ." Soon U.S. forces, massacring tens of thousands of retreating Iraqi forces, many conscript Kurds, occupied parts of southern Iraq and a formal ceasefire was signed

February 27. Encouraged by U.S. radio broadcasts, the Shiite and Kurdish populations, who had dreamt of an Iraq free of the Ba'th party for 22 years, revolted. In a matter of days, the south and Kurdistan were freed from Ba'th rule. The Iraqi army then launched a counter-offensive that successfully suppressed the revolt. President Bush publicly forbade the Iraqi government from using fix-winged aircraft against the rebels, but consciously legitimated the use of helicopter gun-ships.

Fearing extermination, millions of Kurds again fled toward Turkey and Iran. The world knew about the exodus through the snow-covered mountain passes in early April. Thousands of children and elderly people were dying. But the refugees were not allowed to enter Turkey, where their fellow Kurds were ready to give them shelter and food. At Turkish gunpoint the refugees were driven back to die of cold and hunger. Their suffering broke the hearts of millions worldwide, who watched this tragedy on their TVs; though the Kurds who fled and were admitted to Iran did not appear on TV as extensively as those on the Turkish border, nor did the Shiite refugees who fled from the south of Iraq. One sobbing Kurdish woman on the Iraq-Turkey border asked a BBC-TV reporter: "He [President Bush] destroyed Iraq for Kuwait. There are one million Kuwaitis. We are five million. We are dying in these cold mountains. But he does nothing. Why?"

Under pressure of public opinion, European members of the U.S.-led coalition acted to help the refugees. And on April 12, Washington announced the use of U.S. military troops to bring food and provide temporary shelter for the refugees, but again only on the Iraq-Turkey frontier. The Europeans proposed setting up a "safe haven" for the Kurds inside the Kurdish areas of Iraq. A plan which had a high humanitarian profile was undertaken, one that would take enough time to implement that media and public attention would fade. Tent cities were established and coalition forces were stationed in Zakho city and at a number of other locations.

The plan was to remove the Kurdish refugees from the Iraq-Turkey border because they were considered a threat to the stability and security of an important coalition partner and NATO ally, Turkey. Secondly, the plan was to resettle Kurds in their original towns and cities and thus place them again under Ba'th party rule. By mid-June, U.S.-led forces moved the refugees from the Turkish border to Zakho, Dohuk and other locations. On June 15, Iraq regained effective control of Dohuk as the coalition withdrew their last troops.

A British official commented, "we are trapped inside American decisions. We are setting people up for destruction."[16] In late June, coalition forces left northern Iraq and set up a rapid-deployment force in Turkey, supposedly to protect the Kurds in Iraq when needed. Turkey, meanwhile, was not satisfied with simply getting rid of the refugees on the border. Turkey has denied democratic rights of language use and culture to the Kurds under its rule, let alone political autonomy, and predictably this has generated resistance. Unable to suppress a seven year guerrilla operation of a small, but apparently popular, Kurdish Workers Party (PKK: *Partiya Karkeren Kurdistan*), in early August Turkey's army launched air and ground attacks on northern Iraq, ostensibly against the PKK.

Failing to trace their hideouts inside Turkey, one wonders how they can trace the PKK inside Iraq. Not surprisingly, according to the Kurdish Democratic Party of Iraq, Turkey's warplanes bombed Kurdish settlements, killing 11 and injuring 48. Using F-4 and F-104 planes, 92 raids were made between August 5 and August 8 alone, and artillery was used when troops seized some of the mountain areas. According to Turkey's Prime Minister Mesut Yilmaz, a five kilometre deep "buffer zone," extending along the entire 320 kilometre border with Iraq was to be established. Yilmaz said that "everyone who steps into that area [without permission] will be fired upon." Thus the coalition's "safe haven" for the Kurdish refugees became the "safe haven" for Turkey's army.[17]

Nothing could better suit the U.S. Iraq gradually will eliminate the Kurdish revolt, and Turkey will have a free hand in uprooting its own. The U.S. never intended to eliminate the Ba'th party, which it had nurtured throughout the 1980s.[18] Saddam Hussein's regime, unlike that of Ngo Dinh Diem in Vietnam or Manuel Noriega in Panama, was not disposable. Bush's statement above is clear: it calls on the military and the people of Iraq to remove the person of Saddam, not the dictatorial structure.

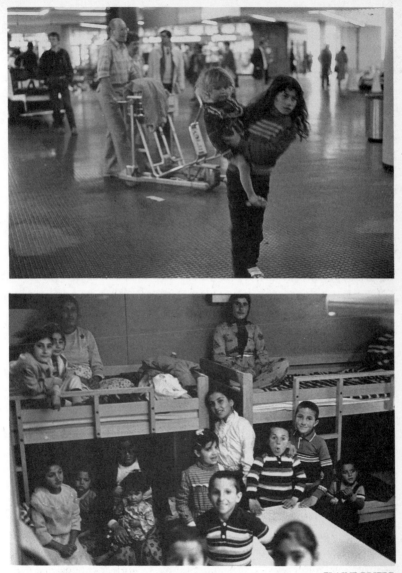

ELAINE BRIERE

Kurdish refugees from Turkey arriving at the Frankfurt airport, where many also lived for a time. Within the tapestry of travellers moving between countries of their own, these people without a country weave their transient existence.

U.S. officials revealed "the secret of it – they want a military coup," not a free and democratic state in Iraq.[19] The U.S. needs a dictatorship that is capable of disarming and suppressing the Kurdish demand for autonomy, so that they will not pose a threat to Turkey. The U.S. needs a dictatorship in Iraq so that it can suppress the Shiites, who might pose a threat to the feudal monarchies of Kuwait, Saudi Arabia and the United Arab Emirates. The U.S. needs a brutal regime that can continue hostilities with the still unpacified Iran. The U.S. needs a regime in Iraq that can be a die-hard enemy of Syria, as long as Syria continues to be a potential threat to Israel.

Given these obvious political imperatives, the U.S. would try to recreate Ba'th rule in Iraq if it is overthrown. It is not surprising, therefore, that the U.S. left the Republican Guards intact with 16 of Saddam's 40 divisions, 700 of his 4,550 tanks, 1,400 of his personnel carriers, plenty of heavy artillery and helicopters.[20] A democratic state in Iraq is a nightmare for the U.S.

Are there lessons?

While apologists disguise or excuse human rights abuses by U.S. client governments, whether the Shah before or Turkey today,[21] official documents provide a clear picture of the primacy of strategic interest over human rights. For example, the State Department 1976 report on human rights records:

> The U.S. security assistance program in Iran [under the Shah] is devoted to developing a militarily strong Iran. This goal, because of Iran's strategic geopolitical location, its long border with the Soviet Union, and the broad similarity of our political-strategic perceptions and security policies in the Middle East and Asia, is a major national interest for both Iran and the United States. It has always been clear to Iranian officials that the military strength of Iran is the overriding purpose of our security assistance program.[22]

In their study of the political economy of human rights, Edward Herman and Noam Chomsky conclude:

The basic *fact* is that the United States has organized under its sponsorship and protection a neo-colonial system of client states ruled mainly by terror and serving the interests of a small local and foreign business and military elite. The fundamental *belief*, or ideological pretence, is that the United States is dedicated to furthering the cause of democracy and human rights throughout the world, though it may occasionally err in the pursuit of this objective.[23]

Human rights will be used as a "card" to be played whenever necessary. The Soviet army's killing of a few opponents in the Baltics leads to threats of economic sanction, while the deaths of thousands of Kurds is considered an internal affair of Iraq, even when the U.S. had occupied a portion of Iraq's territory and had destroyed the infrastructure of the entire country. What horrible irony.

This analysis of U.S. policy, by no means original, may be criticized by pundits as economic determinist or structuralist. Whatever label they attach to it, it is more adequate than psychological explanations which: ignore the relevant evidence gathered by people like Herman and Chomsky; fail to account for the regularity, the pattern of policy, regardless of the decision-makers; and avoid considering the connections of economy and politics on a global basis. To show that U.S. foreign policy is, by its very nature, aggressive and entails violations of peoples' and nations' rights should not make peace activists feel helpless. In a world which will witness more encroachments on the rights of individuals, peoples and nations, accurate analysis of the roots of the problem helps every concerned individual contribute towards building a better world.

There are many lessons for the Kurds. The most important is a critical consideration of Kurdish leadership. Dating back to 1916, a Kurdish leader Sharif Pasha advised the British to form a Kurdish state under their rule. This was a Zionist model of establishing an alliance with foreign imperial powers. In more recent times, Mulla Mustafa Barzani proposed the formation of a Kurdish state in Iraq, which would become the 51st state of the U.S. At present, with the formation of a Kurdish diaspora in the West, a variant of this has found support among a small circle of Iraqi Kurds. The idea is to form a Kurdish state, protected by the U.S., to function in the interest of the West and Israel.[24] Not only do proponents of this fail to see that this road to "emancipation" would turn Kurdistan into a second base for imperial domination of the Middle East, they fail to understand that the Zionist state itself was not created to save the Jewish people, but primarily to act against national struggles by the Arab peoples. In any case, lobbying for this is hopeless.

Kurdish leaders who tie the destiny of their people to that of foreign powers, Western or regional – Iran, Iraq, Israel, Turkey, Syria – betray their cause. While the Kurdish people cannot change Washington's foreign policy by allying with it, they can reject a leadership that attempts just that.

Notes

[1] An article by Ismet Sherriff Vanly provides a Kurdish view. "Kurdistan in Iraq," in Gerard Chaliand (ed), *People Without a Country: The Kurds and Kurdistan* (London, Zed Press, 1980). The book of Edmund Ghareeb, *The Kurdish Question in Iraq* (Syracuse, Syracuse University Press, 1981), provides a pro-Ba'thist view. See pages 105-129.

[2] See also William Safire, "Son of 'Secret Sellout,'" in *The New York Times*, February 12, 1976.

[3] *The Washington Star*, editorial March 14, 1975.

[4] *Ibid.*

[5] "Kurdish Refugees in Iran," in *Information Bulletin No. 1*, published by the British Kurdish Friendship Society, November 1, 1975, p.5.

[6] *Ibid.*, pp.6-9.

[7] Anderson, Jack, "Nixon-Shah legacy haunts the Kurds," *Miami Herald*, March 11, 1978.

[8] U.S. Congress, *New Perspectives on the Persian Gulf*, Hearings before the Subcommittee on the Near East and South Asia of the Committee on Foreign Affairs, House of Representatives, Ninety-third Congress, First Session, June 6, July 17, 23, 24, and November 28, 1973. Washington: U.S. Government Printing House.

[9] *Ibid.*, p.39.

[10] Quoted in Bill, James A., *The Eagle and the Lion: The Tragedy of American-Iranian Relations* (New Haven, Yale University Press, 1988), p.203.

[11] McGaffey, David, "Policy and Practice: Human rights in the Shah's Iran," in David Newsom (ed), *The Diplomacy of Human Rights* (Lanham, University Press of America, 1986), p.71.

[12] See Marvin Zonis's statement in the U.S. Congress 1973 *op.cit.*, p.68.

[13] U.S. Congress, *op.cit.*, p.42.

[14] For a history of the two movements, see Halliday, Fred, *Arabia Without Sultans* (London, Penguin Books, 1974).

[15] Farouk-Sluglett, Marion, *Iraq Since 1958: From Revolution to Dictatorship* (London, I.B. Tauris and Co., 1990), pp.132-34.

[16] Flint, Julie, "Allies abandon Kurds," *The Sunday Observer*, June 16, 1991, p.13.

[17] *The Globe and Mail*, August 8, 1991, A11.

[18] Hitchens, Christopher, "How the U.S. helped create the monster Saddam," *The Toronto Star*, January 12, 1991, pp.D1, D4.

[19] *The New York Times*, April 11, 1991, p.A7.

[20] Siddiqi, H., "Hapless Kurds double-crossed," *The Toronto Star*, April 4, 1991, p.A25.

[21] For critiques of U.S. minimization of human rights violations in Turkey see: "Critique: Review of the Department of State's Country Reports on Human Rights Practices for 1990 – Turkey," Lawyers Committee for Human Rights, 1991 (mimeographed). For a similar critique of U.S. reports on Latin America, see "Country reports on human rights practices for 1981-1987: United States Human Rights Policy," [Harvard] *Human Rights Yearbook*, Vol. 1, Hebenton, B. and Sullivan, E., pp.290-97.

[22] U.S. State Department, *Human Rights and U.S.policy: Argentina, Haiti, Indonesia, Iran, Peru, and the Philippines*, 1976, p.21.

[23] Herman, Edward and Noam Chomsky, *The Political Economy of Human Rights*, Volume 1, (Boston, South End Press, 1979), p.ix. In *Manufacturing Consent: The Political Economy of the Mass Media* (New York, Pantheon Books, 1988), the same authors show how the media promotes this policy.

[24] Khailany, Asad, "U.S. policy toward the Kurdish problem from the Kurdish perspective," in the *Kurdish National Congress Newsletter*, Special Issue on Current Events, Kurdish National Congress of North America, Ann Arbor, Michigan, July 1991, pp.2-3.

Desert Song

Bob Bossin

*Song lyrics, printed out tuneless, read like bad poetry but what can
you do? The best I can suggest is to picture yourself not reading the
words but hearing them, say, in a public square with some five or six
thousand others on a wintry afternoon early in the war – if that is
really the word for the one-sided slaughter our leaders so blithely and
hurriedly joined us to. You feel frustrated, despairing, embarrassed,
mad, cold. Over the speakers, the music perks up: gospel gone angry.
People start to move in rhythm, sing on the chorus. "Desert Song" did
not have a lot of performances, but one of them was like that.*

Last night I had the strangest dream –
I saw Joe Clark flying a CF-18.
An Iraqi shell came whistling by,
said Joe, "Maybe sanctions need another try."

CHORUS:
We won't study war no more!
We won't study war no more!
We won't study war no more!
We won't study war no more!

I dreamed that George Bush and Saddam
Were out in the desert going man to man.
One of 'em won and one of 'em lost
And either way we were better off.

CHORUS

I dreamed I was the guy who picked the ones to fight
So I picked Mary Collins and Bill McKnight.
Then if they still need willing men,
I figured we could send them over Jean Chretien.

Let's send Kim Campbell to Iraq,
Send the Sureté du Québec.
We'll get Mulroney to volunteer –
It might not help there, but it would sure help here.

CHORUS

I dreamed I talked to George about the war.
I said, "How many people have died so far?
And how many more will die today?
Then can you tell me what we won this way?"

Tell me what we won this way.
Tell me what we won this way.
Tell me what we won this way.
Tell me what we won this way.

This song is for our soldiers in uniform.
This song is for the kids that the bombs fell on,
For the poor Iraqi boys trying to run,
And for our pilots gunning them down.

This song is for the Kurds on the mountainside,
This song is for the orphans of Palestine.
For the beast slouching into Bethlehem,
And for the lesson we repeat again and again.

CHORUS:
We won't study war no more!
We won't study war no more!
We won't study war no more!
We won't study war no more!

Canada and
the War Against Iraq
James A. Graff

"NO BLOOD FOR OIL!" THIS RALLYING CRY FOR U.S., CANADIAN AND OTHER anti-war activists expressed a fundamental rejection of *Realpolitik* as the determining attitude of foreign policy. It represented a plea for a world order governed by concerns for justice, for human well-being and compassion. In the present world order concerns for justice, human rights and a humane society appear to constitute the rhetoric which "justifies" war, repression and intervention, motivated by concerns for national, party and individual economic advantage, influence and power.

For a minority of Canadians, the Mulroney government's decisions – to participate in the blockade of Iraq, to work through the Security Council to lay the "legal" basis for war to restore the Al-Sabah family and the Kuwaiti monied elite to power, and finally to join in the "joy of killing" during the last two days of the ground offensive – betrayed a "peace-keeping" image Canada had and should stand for. Was this a misconception? Is the slogan "no blood for oil" misleading? What, in short, has been the *Realpolitik* of Canadian Middle East policy since the late 1940s and what role can considerations of justice play?

The context: Canada and the Arab Middle East

There are two, major, interconnected aspects of Canadian policies towards the Arab Middle East: 1) Canada's positions on the Arab-Israeli conflicts, and 2) its political-economic relations with the countries of the region.

From 1947 until the early 1980s, Canada's official position on the Arab-Israeli conflicts reflected and often echoed U.S. policy. With some notable exceptions, those United States and Canadian policies reflected the positions of their domestic Israeli lobbies.

Former prime minister Lester Pearson, among other prominent Canadians, was personally sympathetic to the Zionist cause, and as minister of external affairs he played an important part in the 1947 partition of Mandatory Palestine.[1] Canada voted for U.N. resolution 181, creating a Jewish and a Palestinian state with democratic constitutions and an internationalized Jerusalem. Doing so, Canada recognized the rights of the Palestinians to self-determination and statehood. However, Canada really was pressing for the creation of a Jewish state in Palestine. Canada's vote never represented a commitment to the equal national rights of the Palestinian and the European Jewish communities in Palestine.

Canada then had no significant economic or political interests in the Middle East. Its foreign economic and political interests lay with the U.S. and Britain. The British supported Jordanian control over whatever Palestinian lands the Israelis failed to take by force in 1948, and the U.S. had no interest in the establishment of a Palestinian state. Domestically, there was considerable sympathy for the sufferings of European Jewry, growing guilt over this, an active Zionist lobby, and no countervailing concern for dispossessed and massacred Arabs. There was no Palestinian lobby. From the perspective of *Realpolitik*, it made sense to allow Canada's implicit 1947 recognition of Palestinian national rights to lapse. Canada was prepared to offer aid to Palestinian refugees, since doing so in no way hurt Canadian interests on the one hand, and promoted a humane image on the other. Canada subsequently established a good record for its financial contributions to the United Nations Relief and Works Agency (UNRWA), whose mandate is to provide basic relief, health care and educational services for

Palestinian refugees driven beyond the expanded "Green Line" borders of Israel, drawn in the 1949 Armistice with its Arab neighbours.

Following the 1956 British, French and Israeli invasion of Egypt, trying to reverse Nasser's nationalization of the Suez Canal, Lester Pearson helped to establish the U.N. peace-keeping force in the Sinai. Prof. Tareq Ismael explains Pearson's role as intended primarily to end the split within NATO, between the U.S. and its British and French allies.[2] The U.S. was replacing Britain and France as the dominant foreign power in the Middle East. At the time, a major U.S. objective, shared by Canada, also was to block the expansion of Soviet influence in the region. Subsequent Canadian interventions, whether under the aegis of the U.N. (in Lebanon and in the Golan Heights) or the U.S.A. (in Sinai after Camp David, and in Iraq) have to be understood in terms of services Canada could render to its American ally, promoting the kind of "stability" it found acceptable. Canada's role as peace-keeper in the Middle East did not begin with any concern for the national rights of Arabs. Commitment to genuine stability and the territorial integrity of the Arab states would have required a vigorous and independent Canadian Middle East policy, firmly rooted in the ideals of the U.N. Charter and the requirements of international law. From the point of view of *Realpolitik*, "to be realistic," such a policy, unsupported by major domestic and foreign economic and political interests, never was an option.

Paul Martin, minister of external affairs when addressing the U.N. General Assembly in 1967, declared the prospect of the return of Palestinian refugees to Israel an "illusion."[3] Thereby Canada officially ignored one of the conditions placed on Israel's admission to the U.N.; namely, that it permit the Palestinian refugees to return. Canada's Ambassador to the U.N. George Ignatieff obligingly removed the definite article from the English version of the 1967 Security Council Resolution 242 so that it called for Israeli withdrawal from "territories" – instead of from "*the* territories" (as in the French version) – it occupied in 1967. Under Mitchell Sharp's tenure as minister of external affairs (1968-73), Canada followed the U.S. and voted against General Assembly resolutions affirming the right of self-determination of the Palestinian people. Canadian policy began to change after the October

War of 1973. This coincided with a rapidly expanding Canadian trade with the Gulf oil-producing states, increasing divisions between the European Economic Community (EEC) and U.S./Israeli policies, and political developments in the region.[4] A change of ministers and the policy review which followed resulted in a shift in Canada's policy. Allen MacEachen, unlike his predecessor Mitchell Sharp, did not represent a constituency where the Israel lobby was active and strong. (It was not until April 1991, when Barbara McDougall replaced Joe Clark as secretary of state for external affairs, that the portfolio was held again by an MP from such a riding – ironically, from what is basically Mitchell Sharp's old riding.)

In 1973, for the first time, Canada joined the majority of EEC members and abstained, instead of opposing a General Assembly resolution referring to the existence of the Palestinians as a people with legitimate political concerns and a right to representation in any negotiations aimed at resolving the Arab-Israeli disputes. Canada continued to abstain on such resolutions for the next 16 years, thereby distancing itself from the U.S./Israeli position. Canada also abstained on resolutions referring to the right of Palestinian refugees to return, though it opposed the General Assembly's vote to grant observer status to the PLO in 1975, opposed establishment of the special U.N. Committee on the Exercise of the Inalienable Rights of the Palestinian People, and, with other Western governments, voted against the Assembly's "Zionism is a form of racism" resolution.

The re-emergence in the mid-70s of official Canadian recognition of Palestinian political claims, however, did not constitute an even-handed approach towards Israeli and Palestinian national and individual rights. In essence, Canada favoured the outlines of a settlement proposed by Israeli Foreign Minister Yigal Allon in the mid-1970s. Under Don Jamieson, whose sympathies lay with Israel, Canadian policy basically ossified.

Joe Clark's promise to move Canada's embassy in Israel from Tel Aviv to Jerusalem brought home the extent to which Canadian regional economic interests now were a factor. Pressure from Canadian business and Arab governments compelled Clark to reverse the embassy decision. By 1978 Canadian export and import trade with the Arab

Gulf states had reached over $1 billion, from a previous $134 million (1973) and $52 million (1968). The sale of Canadian services to the oil-producing Arab states in 1978 may have added almost $1 billion. By contrast, Canadian trade with Israel totalled $126 million (1978).[5] This was the only known instance of direct Arab government pressure affecting Canadian policy towards Israel.

By 1984 Canada was using the voting patterns of Australia, Norway and New Zealand as the point of reference for its U.N. votes. Those countries tended to vote for "moderately worded" resolutions emphasizing the illegality under international law of Israel's annexations of East Jerusalem and the Golan Heights or condemning broadly described Israeli violations of the Fourth Geneva Convention in the occupied territories. The basic outlines of Canada's policy towards the Palestinians remained intact for four years after Israel's 1982 invasion of Lebanon. Until 1986 Canada found itself isolated with the U.S. and Israel in opposing a U.N.-sponsored international peace conference, which presupposed the right of the Palestinians to self-determination, the right of Palestinian refugees to return, and the status of the Palestine Liberation Organization as sole legitimate representative of the Palestinian people. However, Canada finally joined the EEC and (white) Commonwealth countries on this critical issue when it switched from a no vote to an abstention.

When in 1987 millions of Canadians had seen Israeli soldiers beating up Palestinians in their custody, strapping a youth to the hood of a jeep to use him as a human shield and sniping at distant crowds of protesters, Prime Minister Mulroney defended Israeli practices. By 1989, a growing number of mainstream Canadian institutions favoured the recognition of Palestinian national rights largely because of Israeli repression during the intifada. This repression, coming five years after savage Israeli attacks on Beirut and clear Israeli collusion in the Sabra and Shatilla massacres there, generated more sympathy with Palestinians as an oppressed, and colonized people.

On December 6, 1989, Canada joined the EEC and white Commonwealth countries and for the first time supported the U.N.-sponsored international peace conference on the Middle East based on Resolutions 242, 338 and recognition of the Palestinians' right of self-determination. It took 42 years for Canada to return to its official 1947 recognition of Palestinian national rights.

Although from the mid-1970s Canada's position on the political rights of the Palestinians inched away from the U.S. position, Canada's actual policies, like those of the NATO and white Commonwealth countries, acknowledged the U.S. as the dominant Western power in the region. Differences of official formulae neither prompted political pressure on the United States to change, nor threatened U.S. power and influence in the region. Until the late 1980s, when the EEC pushed Israel into permitting direct exports of Palestinian agricultural products to Europe, and cut an academic exchange programme to mark its condemnation of Israel's closure of Palestinian universities, European divergence from the U.S. had no consequences for Israel. To date, Canadian divergence has had no spill-over into practices affecting either the U.S. or Israel.

Given Iraq's open aggression in seizing all of Kuwait in clear contradiction to U.S. interests in the Gulf, the Mulroney government naturally would offer political support for whatever response the Bush Administration made. What took many Canadians by surprise, however, was that Mulroney's support went well beyond rhetoric.

Canada, the U.N. and the 'new world order'

Mulroney joined the U.S.-led blockade of Iraq two weeks before the U.N. Security Council passed Resolution 665 on August 25 authorizing it. Canada's U.N. ambassador Yves Fortier reliably was reported to have been instrumental in securing U.S. agreement to work through the United Nations in pursuing its objectives in the Gulf, and in helping to line up Security Council approval for resolutions the U.S. wanted, among them Resolution 678 setting the January 15 deadline after which the U.S.-led coalition would be permitted to take whatever measures they deemed necessary.

Mulroney, and to a lesser extent Clark, parroted Bush's moralized legalism to justify the blockade and finally the war. Iraq had committed an act of aggression in violation of its obligations under the U.N. Charter. The Security Council fulfilled its obligations under the Charter by authorizing the enforcement of sanctions and, when they failed to secure the restoration of the sovereignty and territorial integrity of Kuwait, authorized the use of force. By joining the blockade and then the war, Canada was fulfilling its obligations under the Charter and upholding respect for human rights and the rule of international law. Speaking to representatives of Ontario-based Arab Canadian organizations, External Affairs Minister Clark stressed both Canada's successful efforts in persuading the U.S. to tailor its Gulf operations to the requirements of international law and international legitimacy, and the importance of that success in building a "new world order." The "new world order" referred to was envisioned as a world in which the rule of international law and respect for human rights would characterize relations among states.

Even if Mulroney's apparently obsequious subservience to Washington genuinely reflected his own views, it is clear that others in the government were well aware that a U.S. which treated international law and the U.N. with contempt whenever it suited its ambitions was a more dangerous U.S. than one which felt that it had at least to keep up a pretence of respect for international law. Bringing the U.S. into the U.N. system would subject it to direct pressures and possibly to some restraints which it could otherwise ignore in pursuing its objectives in the Gulf. It also would strengthen the Security Council when, for the first time, the U.S.S.R. and China could be expected to go along with the U.S.A.'s declared objectives in the Gulf. The rationale presented an image of the U.N. which at last could fulfil its mission.

Persuading the U.S. to follow this route does compel it to adhere to the form of international legality which may in some ways serve as a brake or restraint on its behaviour. In fact, however, the U.S. followed the U.N. route to its advantage, buying and coercing otherwise hesitant votes in the Security Council,[6] totally ignoring the requirement that the sanctions be given sufficient time to work, and that their failure be certified by the Security Council before authorizing military action. The U.S. subverted the U.N. process. Canada had enticed the wolf into the chicken coop. In and outside of the U.N. there was no counterweight to U.S. power.

The "new world order" actually preceded the Gulf war which supposedly was to give birth to it. In itself, the Soviet collapse created the real new world order in which the U.S.A. was the sole superpower. That is why the U.N. could be used to "legitimate" U.S. objectives in the Gulf and why it could be ignored when U.S. objectives could be achieved more easily without it. A U.N.-sponsored international peace conference on the Middle East, for example, would have to be predicated on Security Council Resolutions 242 and 338, and on General Assembly Resolutions acknowledging the right of the Palestinian people to self-determination and the right of Palestinian refugees to return (or be compensated). The last two principles do not suit U.S. policy in part because they are vehemently opposed by Israel and therefore by its lobby in the United States. The rhetoric about the ideal conception of the new world order masked the reality that Canada was engaged in the Gulf to advance objectives set by the United States.

In notes prepared for minister Clark's address to the External Affairs' annual consultation with non-governmental organizations concerned with human rights, he detailed Iraq's "basic violations of human rights" in its occupation of Kuwait.[7] With minor adjustments, Mr. Clark's litany of abuses and open contempt for Security Council resolutions could have applied to Israeli practices in south Lebanon and the occupied Palestinian territories. As he said, they apply elsewhere in the world as well. Most of the items on Clark's list apply to the regime in Kuwait which Canadian forces helped to reinstate and which Canadian entrepreneurs are courting. With suitable modifications, the list applies to a host of U.S. client regimes around the world, which are at no risk of boycotts, let alone blockades or military intervention. The justification for Canadian co-belligerence was at best, incomplete. In such a situation, there are two ploys available to shore up policy against the charge of hypocrisy: 1) to argue that ideals must, in this world, be pursued selectively because other, less noble concerns have to be taken into account when deciding on foreign policy; and 2) to argue that what was true in the past will be overcome in the future because the situation has changed dramatically. Mr. Clark, following Mulroney and Bush, chose the second option.

The first option immediately raises embarrassing questions about the coincidence of interest and principle and the relative weights to be assigned to each in determining policy. The second buys time, a political move which, it is hoped, will delay scrutiny of policy until the issues have become "academic." In the present state of politics in Canada, Mr. Clark's choice is perfectly understandable. To address the issue squarely before major decisions are taken demands a quality of democracy and public political sophistication which Canada, and probably all of the other democratic countries of the world, has not achieved. Certain kinds of academics, diplomats and politicians, but not the general public, are supposed to be at the level where intelligent discussion is possible to address whether selective enforcement of international law and respect for human rights is consonant with or promotes other Canadian interests. The assumption is elitist – and it may be warranted at this point.

For a humanly decent decision, more than a sophisticated understanding of the realities of politics and national interest is required: what is needed is a humane but "realistic" weighing of values. It is not plausible to think that an open discussion of these issues would be digestible or understood by the public at large. This assessment is elitist, but it also raises serious questions about the quality of political education to which most Canadians have been exposed.

Canadian economic interests clearly favoured Canadian alignment with the Gulf states as a whole, though not Kuwait individually, against Iraq. In 1990, Canadian trade with the Gulf states aligned against Iraq totalled $1.04 billion, and the sale of Canadian services approached an additional $1 billion. By contrast, Canadian trade with Iraq in 1989 amounted to roughly $320 million.[8] Reporting on his visit to the Middle East after the war, Mr. Clark stated that he ". . . welcomed the clear assurance [of the Kuwaiti Emir, then still in Taif awaiting the restoration of his palace] that the expertise of Canadian companies will enjoy opportunities commensurate with the important role Canada played in liberating Kuwait."[9] In terms of protecting and enhancing Canadian-Gulf state economic links, Canadian co-belligerency was clearly more profitable than Canadian inaction or mere rhetorical support. That amounts to Canadian jobs and profits for some Canadian businesses. It also means continuing Gulf state investments in Canada, which again convert into jobs and profits. "No blood for oil!" comes at a price. If

Canada had to choose sides, international legality and economic interests in the region clearly demanded a stance against Saddam Hussein's
seizure of Kuwait. But international legality, as we have seen, has not
itself been sufficient for Canadian action.

It was clear from the outset that the Bush administration would
reward those countries which offered material and political support for
its intervention in the Gulf, and would punish those which opposed it.
The bitter attacks by certain members of the U.S. Congress on Germany and Japan for not sending forces to the Gulf despite the fact that
their constitutions forbade such ventures, coupled with enormous
pressure to pay the United States approximately $15 billion to com-
pensate it for its military expenditures, clearly demonstrated the extent
to which the Bush administration and its supporters were prepared to
coerce friends and allies.

There is no evidence that Mulroney's decision to join the U.S.-led
blockade before the Security Council dutifully authorized it was in any
way encouraged by U.S. economic threats. His record of automatic and
enthusiastic support for U.S. military interventions against Third
World "enemies" would suggest an equally enthusiastic support of the
blockade and an eagerness to be "helpful." Whether or not the U.S.
had to wave carrots and sticks to win Mulroney's agreement to
Canadian co-belligerency against Iraq, there were carrots and sticks to
be waved, as others in the Canadian government who must have had
some input on the decision and on subsequent decisions to send aircraft, to interdict shipping and finally to adopt an offensive role in the
war, knew very well.

The Gulf crisis was the first major post-free trade test of Canadian
foreign policy. The Bush administration could, for example, have
pressed for Canadian concessions on the politically sensitive issue of
protecting Canadian cultural institutions against United States competitors and insisted on measures which would have undermined the
Canadian health care system. Economic retaliation for a perceived
Canadian unwillingness to "play ball" would have worsened the deepening Canadian recession and further undermined an already vastly
unpopular Mulroney government. Furthermore, Canada wanted a seat
at the forthcoming U.S.-Mexico free trade talks, to get guarantees that

major agreements under the Canada-U.S. Free Trade deal would not be open to renegotiation. According to a January 12, 1991 front page story in the business section of *The Globe and Mail*, "Trade officials and analysts in Canada, the United States and Mexico credit Canada's Gulf stance with helping to lift U.S. reservations about giving Canada a seat at the table."[10]

So Canadian co-belligerency was rewarded. Neutrality would have threatened Canadian trade with the Gulf states and with the U.S. Rhetorical support without military participation would have cost the sagging Canadian economy profits and jobs. Enthusiastic participation in the coalition, coupled with political services to the U.S. cause at the U.N., paid off economically with the U.S. and with Kuwait. Nor could Canada distance itself from the U.S. intervention in the Gulf without paying a political price in terms of diminished influence in the Organization of American States (OAS) or loss of membership in the G-7. Canada's position in the G-7 is to some extent a matter of toleration by the U.S., Britain, and France which is antagonistic to the Canadian presence. Canada's OAS status also depends in large measure on its "cooperation" with the U.S. In various ways, NATO allies were corralled into supporting the coalition. So by participating in U.S.-led alliances and consortia from which Canada benefits in terms of influence or profits, Canada has insured that its political and economic interests are closely tied to support for policies the U.S. views as vital. Distancing Canada from such policies would carry its political costs and ultimately, its economic costs as well. The human costs to others of such policies cannot be a determining factor so long as such *Realpolitik* sets the criteria for Canadian policy.

Canada's established affinity for "moderate" Arab states was reinforced by significant trade relations with the Gulf states and cordial political relations with Egypt and Jordan, consonant with U.S. policy in the region. Canadian relations with Jordan during the Gulf crisis did not deteriorate perhaps because Canada had nothing to lose by not following the U.S. and in part, because Jordan's record of "moderation" insured its cooperation with the U.S. after Iraq's defeat. Certainly some Canadian leaders understood the trap King Hussein had been forced into and were sympathetic to his plight. There was no comparable sympathy for the PLO which was more firmly enmeshed in the trap, but the PLO never counted as a "moderate" force. A "moderate" Arab state is one which either aligns itself or cooperates with the U.S. Egypt became a "moderate" state when Sadat opened the country to U.S. investment and pressed for a peace agreement with Israel. Jordan and the Gulf states are viewed as "moderate" because of strong economic ties to the U.S., or half-hearted support for the Palestinian cause. Iran before the Islamic Revolution was "moderate"; and Syria seems now to have achieved that status. "Moderate state" status has nothing to do with human rights records or democracy.

When in 1987 the U.S. intervened directly in the Iran-Iraq war to protect Kuwait and others shipping goods to and oil from Iraq, tipping the military scales in Iraq's favour, Canada gave economic support to the U.S. effort. Canadian trade during the Iran-Iraq war is an indicator of actual policy. Canada doubled its over-all trade with Iraq in 1987, while halving its imports of Iranian oil.[11] In effect this meant a shift of Canadian funding for each country's war efforts. It should be noted that in 1983, a year after Israel's invasion of Lebanon, Canada imported over half a billion dollars worth of Iranian oil, thereby contributing at that time to Iran's war effort against Iraq. In 1983 Iran was still on the defensive. By 1987, Iraq was on the defensive and the U.S. intervention assured the Iran-Iraq military stalemate which brought the parties to the negotiating table, and left each with its pre-war borders intact. Canada supported the U.S. intervention knowing full well that it permitted Iraqi attacks on shipping to and from Iran, while protecting shipping to and from Iraq. Neither the Iranian nor the Iraqi regimes could boast of a strong record on human rights, democracy or conformity to the laws of war. From a moral point of view, no tilt would have been warranted. Canada tilted in the same direction as the U.S. leaned. The tilt had nothing to do with democracy or human rights records.

Those who would argue that Canada's support for the "moderate" Arab states against the "radical" Iraqi regime reflects a Canadian preference for less brutal regimes which helps to determine Canadian policy are stretching the truth. The merits for Canada of the "moderate" Arab states are then that they cooperate with the U.S.A., serve

U.S. interests or, what has amounted to the same thing, pose no serious threat to Israeli power and interests in the Middle East. If President Assad of Syria soon finds himself listed among the "moderates," Canadian policy probably will follow suit.

None of this means that sympathies for "moderate" Arab leaders and "moderate" Arab states do not enter into foreign policy decisions on their own, independently of any clear perception of the "moderates" as cooperative with the U.S. or at least, as not in an opposing camp. "Moderates" tend also to be politically conservative, drawn from educated, commercial or military elites, who either reject revolutionary rhetoric or do not take it seriously. They are therefore ideologically congenial and likely to be personally more attractive than their "radical" counterparts. Congeniality has nothing to do with respect for human rights or commitment to democracy, since "moderates" can be just as autocratic and repressive as the "moderate" Al-Sabah dynasty in Kuwait has amply demonstrated.

No blood for oil?

Realpolitik is a perspective on the proper way of conducting foreign (or domestic) policy which places greater weight on economic interests and power, and consequently security interests and strategic advantage over competitors, above moral concerns which focus on the well-being of people – broadly speaking, humanitarian and human rights concerns. A *Realpolitik* perspective seems to characterize the foreign policy of every state. No one can opt out of the *Realpolitik* game, however it may be tempered by humane concerns and limited by basic moral principles. For some governments, there are limits to what they are prepared to do to secure economic advantages or power or influence. For most governments, there are no limits except those set by considerations of "hardball" *Realpolitik* itself.

"Hard-ball" *Realpolitik* determines policies promoting human well-being by reference to economic or power interests. "Soft-ball" *Realpolitik* represents a different, more humane attitude which tends to subordinate humane concerns to economic or power interests, but acknowledges those concerns as representing legitimate objectives of domestic or foreign policy. For almost 40 years, Canada's version of *Realpolitik* had been tempered by moral concerns. In the Middle East and elsewhere, its aid programmes have come with few strings and have generally been aimed at promoting the welfare of the population they were designed to serve. From the U.S.-led war in Korea until Mulroney's decision to join in the Gulf war, Canada has not been prepared to participate in massive killing, maiming, injuring and devastation to secure Canadian economic and/or power interests. The U.S.A. as superpower, like the U.S.S.R., had played "hard-ball" *Realpolitik*, demonstrated by the two million dead and the massive destruction in Vietnam, the "small-scale" butchery of Panamanian poor, Irangate, support for the murderous regimes of El Salvador and Chile, to mention only a few examples. Now the Mulroney government, it seems, has joined the "big leagues," albeit as a junior partner, but not without resistance within its own ranks from those like Joe Clark, who sought to maintain *Realpolitik* within the confines of moral principle.

"No blood for oil!" The central issue is not the total abandonment of *Realpolitik*, but the weights which should be given to human well-being and therefore to human rights and considerations of justice when determining Canadian domestic and foreign policy. The real choices are not between a suicidal commitment to high moral principles on the one hand or the total subordination of principle to economic and power interests on the other, but a standing preference for humane values to which economic and power interests should be subordinated when determining policies which, in the long-run or from a broader perspective, will serve Canadians well. Realism may require that principle give way to economic and power interests, but the points at which principle crumbles mark the moral character of a government.

Canada could declare itself neutral in any conflict which did not threaten its existence as a democratic country. Such a declaration, which would make Canada a kind of North American Switzerland, would eminently suit its multi-ethnic composition and permit it to pursue a humanly decent foreign policy. No doubt the U.S.A. would retaliate but ultimately it would have to accommodate such a Canadian stance because it needs Canadian markets and needs Canadian water, energy and raw materials. From a *Realpolitik* perspective, Canadian neutrality and independence openly grounded in commitments to human rights, justice, human well-being and international law would probably bring shorter-term economic losses. In the longer run, however, what the U.S. wants economically from Canada still will be wanted.

The key issues concern the kind of society, the independence and moral character of Canadian foreign and domestic policy. Canada's co-belligerency in the Gulf war spurred anti-Arab and anti-Muslim racism, encouraged support for the massive use of force to resolve international conflicts and strengthened the perception of the U.S. as properly setting the course for Canadian foreign policy. Erosion of identity, of a sense of independence, of tolerance and commitment to humane values were among the costs of Canada's co-belligerency. The central issue is the very character of Canadian society, its integrity and its survival within the new world order.

In many ways, Canada's participation in the Gulf war encapsulated Mulroney's vision of politics, of the new world order and of Canada: "Blood for oil" provided that it is the blood of foreigners, and other goods and good things can be substituted for oil. "No blood for oil!" The slogan tells us that human decency should take precedence over greed, pride and ambition. Human decency required sanctions and patience, and should warfare have been necessary, far less devastating than the reduction of Iraq to a pre-industrialized status. Respect for democratic values required an open discussion of the real issues before decisions were taken. Human decency required respect for democratic process. We must think through the costs of human decency and of *Realpolitik*. We must also decide on the character of the society we, as Canadians, may still be able to build. The Gulf war epitomizes a human obscenity. From a moral point of view, "No blood for oil" expresses a human necessity.

"No blood for oil!" could serve as the rallying cry for Canada's future, a future which those who are "politically wise" would rule out as unrealistic. The problem with realism is that it is anti-human – its values are skewed. However misleading, "No blood for oil!" poses the real issues and offers the only solution people of conscience could accept.

Notes

[1] Ismael, T.Y., "Canada and the Middle East," *Canadian Arab Relations: Policy and Perspectives*, T.Y. Ismael (ed) (Ottawa, Jerusalem International Publishing House Inc., 1984).

[2] *Ibid.*

[3] Nobel, Paul, "From Refugees to a People?," in *Canada and the Arab World*, Tareq Ismael (ed) (Edmonton, University of Alberta Press, 1985), pp.91-95.

[4] Nobel, Paul, "Where angels fear to tread: Canada and the status of the Palestinian people 1973-1983," *op.cit.*

[5] Kubursi, Atif, "Canada's Economic Relations with the Arab World: Patterns and Prospects," in Ismael, Tareq, *op.cit.* The figures are taken from tables using Statistics Canada data.

[6] Third World countries on the Security Council either received U.S. aid or were given guarantees of aid, on the one hand, or faced withdrawal of aid on the other. U.S. aid was suspended to Yemen, for example, after it opposed Security Council Resolution 678. China found that compliance with U.S. intentions in the Middle East contributed to normalizing relations with the U.S. and its consideration as a "most favoured nation." In addition, Egypt was rewarded for its role in the U.S.-led coalition by being forgiven almost half of its $50 billion debt. Besides a "green light" to consolidate its influence in Lebanon, strengthening the central government there and disarming the militias, Syria received assurances of billions of dollars in Saudi aid and established cordial relations with the U.S. For its opposition to the full blockade and the war which followed, Jordan, like Yemen, found its U.S. aid cut, its staggering losses because of the blockade uncompensated, its weakened economy strained further by massive unemployment and the influx of over 100,000 Palestinians fleeing Iraqi-occupied Kuwait.

[7] "Notes for a statement by the Rt. Honourable Joe Clark, P.C., M.P., Secretary of State for External Affairs, on the occasion of the annual consultations on human rights with Canadian Non-governmental organizations, January 21, 1991." The document carries the caveat: "check against delivery."

[8] Statistics Canada, "Canada/Middle East Trade," updated April 11, 1991.

[9] "Notes for a statement by the Rt. Honourable Joe Clark, Secretary of State for External Affairs, in the House of Commons, on his visit to the Middle East, Ottawa, Canada, March 15, 1991." The document carries the caveat: "check against delivery."

[10] The headline was: "Canada Invited to Free Trade Talks, Gulf Stance Called Key to Mexico."

[11] This is based on Statistics Canada data for Canadian trade with Iran and Iraq for 1986-1988.

Part 3: OBSTACLES TO UNDERSTANDING

Old Familiar Tunes

When some people mistreat others, they have their "reasons." One familiar reason is: the mistreated are different. "They" don't have the same needs, the same responses, the same qualities that "we" do. It may be patronizing: "they" are more primitive and need our guidance, at least for some time, and sometimes for ever. It may be contemptuous in a different way: "they" are a barbarous threat from which our civilized world needs to protect itself.

Frank Rutter, syndicated Southam News foreign affairs columnist, used this latter mode of contempt in an article on the current U.S.-planned peace conference. Lumping all "Arab countries" together, Rutter wrote:

> None of them is in any sense of the word "western" in outlook, history, thought or behavior . . . Saddam demonstrated that an Arab country does not necessarily play by the "rules" – that is by the conventional norms established in western thinking.[1]

"They" think differently and "they" are dangerous. Stereotyping has become the neutered word for this process of dehumanization, this

The Descent of Man

By David Levine

An elite publication for the U.S. intellectual community, The New York Times, printed this racist cartoon February 1, 1991. Called "The Descent of Man" it depicts Clark Gable as the apogee of evolution and Saddam Hussein as the member of some filthy, sub-human, sub-snake species. This is a high-brow parallel of the dehumanized metaphor used by U.S. pilots, that their bombing missions against Iraqis were like killing stunned "cockroaches."

denial, whether by disguise or rationalization, of another group's human capacities to think and feel in recognizable ways worthy of respect.

Stereotyping is more readily conceded when it appears in Hollywood cinema and television serials, and anti-Arab racism certainly has been well-documented in these domains.[2] But one need not go to the local cinema to view them. A visit to the Canadian literary section of the local library will do, as the next essay argues. For stereotyping is not the peculiar diet of the poorly educated. As Noam Chomsky painstakingly has documented, there is a persisting dishonesty and moral failure in liberal North American intellectual circles' portrayals of the Middle East.[3] In fact, these circles are very important in the stimulation of contempt for Middle East peoples.

Pernicious in itself, routine "peace-time" stereotyping then swells into waves of war-time propaganda. This interplay was brought home in miniature by a recent experience. Justly proud of their literacy students, some teachers at a college in British Columbia had selected several examples of their students' writing, and enlarged them for public display. One was titled "Haifa." The student-writer recollected migrating from Russia to Haifa as a child. The penultimate line read: "We always had to walk right beside our mom because Arabs would steal children and sell them."

In the midst of a war demonizing the Arab world and sowing hostility toward Canadians of Arab ancestry, how could caring professionals unthinkingly advertise this classic racist canard? Had a student chosen to identify a different "terrifying outsider" who steals innocent children – Gypsies, Jews, or Indians – would it have been selected for display? But the combination of peace-time and war-time propaganda allowed the racism in its Arab form to pass without questions. It took the protest of a Canadian Arab, visiting the campus, to jar the teachers into recognition of the consequences of their display: the hatred that was encouraged here against Canadian Arabs, and the reinforcement it added to the massacre of Arabs in the Middle East by the U.S., Canadian and allied governments. But once recognizing the pattern of anti-Arab racism, these teachers willingly gave a public apology and withdrew the piece from display and further circulation.

Notes

[1] The *Vancouver Sun*, August 6, 1991.

[2] Shaheen, Jack G., *The T.V. Arab* (Bowling Green State University Popular Press, 1984). Jack Shaheen also has written on movie and cartoon depictions of Arabs.

[3] Chomsky, Noam, *The Fateful Triangle: The United States, Israel and the Palestinians* (Boston, South End Press, 1983).

Sand in the Snow: Canadian High-Brow Orientalism

Mordecai Briemberg

LOUIS JACKSON, A CAUGHNAWAGA INDIAN FROM MONTREAL, CAPTAINED boats on the Nile in 1884. He and other Caughnawaga and Iroquois people were part of a British Expeditionary force to rescue the besieged General Gordon in Khartoum.

In all, 386 Canadian river boatmen and pilots had been recruited to carry out a speedy ascent of the white-water rapids of the upper Nile River, under the command of Lord Wolseley, who had led the Red River Expedition against Louis Riel. Before they left Canada on the imperial venture, the recruits were photographed in front of the Centre Block of the Ottawa Parliament Buildings.

The newly independent Canadian government, then headed by Prime Minister John A. Macdonald, had given the British the green light to recruit in Canada, with one proviso; it had to be made clear that the mercenary force was in the employ of the British, and not the Canadians. This "yes-and-no" arrangement aimed to satisfy both the pro- and the anti-imperialist constituencies in the country.

The British Governor General of Canada willingly complied with Macdonald's caveat, organized the necessary advertising, and recruited – with the assistance of lumber merchants – workers with the requisite

238

skills: the shanty-men who guided log rafts to sawmills down the swollen spring rivers of the Ottawa, Gatineau and Saguenay.[1]

Such manoeuvres have modern analogues. Canadian cabinet documents reveal that in 1956 the St. Laurent government secretly delivered arms to Israel, and considered selling them a squadron of Canadian F-86 aircraft. This was at the behest of the United States. But on the public side, Canada supported United Nations negotiations for an Israeli-Arab settlement and feared arousing popular criticism if its arms supplies to Israel became known. External Affairs Minister, later Prime Minister, Lester Pearson argued in cabinet privacy that the sale of the aircraft would give Israel greater confidence. Meanwhile, his public U.N. role won him a Nobel prize for peace-making.

High schools

The story of the Canadian river boatmen is not one of those "adventures" embedded in the cultural consciousness of Canadian school girls and boys. Few high school graduates might even recognize the name Khartoum, let alone a Canadian connection. What images dominate their Middle East reflexes?

Facing me were high school students, in their graduating year. It was a modern history class in a quite unexceptional Vancouver-area school. They had not yet studied any of the optional curriculum on the modern Middle East.

"Just shout out the first thing that comes to mind after I give you a word. Fill in a blank after the word." Those were my only instructions. This was the outcome.

"Arab." – "Oil. Rich clothes. Mercedes. Gold."

The class was like a Hallowe'en sparkler; one voice ran into the next, which in turn ran into a third, bright and rapid.

"Where is the Middle East?"

The sparkler had burnt out. The students were groping in the dark, very, very slowly.

"Muslim." – "Cult. Black. Ayatollah."

Another sparkler-spray of responses.

I printed "P-a-l-e-s-t-i-n-i-a-n" on the blackboard. "Refugees. Barbarians. Terrorists. PLO."

Then I printed "I-s-r-a-e-l-i-s." "Lebanon. Bible. Jerusalem. Jews. Freedom fighters. Concentration camps. Promised Land."

The stimulus of a single word evoked a cascade of images, even though they had declared at the outset that they "knew nothing" about the Middle East. "Nothing," clearly, is not a clean slate.

But I asked myself: vocabulary and grammar aside, how different is the Middle East mental world of the Canadian intelligentsia, the cultural elite, the writers, commentators, creators and guardians of magazines and journals? What images of "Arabs," of "Muslims," of "Palestinians" and "Israelis" does a literate Canadian encounter as she turns the pages of Canadian novels, short stories, poems, thrillers, travel essays, cultural magazines and book reviews? My research exposed a lack of qualitative difference between the imagined Middle East of those high school students and that of the high-brows.

Blood libels and high-brows

One of the most vicious lies of anti-semitism is the "blood libel": a fear and hate-promoting fantasy that Jews, as part of religious ritual, slaughter and then use the blood of Christian children. What would be the response to books, written by and for the Canadian intelligentsia, that give the slightest credence to even the most attenuated version of such slanders? The question need only be posed to know the answer.

But what are Canadian intellectual sensibilities when the victim of parallel enmity is Arab? This question rarely ever is posed. But once posed, the answer is far from flattering.

Professor David Bercuson, a nationally known academic figure wrote *The Secret Army* in 1983. This book is an account of the mainly Jewish volunteers, the *mahal*, who came from outside Palestine to fight with the Israeli military in the 1947-49 war. Bercuson's larger political objective is to demonstrate that Israel is the client of no power, that her creation was the independent, heroic effort of Palestine-resident and diaspora Jews.

A bold heading in quotation marks dominates the book's first page: "We Shall Drink Jewish Blood." Who shall drink Jewish blood? The "Arab mob" we are told in breathless prose.

The ancient stones of the holy city of Jerusalem rang to the cries
of street hawkers and peddlers in the Arab market. Children
played in the narrow streets under the bright sun of a glorious
spring day in Palestine. It was April 4, 1920. As Jews prepared
for the Passover festival due to begin the next day and Christians
began to gather for the Easter pilgrimage, Moslems poured into
the city for the celebration of the Feast of the Prophet Moses.
The Moslem religious authorities had requested and received
permission from the British military government to hold a parade
through the streets of the ancient walled city. As a British
military band led the procession, the Military Governor watched
with interest from a balcony. The parade ended at the golden
dome of the Mosque of Omar on the temple mount. There an
Arab nationalist leader gave a violent harangue against the Jews.
Suddenly a mob, wielding knives and screaming "we shall drink
Jewish blood," broke from the crowd and ran through the streets
to the Jewish quarter where it swept down on startled and
unsuspecting Jews. Within minutes Jewish dead and wounded lay
in the streets, and Jewish homes and shops were looted and set
ablaze. Three days of rioting had begun.[2]

Whereas the writer of fiction can be the arbiter of the plot, the evidence of past actualities sits in final judgment of written history. On
what evidence, then, does Professor Bercuson rely for his racially
inflammatory account of April 4, 1920 in Jerusalem, the event he
proclaims as the "pattern for the Palestine war"?[3] He provides only one
reference: Israeli military commander Yigal Allon's *Shield of David*. A
sympathetic reviewer wrote of this book: "Handsomely printed and
illustrated with superb color pictures, the book, I would guess, is destined to enjoy success as a bar mitzvah gift."[4] Meanwhile Bercuson, a
professional historian, ignores Israeli, American and Canadian schol-
arly accounts, based on original documents, that do not mention, let
alone feature, the cry "we shall drink Jewish blood." Indeed a reading of
these historical works shatters Bercuson's archetypes.[5]
    Throughout his book, Bercuson uses the technique of dramatizing
his history, imagining and injecting conversations for which there is no

documentation. It is intriguing to see how he transforms even the partisan sources favorable to his objective. Consider the 1947 event with which he begins his second chapter. Bercuson's only source is an unfootnoted official Israeli military history. There Lt. Col. Natanial Lorch wrote:

> On the day after the Partition Resolution a Jewish bus was driving along the highway from Natanya to Jerusalem. Near Lydda Airport Arab riflemen standing by the roadside suddenly opened fire. Three women and two men were killed.

Here is how Bercuson rewrites his source material.

> On November 30, 1947, a bus crowded with Jewish passengers trundled over the two-lane road on its way from Netanya to Jerusalem in Palestine. The small knot of Arabs in *keffiyahs*, standing by the road, was not an unusual sight, and the driver probably paid no heed to them. As the bus drew alongside the group, however, the Arabs shouldered rifles and opened fire at close range. The driver quickly shifted gears and kicked the accelerator down as screams of panic mingled with cries of pain and the blood of dead and wounded passengers collected in pools on the rough wooden floors.[7]

And the professional Canadian reviewers? In the *Canadian Historical Review* Bercuson is complimented for his "clear, felicitous prose" that "retells a story of human interest in an engaging way while conforming to the canons of scholarship."[8] In another journal Bercuson is commended for his "fascinating and dispassionate model of historical writing."[9] In Canada's prestige newspaper, *The Secret Army* again is praised for its "meticulous" historical scholarship.[10]

The Secret Army is built upon two archetypes: the cruel Arab and the innocent Jewish settler, where the cowardice and venality of the former is overcome by the courage and purity of the latter. History is reduced to a morality tale that simply repeats.

Were Bercuson not a prominent intellectual and his publisher one of Canada's most prestigious, the absence of critical response might be considered as a singular event. But given the reputation of both author and publisher, the absence of response to a litany of crass racial stereotypes is a broader measure of the contempt in which considerable numbers of the Canadian intelligentsia hold the real people of the Middle East.[11]

Kattan and Klein: the European mould

Naim Kattan is a Canadian novelist born in Iraq in 1928. He attended university in Baghdad (1945-47), studied at the Sorbonne (1947-51), emigrated to Canada (1954), and became a professor and newspaper literary critic in Quebec. Appointed head of the Writing and Publication Section of the Canada Council, he has been honoured with the Order of Canada.

The first in his trilogy of autobiographical novels opens, like Bercuson's book, with a scene of throat-slitting murders; rape and plunder of defenceless Baghdad Jews by "unbridled, chaotic" and "tribal" Moslem Bedouin for whom "instinct was the law." "As they advanced, their ranks swelled, teeming with women, children and adolescents who ululated as they did on great occasions such as weddings and feasts."[12]

The second volume of the trilogy opens with news of the declaration of the state of Israel and the war of 1947-49. In Baghdad anti-Jewish persecution is rampant. Moreover, Baghdad is transformed by Kattan into Warsaw under the Nazis. "Where was Baghdad? My brother? The Jews in prison? We were all in Warsaw, we were all Warsaw Jews, and death lay in wait for us."[13] This dubious Europeanization of Iraqi history comes to a full halt at a critical juncture, however. In Paris Kattan learns to overcome his "fear of Germans," but by contrast he remains resolutely antagonistic to Iraqi society.[14]

In this same novel, Kattan sketches two scenes in which Iraqis, one pro-fascist, the other pro-communist, are reduced as characters to a single dimension of repugnant male lechery. This theme recurs in a Kattan short story where Ottawa-in-winter is contrasted with sexual and hedonistic fantasies of Baghdad, a world dominated by the dimension of sensuality. In another short story, the Egyptian male figure is characterized by a blend of cruelty, stupidity and servility.[15]

Again book reviewers did not comment on any of this. Kattan's Mid-

EYELESS IN GAZA

After the invasion of Egypt by the combined forces of Britain, France and Israel, Canadian Forum, a major journal of the Canadian academic and literary community, printed this April 1957 cartoon. John Foster Dulles, U.S. Secretary of State, is portrayed walking blindfolded between Israeli and Egyptian forces, leading an equally blindfolded U.N. and U.N. military forces. What is particularly significant in this high-brow journal is the crude and degrading depiction of the Arabs: with hooked noses and threatening demeanor, something very similar to anti-semitic depictions of Jews. Contrasting with the Arabs, the Jewish-Israeli forces in this cartoon are facially nondescript.

dle East stereotypes were so common-place, and his unhistorical Europeanization of Iraqi Jewish experience "natural" enough, not to have astonished any of them.[16]

Another highly regarded Canadian writer also bent Jewish experience in the Arab world to fit a European mould. A.M. Klein did this on the basis of a three-day visit to Morocco in 1949, which he made as a Canadian Zionist functionary. Three days were sufficient to fuel the fantasies of this Joycean scholar and 1948 recipient of the Governor General's award as Canada's outstanding poet.

For Klein, Casablanca was but a microcosm of Morocco, and Morocco a microcosm of the entire Moslem world. Among the "swarthy and sinister" Arabs, where "life [is] held to be the cheapest of commodities," disaster is imminent.[17]

> The pit: has it not been this same pit which in Europe yawned annihilation to our European brothers?...From that edge and precipice it was saved, and see! a new ordeal in another area reveals itself. Deadlines swing back and forth over the heads of a million Jews who lie shackled and fettered on Moslem boards. It is a scimitar which hisses over them, and they must escape or be carved to death![18]

An important section of Klein's novel, *The Second Scroll*, derives from his visit to the Jewish quarter of Casablanca, where the "Moors"

> ...lived well...too well; the thigh-filled pantaloons that waddle along the street; the Negress with scarves...knotted about her large hips; the paunch-proud merchant...these spoke eloquently of past banquets, of many-coursed meals digested reposeful upon soft pillow and divans beneath the gauze of golden slumber, the brocade of the gold snore.[19]

For Klein the tragedy is that the supposed hedonistic Moslem has infected the Jews of Casablanca with "oriental obeisance" and "resignation." Klein writes that the Jews have become "like the culture (sic) in the midst of which they live, fatalists."[20] Klein, by his interjection of a "(sic)," denies even culture to the Moslems.

One might not expect other than this from a life-long publicist for the Canadian Zionist movement. He also was a speech-writer for the Zionist founder of the Bronfman financial empire, as well as a two-time unsuccessful candidate for the social-democratic CCF party. But that the brazen racism of this established Canadian literary figure stirred no critical literary comment, is far more telling.

Indeed after his death in 1972 there was a Klein revival: his literary and political writing was gathered and published and made more widely accessible than ever before. The *Journal of Canadian Studies* devoted a special issue to Klein in 1984; and the Casablanca section of *The Second Scroll* was reprinted in 1986 in a volume of high-brow Canadian travel writing. Bypassing Klein's bigotry, the literary reviewer for Canada's national newspaper nonchalantly wrote of Klein's "discovery of anti-Semitism in Casablanca."[21]

Laurence and MacEwen

It is a relief then to turn to the writings of Margaret Laurence who extends to the stranger, even from the world of Islam, the kinship of a common humanity. Laurence, who died recently, was deservedly respected internationally for her thoughtful, humane and brilliant novels. She was born in a small town in Manitoba. As a young married woman she lived in Somalia and in Ghana. The struggle for independence from imperial Europe, as well as the ambiguities consequent upon its achievement, were the centerpiece of her initial literary work.

Her first book was *The Prophet's Camel Bell*. It is a direct account of her personal experiences living for two years in an Islamic society, Somalia. Laurence explores the universal tension between acceptance and activism, and in the particular circumstances of Somalia she seeks to understand better how the range of practical consequences an individual can effect shapes their beliefs. Certainly she is more informative than Klein's stereotypical condemnation of "oriental fatalism," and his ignorant equation of Arab and Moslem.

Heart of a Stranger, a better known collection of her travel writings, includes two pieces on Somalia. Laurence manifests a persistent and brave desire to penetrate the experiences of others who people our one world, without the pretence and conceit of speaking for them. She moves beyond those misrepresentations of the native as an alien in her/his own land, a fringe to some other centre, a threatening spectre to be exorcised.

Perhaps this is clearest in her essay "Poem and Spear," on the turn-of-the-century Somali rebel and poet Mahammed 'Abdille Hasa. The British colonialists dubbed him the "Mad Mullah" and (shades of Bercuson, Kattan and Klein) portrayed him as a "kind of grossly exaggerated Arabian Nights figure: unvaryingly and diabolically cruel, a profligate of the worst order, a man who spent his days and nights in riotous living, a glutton and a lecher in the grand style."[22]

But for Laurence, Hasa's letters and poems, considerable parts of which she translates, reveal an intelligent anti-colonialist, reminiscent of Louis Riel on the Canadian prairies. Both faced a power that possessed "only one superior quality, namely superior means of slaughter."[23] Laurence counterposes the heroic individual, part of a disappearing communalism, to the ruthlessness of empire, machine and modernity, which she reworked in a novel when writing of the Highland clans in Scotland and the Metis of the Canadian prairie.[24]

Yet critical as she is of French and British machinations in Suez (1956), Laurence's travel essays still moved within the parameters of propaganda when it came to Israel. Oblivious of Israeli expansionism, Laurence depicts Nasser's Egypt as the regional power with a "pharonic and unhealthy desire to expand."[25]

Gwendolyn MacEwen was striking and utterly individual for taking the Arab revolt as her poetic subject, albeit mediated by the persona of Lawrence of Arabia. In the aftermath of the massacres of Palestinians at Sabra and Shatila, MacEwen wrote "Letters to Josef in Jerusalem." These seven letters were not written as a political tract; certainly they are not without ambiguities; but it is clear that MacEwen, in sombre and plaintive voice, engages herself with the Arab and the Jewish-Israelis in the Middle East.

She explains she first met Josef, an avant-garde Israeli playwright, before 1967 in West Jerusalem. For MacEwen, Israel's military conquest of East Jerusalem is illusory. "Death has sucked your brains out," she writes to Josef who took part in the Israeli invasion. War follows war. And so Israel's invasion of Lebanon in 1982, its bombing siege of Beirut, fuses for MacEwen with images of Vietnam and Hiroshima. "The truth is Nuclear Night, the truth is Shatila fat with death . . ."[26]

Richler and Rambo

But unlike MacEwen, the prevalent literary discourse propagates and presumes a Zionist ideological conditioning. In "Promised Land/Newfoundland," Martin Avery parallels the paranoia of a Jewish wife in the Palestinian quarter of old Jerusalem with that of her husband surrounded by hunters in a provincial park.

> She is alone in the Arab Quarter of the Old City of Jerusalem.
> Alone except for Arabs. It is dusk.
>   I am alone, working in the woodlot of a provincial park...
> during the hunting season. There are not many deer this year.
> The hunters will shoot at anything that moves.[27]

In a Mordecai Richler story, Arabs exist as both historic and present threat; they live in filth out of their own miserliness and harbour illusions of pan-Arabism. Reduced to legend they can be a marketable logo, hence the story title "This Year at the Arabian Nights Hotel." But they do not exist in their own name and concreteness, solely through the imagination of the Israeli.

Seymour Mayne paints an Israeli landscape, including "Judea" (the West Bank of Israeli-occupied Palestine), from which the overt presence of Palestinians has been excised, but where Jews have taken "eternal root." Even the site of destroyed Palestinian villages has been metamorphosed into a mere artistic interplay of light and stones.[28]

Overtly removed, covertly threatening, the "Arab" constantly must be countered. Hence the promethean image of Israel, a state whose transformation of Jewry moves its exercise of power beyond the reach of moral criticism. Several of Irving Layton's poems are shameless eulogies of this Israeli military might. In a poem to his two sons, published September 1967, Layton urges them to "Be gunners in the Israeli Air Force." In a poem a few months later, he writes: "repentance, my son,/is short-lived;/an automatic rifle, however,/endures/a lifetime."[29]

Equally devoid of subtlety are the murder-spy-thrillers, best-sellers of Deverell, Rohmer, Jonas. Viciously anti-Arab prejudices are moulded to serve contemporary imperial politics: like the Coleco children's toy Rambo, and his enemy "Nomad" with swarthy features, unmistakable head-dress, and Arabic writing on his cloak. The packaging tells us: "The desert is the country of the treacherous soldier Nomad. He is as unreliable as the sand, as cold as the nights and as dangerous as the deadly scorpions that live there. His family is a gang of assassins and wandering thieves. They are men without honour, who use their knowledge of the desert to attack innocent villages..."[30]

And so we turn full-circle, from literature to Rambo marketing: Arab/Moslem ruthlessness, treachery, irrationality and Israeli innocence and honour, reliving the carbon-copy of European pogroms; not to forget the stereotype of Arab lustfulness.

Nurit Gretz, an Israeli literary critic, has written a thoughtful article on the failure of Israeli Hebrew literature to present the Arab as a person of "flesh and bones." She shows how myth destroys life, empties even personal memories of their authentic concreteness, then reconstructs them to fit the requirements of a political model. She considers the battle to "free the facts from the myths," not to substitute new myths for old, a pressing responsibility of her country's Jewish-Israeli and Palestinian intelligentsia.[31]

In the Canadian literary imagery of the Middle East, with few odd exceptions, the same abstractions overwhelm the concrete, the same cardboard persona displace the living, the unchanging morality play cloaks the historical record.

Admittedly, in the Canadian literary context, representations of Middle East realities often appear as small fragments. Still, psychiatry and archeology have shown how fragments can be signposts to structures, structures that sustain all too well the war-time propaganda we have just witnessed.

Notes

This essay is adapted from a more comprehensive monograph which examines Canadian periodicals and book reviews, as well as literature, which is the focus of this article. "Sand in the Snow: Images of the Middle East in Canadian English-language Literature and Commentary," Near East Cultural and Educational Foundation of Canada, Occasional Paper No.8, 1986.

[1] Knight, Rolf, *Indians at Work* (Vancouver, New Star Books, 1978), p.163. MacLaren, Roy, *Canadians on the Nile: 1882-1898* (Vancouver, University of British Columbia Press, 1978), Chapter 6.

[2] Bercuson, David J., *The Secret Army* (Toronto, Lester and Orpen Dennys, 1983), p.1.

[3] Bercuson, *op.cit.*, p.76.

[4] Schoenbrun, David, *Saturday Review*, February 6, 1971.

[5] There is a review of this literature in *Sand in the Snow, op.cit.*, footnote 10, p.55.

[6] Lorch, Lt. Col. Nataniel, *The Edge of the Sword: Israel's War of Independence 1947-1949* (Jerusalem, Masada Press Ltd., 1968), p.46.

[7] Bercuson, *op.cit.* p.13.

[8] Hundert, Gershon, *Canadian Historical Review*, Volume 65, September 1984, pp.430-31.

[9] Kuczewski, Andre G. *Journal of Palestine Studies*, Volume XV, No.2, Winter 1986.

[10] Gellner, John, *The Globe and Mail*, February 18, 1984.

[11] Bercuson first established his academic reputation as a labour historian. For several years he was a co-editor of the *Canadian Historical Review*. Then he turned to writing on questions of Zionism, a shift in focus that parallels another influential Canadian intellectual, Professor Irving Abella who has been an editor of *Middle East Focus*.

[12] Kattan, Naim, *Farewell, Babylon* (Toronto, McClelland and Stewart, 1977), pp.13-21.

[13] Kattan, Naim, *Paris Interlude* (Toronto, McClelland and Stewart, 1977), p.107.

[14] Kattan, *op.cit.*

[15] Kattan, Naim, *The Neighbour and Other Stories* (Toronto, McClelland and Stewart, 1982), pp.63-67, 79-104.

[16] For alternatives to this Europeanization and distortion of Iraqi Jewish history, see *Sand in the Snow, op.cit.*, footnote 16, pp.56-57, for writings by other Iraqi Jews.

[17] Klein, A.M., *Beyond Sambation: Selected Essays and Editorials 1928-1955*, Steinberg M.W. and Usher Caplan (eds) (Toronto, University of Toronto Press, 1982), p.383, p.449.

[18] *Ibid.*, p.397.

[19] Klein, A.M., *The Second Scroll* (New York, Alfred Knopf, 1951), pp.68-69.

[20] Klein, A.M., *Beyond Sambation, op.cit.* p.361.

[21] See William French's review, *The Globe and Mail*, March 1, 1986 of Dobbs, Kildare (ed), *Away From Home: Canadian Writers in Exotic Places* (Deneau, 1986).

[22] Laurence, Margaret, *Heart of a Stranger* (Toronto, McClelland and Stewart, 1976), p.69.

[23] *Ibid.*, p.74.

[24] *Ibid.*, p.37.

[25] *Ibid.*, p.115.

[26] MacEwen, Gwendolyn, *The T.E. Lawrence Poems* (Oakville, Mosaic Press, 1982) and "Letters to Josef in Jerusalem," *Canadian Forum*, December 1983, pp.25-28.

[27] Avery, Martin, *The Singing Rabbi: New Stories* (Oberon Press, 1983), p.72.

[28] See for example the poem "Ein Kerem," which was a destroyed Palestinian village in the district of Jerusalem and "Hills of Judea" in Seymour Mayne, *Name* (Erin, Press Porcepic, 1975), pp.46-7.

29 "For My Two Sons, Max and David," *Canadian Forum*, September 1967, and "After Auschwitz," *Canadian Forum*, March 1968. Also see Irving Layton, "Israelis," in Sinclair, Gerri and Morris Wolfe (eds), *The Spice Box: An Anthology of Jewish Canadian Writing* (Toronto, Lester and Orpen Dennys, 1981), p.191.

30 Antonius, Rachad, "Catégories politiques, groupes ethniques et distortion des faits dans le discours sur les Arabes," Centre d'études arabes pour le developpement, Montreal.

31 Nurit Gretz, "Shot on the Bridge," *Ha'aretz*, January 17, 1986, translated by Dr. Israel Shahak in his collection of translations titled "Between Equality and Apartheid."

Covering Islam

Edward Said wrote a book with this title, a book that explores Western, and specifically United States, responses to the world of Islam since the 1970s.[1]

The words "Islam-Moslem" have been so moulded in current usage that they now reveal more about the speaker's psychology than the complexity of those being spoken of. Thus, for example, the simple fact that the country with the largest number of Islamic religious adherents is neither Arab nor Middle Eastern surprises many people. Too few think of the Indonesian archipelago. Too few recognize that 20 per cent of Palestinians are Christian adherents, and that the majority of today's Israeli-Jews migrated from centuries of existence within Arab societies in the Middle East, not from European societies. Instead, common knowledge equates Arab with Moslem with Middle East, forming a single pool, a common cultural reservoir of fears, suspicions and antipathies, that have been manipulated for the political and war-making agendas of our leaders.

To recapture the complexities of "Islam" – as belief and as

practices – requires that we first disconnect ourselves from the psychology of fear, suspicion, and antipathy we have imbibed. We must disconnect ourselves from a symbolism that has been manipulated by our leaders, as it has been manipulated as well by leaders such as Saddam Hussein.

The following essay by Dr. Hanna Kassis outlines some features of Islamic religious belief, and then traces the obscuring and distortion of this within the Christian religious tradition, a tradition that has influenced secularists as well.

Notes

[1] Said, Edward W., *Covering Islam: How the Media and Experts Determine How We See the Rest of the World* (New York, Pantheon Books, 1981), p.x.

Christian Misconceptions
of Islam

Hanna E. Kassis

FOURTEEN CENTURIES AGO IN A CAVE OUTSIDE A DUST-RIDDEN CARAVAN centre in the Arabian Peninsula, an illiterate, disinherited but mature (probably forty year old) man was prompted by a mysterious voice to accept and proclaim the sovereignty of God and to rejoice in obedience to Him. The man's name was Muhammad and the message of obedience he received and proclaimed came to be known as *islam* ("submission"). Since then, Christians have responded to the phenomena that was to have a constructive impact on the lives of millions of people over the centuries, either by misrepresenting the faith or by reviling its scriptures and prophet. Sadly, this negativism has come to colour and condition our entire relationship with and understanding of every aspect of Muslim or Arab life, socially, politically, economically and religiously.

What is Islam?

Islam is a state of total submission to God, whose majestic name in Arabic is Allah (a name which is employed not only by Muslims but by Arabic-speaking Christians and Jews as well). Simply put, Islam is a response (*talbiyah*) to the divine call (*da'wa*) for loving, unquestioning obedience (*ta'a*) to God. Such obedience can be achieved only through the discipline of abiding by God's law (*shari'a*) which He established for humankind.

According to Muslim doctrine, the first Muslim was Abraham, and the first act of islam (or "submission") was his obedient response to God's command (*amr Allah*) to offer his beloved, unnamed son as a sacrifice (See Genesis 22) and the son's parallel willingness and cooperation.

> And We gave him the good tidings of
> a prudent boy;
> and when he had reached the age
> of running with him,
> he said, "My son, I see in a dream
> that I shall sacrifice thee;
> consider, what thinkest thou?"
> He said, "My father, do as thou art
> bidden; thou shalt find me,
> God willing, one of the steadfast."

The Qur'anic narrative, typically brief and evocative in style, differs from its Biblical counterpart in some details. Two of these differences (the call in a dream and unnamed son) are minor; the third (the son's willing response) is quite significant and is highly emphasized by the Muslims. The response to God's command is not only that of him who is to sacrifice, but also of the son who is to be sacrificed. And as Abraham is called *khalil Allah* ("God's intimate friend"), this entire act of an obedient father and willing son must be seen as Islam's expression of God's love for humanity and humanity's loving obedience to God. This loving obedience of Abraham and his son is Islam's archetypal or primary event (or myth) and is celebrated as the highest feast (*'id al-adha*, "the feast of the sacrifice") in the Muslim calendar. Regrettably, the Christian, to whom such vocabulary is common parlance, has remained incapable of comprehending it or respecting its symbolism.

The Muslim is called upon to recollect this "primary event" and to realize it in his or her own life through the discipline of action and belief.

Action

In obedience to God's law (*shari'a*), which is the primary law for individuals and society, and guided by the example of the Prophet, who epitomizes God's law in his practice (*sunna*), a Muslim is required to fulfill two sets of obligations as a matter of discipline: ordinances of divine worship (*'ibadat*) and acts of piety (*taqwa*). Among the former, one is called upon to do the following:

- to restate the principles of faith by testifying (*shahada*) that there is no god other than God and that Muhammad is His Apostle;
- to perform the ritual prayers (*salat*) five times daily;
- to pay the ritual tax (*zakat*) and give alms (*sadaqa*) to the needy;
- to fast (*sawm*) during the month of Ramadan, the month of the revelation of the Qur'an;
- to make an effort to perform the pilgrimage (*hajj*) to Mecca at least once in one's lifetime.

Among the acts of piety, a Muslim is required:

- to do those things that are lawful (*halal*) and to refrain from doing those things that are forbidden (*haram*);
- to give of one's treasured substance to kinsmen, the orphan, the needy, the beggar, the traveller;
- to ransom the slave;
- to fulfill one's covenant when one has engaged in a covenant;
- to perform the struggle (*jihad*) within oneself to overcome the devil's temptation, and with the community against the enemies of God and of Islam, and to endure misfortune, hardship and peril with fortitude;
- to fulfill one's obligations in this world, without it becoming an end in itself, and to direct all of one's thoughts and actions toward obtaining God's pleasure and the rewards of the world to come;
- to seek to understand the law of God; to expand one's mind to the knowledge of all aspects of God's creation and to expand one's heart to the grace of God;

- to ask God's forgiveness for all one's sins, known and unknown;
- to mention the name of God frequently (*dhikr*) as a self-reminder of His sovereignty, and to praise God (*tasbih*) and proclaim God's greatness and sovereignty (*takbir*) in every circumstance and on all occasions.

A Muslim should also recognize that the human being (male or female) is God's supreme act of creation, superior even to the angels. Consequently, every Muslim is a brother or sister to every other Muslim. Male and female are equal in the eyes of God; to each, however, is given a set of responsibilities and obligations (socially and economically) and hence differing privileges (economic and social). Moreover, in the community of faith (*umma*) no person of any class or race is superior to any other; superiority is measured only by God in terms of piety and obedience.

Belief

The primary article of faith in Islam is to believe in the oneness and uniqueness of God (*tawhid*), who is without associate or compeer (*la ilaha illa Allah wahdahu la sharika lahu*), and that Muhammad is His Apostle (*rasul Allah*) and Prophet (*nabiy*). Equally important is the belief that the Qur'an is the uncreated speech of God revealed through Muhammad as the divine gift of guidance (*al-huda*) to humanity, and that it contains the basis of all that is needed to govern human existence and being. In addition, the Muslim is called upon to believe:

- that this world is finite and passing (*dar al-fana*) but that the world to come is the world of permanence (*dar al-baqa*);
- that there is a day of resurrection (*yawm al-qiyama*) and of judgment (*yawm al-din*) on which the living and the dead shall answer for their thoughts and actions; that paradise (*al-janna*) is the reward of those who abide by God's law, and that hell (*jahannam*) is the penalty for those who rebel against it. The Muslim is further called upon to believe in the existence of angels, the *jinn* (guiding spirits that can lead one to either good or evil, depending on one's will) and *Iblis*, the fallen angel who disobeyed God and who tempts human beings to rebellion and disobedience.

Islam teaches that God revealed His word through earlier apostles and prophets, notable among whom were:

- Moses (bearer of the Torah) who was succeeded by other prophets bringing God's promise of deliverance to the Children of Israel and warning them as they swerved from obedience to God's law;
- Jesus (bearer of the Gospel) who, by God's command, was born of the Virgin Mary but who, contrary to the affirmation of the Christians, was neither divine nor the Son of God. According to Islam, God did not beget nor was He begotten and has no compeer (*lam yalid wa-lam yuwlad wa-lam yakun lahu kufu'an ahad*). By God's command, Jesus healed the sick, raised the dead and breathed life into formed clay birds. He taught righteousness and the worship of the true God and foretold the coming of Muhammad. According to Islam, although people thought otherwise, Jesus was neither crucified nor did he die.

But for profound differences in matters of christology, Islam and Christianity are very similar. And not unlike Christianity, Islam sees its revelation as supplanting and superceding those that preceded it.

It goes without saying that the precepts summarized here constitute the ideal of Islam and that not all Muslims abide by them. As students of history, we must be aware of the fact that there is an abyss that separates our ideals from the reality of our life. This is true as much of Islam and the Muslims as it is of Christianity and the Christians. By and large, however, Christians – not without self-righteousness – have condemned Islam either out of ignorance of the elements of that faith or through focussing on selective negative illustrations from history (factual or legendary) of the Islamic peoples. Even when they do understand the basic tenets of the faith, Christians historically have vilified Islam in an expression of what I shall call "religious racism."

Religious racism

Religious racism is more than the conscious affirmation of a perceived ethnic or cultural superiority of Aryans to non-Aryans, or of white to blacks or – in the Canadian context – to Indians (native or Asian). By religious racism I mean the inability or unwillingness of the religious

Traditional angular script: the black area spells the name of the Prophet Muhammad; the white area spells the name of his son-in-law and the first Imam, 'Ali. Each name is repeated in all four directions.

individual or community to comprehend the "other," whose way of life, beliefs and customs, colour of skin, or language are different from the "norm."

Religious racism is the rejection of the "otherness" of the "other." It is the affirmation that one's religion and religious life are superior to those of another. It is the unspoken consciousness of one's religious chosenness, of the preference of Shem over his brothers Ham and Japeth, of Israelite over Canaanite, of Christian over non-Christian, of

Jew over gentile, of Muslim over "infidel." The absence of this racism does not, however, require the abandonment of one's own religious way of life and the adoption of that of the "other." Rather, it indicates the acceptance of the simple fact that there is an "other" – another person, another race, another set of religious customs and traditions, another religious language and way of life – and that this "otherness" is, moreover, both valid and enriching to one's own faith. Accepting the "other" is a recognition of the fact that God's revelation of His will transcends the exclusiveness of any ethnic or religious community.

Muslims as Samaritans

In biblical categories, the Muslims are "neither Jews nor gentiles" as far as Christianity is concerned. Thus, they have been and continue to be the Samaritans of Christian exclusiveness. The history of the Christian attitude toward Islam and of the relationship of Christianity with that Samaritan offers a very good illustration of religious racism. I have chosen the Samaritan motif because the manner in which the people of Jesus treated the Samaritans offers an excellent parable for Christian attitudes toward and treatment of Islam. At the same time, Jesus' response to the Samaritans is the yardstick against which the conduct of the Christians throughout history should be measured. The judgment is severe!

The conflict of Christianity with Islam

The rise of Islam in the seventh century brought with it for Christianity, then barely emerging from the confusion of its many councils dealing with metaphysical issues of little or no concern to the people of the Near East, its most serious problem to date. The Muslim conquest of the heartland of Christianity and its major sacred centres (Palestine, Syria, Egypt, North Africa and Spain) created an atmosphere of a collapse of a political order which perceived itself to be divinely ordained. It would be naive, however, to assess the crisis of Christianity in its confrontation with Islam strictly in terms of military gains or losses or in terms of land or cities lost – although the seriousness of the latter should not be minimized. It was more the doctrine of Islam that confounded the Christians than the military victories it won. The Christian reaction was, at best, negative and self-destructive.

Attitude towards the Prophet and the Qur'an[1]

I cannot recall a single person in the history of humanity who has been such a focus of hostility as Muhammad has been in the thought and writings of the Christians. Examples of this attitude are many, from various periods and regions. It may be best illustrated in the writings of the leaders of the ninth-century Christian (Mozarabic) rebellion in Muslim Cordoba. Such writings are archetypal. To these writers (Eulogius and Alvarus) Muhammad was "the eleventh king to arise after the Fourth Beast" who "shall speak words against the Most High, and shall wear out the saints of the Most High, and shall think to change the times and the law; and they shall be given into his hand for a time, two times, and half a time" (Daniel 7:24f). They concluded that Muhammad's death in the year 666 (a date arrived at by employing the chronology on the Era of Spain), complied with the prophetic value of the number (Revelation 13:18) and established him as the "Beast of Revelation" or the Antichrist.

Among those holding the view that Muhammad was the Antichrist was even the "enlightened" Peter the Venerable, the Abbot of Cluny, who had commissioned the translation of the Qur'an into Latin in order that Islam might be combatted as a heresy. A similar – though particularly vulgar – attitude was that of Simon Simeonis, the Irish Franciscan who travelled to Palestine in 1323. He used vile vocabulary in his references to Islam, Muhammad and the Muslims: sodomites, beasts, pigs, etc. ("that circumcised dog" of Shakespeare's Othello).

In the period that followed – the age of William of Ockham, Meister Eckhart, St. Francis, etc., a time richly endowed with Christian spirituality – there was no desire to come to grips with Islam. The Muslims continued to be viewed as "war-mongers," "luxury-lovers" and "sex-maniacs." The tender prayers of peace by St. Francis are countered by the blind zeal of his friars in their insistence on publicly insulting Islam, Muhammad and the Qur'an in a mission of hate to Muslim Seville and

Marrakesh. When, after provoking the Muslims beyond endurance, they could not be dissuaded by counsel, bribery, imprisonment or expulsion from publicly debasing Islam, they were executed. Misinterpreting the teaching of the founder of their order, these bigots were hailed as martyrs.

The problem was not confined to the Roman or the Medieval Church. In his later years Martin Luther translated a well-known work of Ricoldo, *The Confusion of the Qur'an*, which he had earlier dismissed as a compendium of papist lies. Luther was by now convinced that the Muslims were hard in their hearts, rejecting the Scriptures and clinging to the "lies" they learned from Muhammad and the Qur'an.

I have excluded from this discussion the images of Muhammad, the Qur'an and Islam as these were misconstrued in the secular writings of Christendom: the French romances or *chansons de geste*, Dante and others. I have also excluded the similar negativism in the writings of non-traditional Christians such as John Wycliffe.

A fleeting glimpse of hope

Little impact was to be had from fleeting moments of hope in which a true charitable and enlightened attitude prevailed. For example, little is said of a dialogue in the eighth century between the Bishop of Baghdad and the Muslim caliph,[2] in which the bishop concludes that, in spite of the profound differences on matters of christology, Muhammad was a prophet who followed in the path of biblical prophets.

In the West, it was a sagacious and charitable man of the School of Salamanca (Spain), John of Segovia, who ushered in a brief "moment of vision." In communications with men who shared his vision he sought to examine Islam for the purpose of discovering the common ground it shared with Christianity. Assisted by a Muslim from Salamanca, he began a new translation of the Qur'an. He had the vision of establishing a dialogue with Islam. John of Segovia's efforts, however, were unsuccessful.

It was in fact left to secular individuals of the Age of the Enlightenment and beyond to view Muhammad and Islam in a brighter light. It is true that at times (such as in the case of Voltaire) this was motivated more by a prevailing hostility toward the church than an appreciation of Islam. At other times (such as in the case of Carlyle) it reflected an enlightened understanding of history. Others still (such as Goethe) saw Muhammad positively but romantically.

Modern historians and analysts of Islam follow one or other of these paths. One may wish to compare the work of such historians as Bernard Lewis and Maxime Rodinson. The latter – an enlightened and objective historian – correctly describes Muhammad as "one of the rare men who have turned the world upside down"[3] and, I add, for the better. As a human being, Muhammad shared human strengths and weaknesses.

MIDDLE EAST REPORT

Contemporary calligraphy by Nja Mahdaoui (Tunisia).

In that he is, as Rodinson (a Jew with Marxist inclinations) says, "our brother." As one who received and transmitted God's law to humanity, he is – as the eighth-century Bishop of Baghdad affirmed – a prophet of God. Having said this, I am cognizant of the fact that when Uthred of Boldon argued that salvation was not the monopoly of Christianity, he was condemned.

Notes

[1] I have learned much of what I have to say here from the writings of Norman Daniel, especially his *Islam and the West: The Making of an Image* (Edinburgh, 1960), and R.W. Southern, *Western Views of Islam in the Middle Ages* (Harvard University Press, 1962).

[2] Caspar, R., "Les versions arabes du dialogue entre le catholicos Timodthee I et le calife al-Mahdi (IIe/VIIIe siecle), 'Mohammed a suivi la voie des prophétes,'" *Islamocristiana*, 3 (1977), pp.107-175.

[3] Rodinson, Maxime, *Mohammed* (Pelican Books, 1971), p.313.

Absence of Comparison

What's good for the goose is good for the gander, or good for neither –
if we apply a single standard. But where there are inequalities of
power, double standards are common: between male and female,
between parent and child, and between nations. Because the
criticism of a double standard is so devastating once one recognizes
its existence, those who benefit from the inequity do all they can
to forestall comparison, to block recognition.

Norman Finklestein read the *New York Times* lead editorial for
August 25, 1990. He did not contest the editorial's comprehensive
indictment of Saddam Hussein for violating Nuremberg Principles.
Rather, he took the editorial indictment, part by part, and
examined how the same principles applied to the actions of the
Israeli state. "It is not that Israel is worse than Iraq, but that it is
the beneficiary of a double standard," wrote Dr. Finklestein.[1]

The structured absence of comparison between criticisms of Arab
state and Israeli state actions has been one of the major
impediments to popular understanding of the Middle East. That is
why Dr. Finklestein's lucid, methodical and documented article has
significance even beyond the particular comparisons he makes.

Pervasive double standards complement anti-Arab cultural stereotypes: both are major mechanisms for distorting the presentation of events in that region. After comparing Iraq's crimes against peace with Israel's crimes against peace, Iraq's war crimes with Israel's war crimes, Iraq's crimes against humanity with Israel's crimes against humanity, all violations of Nuremberg Principles, Dr. Finklestein compares decisions of the United Nations on Iraq and on Israel. It is this section of his article which follows.

Since Dr. Finklestein wrote his analysis, the leaders of the G-7 countries issued a communique at the end of their London meetings. They called for a "stronger peacekeeping role for the United Nations" in the aftermath of the war against Iraq.[2] In the very same communique they endorsed the U.S. plan for a Middle East peace conference in which, at Israel's behest, the role of the United Nations is weakened as much as possible. In the U.S. proposal, the role of the U.N. will be entirely ceremonial, restricted to the opening session, and without even a speaking right on that occasion. The media predictably ignored this glaring contradiction. The minimalist role for the U.N. in the Middle East is intended to divert attention away from precisely the comparisons Dr. Finklestein makes between Iraqi and Israeli state actions, incriminating both equally.

Notes

[1] "A Double Standard in the Application of International Law," *Monthly Review*, Volume 43, No.3, July-August 1991, pp.25-54.

[2] *New York Times*, January 17, 1991.

The 'Newly United' United Nations

Norman Finklestein

I WANT NOW TO RETURN TO THE TITLE OF THE NEW YORK TIMES EDITORIAL, "THE World v. Saddam Hussein." This theme has become a staple of commentary on the Gulf crisis. Scarcely a day passes without the media or U.S. administration officials invoking the moral authority of international opinion against Iraq. The now-standard refrain is, in Mr. Bush's words, that "this is not a matter between Iraq and the United States of America. It is between Iraq and the entire world community." [1]

The evidence of a global consensus is, of course, the succession of Security Council resolutions condemning Iraq. Indeed, this – we are told – is the silver lining in the cloud hanging over the Gulf. With the end of the Cold War and the Soviet veto, in the face of Iraq's egregious violations of international norms and law, the "newly united" United Nations is finally functioning as it was designed to. "The level of world cooperation and condemnation of Iraq is unprecedented," Mr. Bush informed a joint session of Congress. "We're now in sight of a United Nations that performs as envisioned by its founders." [2]

Yet, the historical record reveals this is not the first time the United Nations has reached a consensus on a regional conflict. It is the first time in recent memory, however, that the United States has shown such respect for international opinion. The U.N. has agreed for years that Israel has been guilty of the same transgressions against international law for which it condemns Iraq. The difference now is that the U.S. gladly joins the criticisms of Iraq, whereas it previously sought to downplay or even defy the international consensus in criticisms of Israel. Consider the U.N. resolutions on the two conflicts.[3]

Aggression

On August 2, 1990, the Security Council condemned Iraq's invasion of Kuwait and on September 16, 1990, it condemned Iraq's "aggressive acts" against diplomatic missions in Kuwait. During the past fifteen years, the Security Council has adopted eleven resolutions condemning Israeli aggression against Lebanon and other Arab countries. Four more such resolutions were vetoed by a lone U.S. vote. The General Assembly has also overwhelmingly condemned Israeli aggression; for example, 143 countries supported a December 1982 resolution deploring Israel's invasion of Lebanon, with only the U.S. and Israel voting no.

Annexation

On August 9, 1990, the Security Council declared Iraq's annexation of Kuwait "null and void" under international law. In August 1980, the Security Council likewise declared Israel's annexation of Jerusalem "null and void" and, in December 1981, declared its annexation of the Syrian Golan Heights "null and void." On a related issue, the Security Council condemned Israeli settlements in the occupied territories in March 1979 to be "a serious obstruction to achieving...peace in the Middle East." The General Assembly has also repeatedly condemned the Israeli annexation of Jerusalem (a December 1980 resolution was supported by 143 countries with only Israel casting a negative vote), the Israeli annexation of the Golan Heights (a December 1988 resolution was supported by 149 countries with only Israel casting a negative vote), and the Israeli settlements in the occupied territories (a December 1988 resolution was supported by 149 countries with only Israel casting a negative vote).

Occupation

The August 2, 1990, Security Council resolution condemning Iraq's occupation of Kuwait demanded the immediate and unconditional withdrawal of Baghdad's forces. In the same manner, three Security Council resolutions have demanded Israel's immediate and unconditional withdrawal from Lebanon. Moreover, only the U.S. vetoed Security Council resolutions in January 1976 and April 1980 calling for Israel to withdraw to its pre-1967 borders as part of a two-state settlement of the Israeli-Palestinian conflict that would guarantee the "sovereignty, territorial integrity and political independence of all States in the area and their right to live in peace within secure and recognized borders." The General Assembly has repeatedly deplored the Israeli occupation of the West Bank and Gaza (a December 1985 resolution was supported by 153 countries with only the U.S. and Israel casting negative votes), and urged a two-state settlement of the Israeli-Palestinian conflict under the auspices of an international peace conference (a December 1989 resolution was supported by 151 countries with only the U.S., Israel, and Dominica casting negative votes).[4]

Human rights violations

On August 18, 1990, the Security Council condemned Iraq's detention of foreigners and on October 29, 1990, condemned Iraq's hostage-taking and mistreatment of Kuwaitis. The Security Council has repeatedly condemned Israeli human rights practices as well, including seven resolutions deploring its deportation of Palestinians living in the occupied territories and two resolutions deploring its "opening of fire... resulting in the killing and wounding of defenceless Palestinian civilians." A lone U.S. veto has blocked the adoption of fourteen more such Security Council resolutions in the past decade alone. The General Assembly has similarly condemned Israeli human rights practices, including Israel's refusal to recognize the applicability of the Geneva

Conventions in the occupied territories (a December 1988 resolution was supported by 148 countries with only Israel casting a negative vote), its forcible removal and resettlement of Palestinian refugees living in the occupied territories (a December 1988 resolution was supported by 152 countries with only the U.S. and Israel casting negative votes), and its "continued massacre" of Palestinian civilians in the occupied territories (an October 1989 resolution was supported by 141 countries with only the U.S. and Israel casting negative votes).

Sanctions

On August 6, 1990, the Security Council authorized an arms and economic embargo against Iraq. It added an air embargo on September 25, and on November 29 authorized the "use of all necessary means" (after January 15, 1991). The Security Council has tried several times to authorize sanctions against Israel, but the United States, using its veto power and standing alone in opposition, has blocked the way. In January 1982, the U.S. alone opposed a Security Council resolution calling for an arms and economic embargo against Israel for its annexation of the Golan Heights. In June 1982, the U.S. alone opposed a Security Council resolution threatening sanctions against Israel for its failure to withdraw from Lebanon. In August 1982, the U.S. alone opposed a Security Council resolution urging an arms embargo "as a first step" against Israel for its failure to withdraw from Lebanon. And in August 1983, the U.S. alone opposed a Security Council resolution threatening sanctions against Israel for its settlements policy.

Each time the Security Council adopted a resolution condemning Iraq it was the lead front-page story and subject of much commentary. Compare how our two national newspapers [in the U.S.] covered the resolutions against Israel.

In 1989, the Security Council deliberated on five resolutions condemning Israel. Two were adopted and three vetoed by a lone U.S. vote. The *Washington Post* index for 1989 does not list any of these deliberations in its extensive entry for "United Nations Resolutions" and only three of the resolutions received even fleeting mention in the *Post*'s daily "Around the World" column.

Consider the *New York Times*. In December 1986, the Security Council adopted a resolution "strongly deplor[ing]" Israel's killing and wounding of "defenceless [Palestinian] students." The U.S. newspaper of record did not report the story.[5] Coincidentally, it did carry a major front-page article on the United Nations just as the Security Council was deliberating this resolution. Entitled "A Tempest in a Carafe: U.N. Debates Ice Water Question," it reported that the United Nations Advisory Committee on Administration and Budgetary Questions was debating the "implications of restoring drinking water jugs to U.N. committee rooms" (December 8, 1986). In January 1988, a Security Council resolution "call[ing] again upon Israel to desist forthwith from its policies and practices which violate the human rights of the Palestinian people" was vetoed by a lone U.S. vote. The newspaper of record did not report the story. Ironically, it did feature an article entitled "Israeli General describes Charges of Brutal Beatings as 'Just Stories'" (January 28, 1988) as the Security Council was deliberating this resolution. In May 1988, a Security Council resolution "condemn[ing] the recent invasion by Israeli forces of southern Lebanon" was vetoed by a lone U.S. vote. The newspaper of record did not report the story. However, just as the Security Council adopted this resolution, it featured an article entitled "Lebanon Again – And the Israelis are Quiet" (May 8, 1988) reporting that many Israelis were reluctant to talk about the army's "latest victory" because the "Lebanon experience in 1982" so wounded Israel.

In November 1989, a Security Council resolution "strongly deplor[ing]" Israel's "siege of towns, the ransacking of the homes of inhabitants. . .and the illegal and arbitrary confiscation of their property and valuables" was vetoed by a lone U.S. vote. The newspaper of record did report this story – on the inside pages in three paragraphs. It also chose to run an editorial that same day entitled "A Welcome Inch in the Mideast" (November 8, 1988) that urged "praise" for Prime Minister Shamir for advancing the peace process. In December 1989, 151 countries supported a United Nations General Assembly resolution calling for a two-state settlement of the Israel-Palestine conflict under the auspices of an international peace conference, with only the United States, Israel, and Dominica casting negative votes. The newspaper of record did not report the story. Instead, it featured an article on these same General Assembly proceedings entitled "U.N. Puts Off Its Vote on P.L.O." which reported that, under "broad international" pressure, the Arab states deferred an Assembly vote on recognizing the Palestine Liberation Organization as representative of a Palestinian state. The "broad international" support for a two-state settlement of the Israel-Palestine conflict and an international peace conference was not deemed newsworthy.[6]

Moral authority is indivisible; it cannot be selectively invoked. The consensus of the United Nations cannot be acclaimed in the Iraq-Kuwait conflict and – as is typically the case – contemptuously dismissed or simply ignored in the conflict between Israel and Palestine.[7]

Notes

[1] Transcript of President Bush's news conference, *New York Times*, August 23, 1990. [In the original footnote, Finklestein provides several additional references.]

[2] Transcript of President Bush's address to Congress, *New York Times*, September 12, 1990. [In the original footnote, Finklestein provides several additional references.]

[3] The adopted Security Council resolutions can be found in the annual Resolutions and Decisions of the Security Council, United Nations. The vetoed resolutions are only available in the United Nations archives. The General Assembly resolutions can be found in the annual Resolutions and Decisions Adopted by the General Assembly, United Nations.

[4] A December 19, 1990, *New York Times* editorial ("Israel and Iraq, Unlinked") avers that there is "no parallel" between the Iraqi and Israeli occupations because Iraq occupied Kuwait through aggression while Israel occupied the West Bank and Gaza in a war of self-defence. Yet the most basic parallel is that both are occupations. Even if one credits Israel's highly dubious claim that the West Bank and Gaza were occupied in the course of a defensive war, it still has no legal title to them. As R.Y. Jennings observes in his classic study (*The Acquisition of Territory in International Law*, 1963), "it would be a curious law of self-defense that permitted the defender in the course of his defence to seize and keep the resources and territory of the attacker" (55). Indeed, Israel itself has conceded this point. In the wake of the June 1967 war and Israel's occupation of the West Bank and Gaza, the Security Council adopted Resolution 242 and, in May 1968, the Israeli government officially endorsed it. The resolution called inter alia for the "[w]ithdrawal of Israel armed forces" in accordance with the principle – listed first in the preambular paragraphs – of "the inadmissibility of the ac-

quisition of territory by war." Recall further that President Bush invoked precisely this principle in his condemnation of the Iraqi occupation of Kuwait: "The acquisition of territory by force is unacceptable" (*New York Times*, August 9, 1990).

[5] The *New York Times* made a passing reference to this resolution a year later on December 23, 1987.

[6] Predictably, the *New York Times*' coverage of the U.N. Secretary General's "Report to the Security Council" following the Al-Aqsa Mosque killings did not mention the report's repeated reference to resolutions on the Israel-Palestine conflict that "could not be adopted owing to the negative vote by a permanent member of the Council." (The report was officially issued on October 31, 1990, and the *Times*'s story appears on the same day.)

[7] In this respect, Israel is as vulnerable to the claim of hypocrisy as the U.S. Israel has repeatedly invoked the authority of the November 1947 General Assembly resolution (181) recommending its statehood. (It passed with 33 in favor, 13 opposed and 10 abstaining – and not without considerable U.S. arm-twisting.) The Israeli declaration of independence referred to the legitimacy conferred on the state by Resolution 181 as did Zionist leader Chaim Weizmann who deemed it a "grant of independence." In an address before the General Assembly, Abba Eban called Israel "the first state to be given birth by the United Nations." Yet, recent General Assembly resolutions which seem to command as much authority – for example, the December 1989 resolution calling for a two-state settlement and an international peace conference, passed with 151 in support, three opposed and one abstaining – are typically ridiculed by Israel. Indeed, the numerous General Assembly resolutions on the Middle East conflict ignored by Israel apparently command as much authority as Security Council resolution 242, the most widely cited of the relevant U.N. resolutions. The Security Council adopted 242 under Chapter Six of the U.N. Charter, which gives it the power to recommend solutions for disputes. The Council did not act under Chapter Seven, which gives it the power to make decisions binding on member states to resolve breaches of the peace. Thus 242, like the General Assembly resolutions, has the status of a recommendation. See Sydney D. Baily, *The Making of Resolution 242* (Dordrecht, 1985), p.151 [. . .] [A]s Abba Eban observed in the *Jerusalem Post* – current Israeli Prime Minister Shamir "has never allowed any mention of 242 to pass his lips except in tones of rejection. . . While some governments have not explicitly endorsed 242, Mr. Shamir is the only prime minister in the world who has actually turned it down" (international edition, December 3, 1988). The opinion Eban expresses in the same article about the purported bias of the U.N. against Israel is also worth reporting: "The U.N. has spoken much virulent nonsense on Israel as on many other issues, but the overwhelming balance of its influence on Israel's destiny and status is dramatically positive. No nation involved in a struggle for legitimacy has received such potent support from the overall jurisprudence of an international organization."

Missing Voices

Not a lot is translated. What is translated is not always known. And even what is known to be translated often is not easily available. In the end we have far too little sense of the variety of voices, particularly dissenting voices, in the Middle East.

In the war against Iraq, we didn't hear the voices of the Iraqi opposition to Saddam Hussein because they also opposed the U.S.-led war against their homeland and people. Those who waged war against Iraq manoeuvred and still manoeuvre for a military coup, not a participatory, pluralist democracy; so these dissenting Iraqi voices are unavailable, for all practical purposes, to citizens here.

An Iraqi woman, Salma Khadra Jayusi, a distinguished literary figure in the Arab world, has initiated and directs a major Project of Translation from Arabic (PROTA). Her collections of modern and classical poetry, fiction and drama are being published in North America and England, but still are known only to a very limited audience. In cooperation with Salma Jayussi, a Canadian, Olive Kenny, last year translated the autobiography of one of Palestine's most admired women poets, Fadwa Tuqan's A

Mountainous Journey. Nawal el-Saadawi's feminist novellas about Egyptian women, like *Woman At Point Zero*, are a little more known. But even when the Egyptian novelist Naguib Mahfouz was awarded the Nobel Prize for Literature in 1989, the first Arab writer to receive it, his books were less than prominently promoted. Our ignorance of the artistic and dissenting voices in the Middle East obviously impedes our understanding of the contradictoriness of reality there, as well as the discovery of democratic allies. A collection such as this cannot compensate for that ignorance; at best it can let the reader overhear snatches of conversations.

Here are a few cartoons of Naji Ali. His often poignant drawings were published and widely admired in the Arab world. Every drawing featured a small boy, whom we always see from behind, representing the dispossessed Palestinians, like Naji Ali himself. Only when Palestinians have a homeland would the boy's face be visible, he said. An uncompromising critic of the wealthy and dictatorial Arab regimes, Naji Ali portrayed them in the persona of short, fat men. A courageous advocate for the democratic tolerance of political differences, Naji Ali was assassinated by an unknown enemy: some say Israel, some say an Arab regime.

The Islamic Republic of Iran is not a place we are led to expect to find a best-selling, feminist novelist. Sharnoush Parsipoor's works have not been translated from her original Farsi. Few on this continent, other than exiles, know her portrayals of Iranian patriarchal structures, and Iranian struggles for national and democratic rights. An Iranian woman exile provides us with a flavour of Parsipoor's work.

Lastly, there is an introduction to the Israeli Hebrew press which, even with its institutionalized censorship, encompasses pungent discussions. These conversations effectively are suppressed on this continent because they are too deeply embarrassing to Israel's supporters here. Dr. Israel Shahak, a human rights activist in Israel and a holocaust survivor, regularly translates the Hebrew press to stir North Americans out of popular fantasies about his society.

Naji Ali

Some examples of Naji Ali's cartoons. The dispossessed Palestinian child with his back toward the viewer was Ali's signature; he said he would never show the child's face until the Palestinians had won their independent homeland.

Sharnoush Parsipoor:
A Best-Selling Feminist

Shahla Sarabi

SHARNOUSH PARSIPOOR WORKS TRANSLATING, FROM ENGLISH AND FRENCH into her native Farsi, but her own writing never has appeared in any other language. She lives with her son and mother in a small Tehran apartment, and at 45 continues writing literature as she has done since the age of 14. Her most famous novels and short stories are *Dog and the Long Winter*, *Tooba and the Meaning of Night*, and most recently *Women Without Men*.

Parsipoor's protagonists are very ordinary women who challenge social conventions and social power. In an interview in a Tehran literary magazine, Parsipoor has said:

> Being a woman is a "value." A woman has to bear the burden of
> the society and be patient. She is physically weaker. By
> discovering this weakness as a negative point in women, they
> have been labelled as the weaker gender. But weakness is an
> honour. Only a weak human being can create. A man who is
> creative is definitely growing a woman within himself.

Neither the current Iranian government, nor the previous regime of the Shah, have welcomed her work. Yet despite harassment and imprisonment, even with the legal codification of a highly patriarchal order, Sharnoush Parsipoor's books not only are published, they have become best-sellers in the Islamic Republic of Iran. Parsipoor's works focus on women's deepest feelings, a new, strengthening trend in Iranian literature, matching the deepening oppression of women under the Islamic Republic. Parsipoor challenges many traditions, like the confinement of women to the house and the taboo of virginity, and in her stories men fall from positions of power to complete powerlessness.

The enmity and frustration of the authorities is evident in these comments, published for circulation to government officials only.

> Before the [Khomeini] revolution there were [Parsipoor] works . . . identified as not suitable for sale because of extreme obscenity, and they were destroyed. A while after the revolution, Parsipoor was arrested and sentenced to prison. During her prison term she consistently declared her hatred for veiling and proper clothing for women! She has been out of jail about three years now, and has been collaborating with anti-revolution magazines inside the country. In her works, she has attacked the values and ideals of the Islamic Revolution in different and subtle ways . . .
>
> In her letter [to a Tehran literary journal], Parsipoor strongly criticizes the Ministry of Islamic Guidance and describes what she calls the Ministry's trouble-making, saying her book is being sold on the black-market for 15,000 rials [Cd$12], while the assigned Ministry price is 2,500 rials. She writes: "In these cases one thinks about selling the books abroad, and making a living from translating them. But, if my book is translated and I profit, since this is unusual in Iran, suddenly 83 historical dwarfs will appear from nowhere and say: 'Oh, yes. It's clear that this person has relations with suspicious circles.'" (Cultural-Social Newsletter, no. 71, 20-Azar-1368 [December 1989])

Her best-selling *Tooba and the Meaning of Night*, a 500-page novel, spans three generations of the most crucial events of 20th century Iran, starting with the 1906 constitutional revolution. One focus is the deeply rooted traditions that maintain patriarchy, and for the first time in Iranian literature there is detailed exploration of the killing – by fathers, brothers, uncles – of "dishonored" women.

An anti-monarchist activist murders his 14-year-old niece when he discovers she was raped by the King's soldiers and has become pregnant. Mirza, the uncle, is an estate manager in Azerbaijan for a poor prince, and flees to Tehran with his sister and her children, one of them his niece Setarah, when the constitutional revolution he supported is bloodily defeated. The main protagonist of the novel is Tooba, the prince's untraditional, self-educated and idealistic wife. When her husband takes a young peasant girl as a second wife, Tooba is heart-broken. She dreams repeatedly of killing her husband and develops a hatred for young women, including Setarah who has come to live with her uncle in Tooba's household. In her moving description of Setarah's murder, Parsipoor exposes the web of social taboos that leads to this tragic deed. Tooba and Mirza secretly bury Setarah under a pomegranate tree, whose shadow is cast over Tooba's life. The children of Tooba's household follow both conventional and oppositional paths. The novel offers a compelling portrayal of the psychology of activists who have chosen alternative ways of living.

Women Without Men is Parsipoor's latest book; published in Tehran in 1989 it also is a best-seller. She was arrested, apparently interrogated on the book, held for a month, then released. While set in the 1950s, in the time of the U.S. organized coup against the nationalist government of Mossadegh, the attitudes of *Women Without Men* are very contemporary.

Five main characters appear in the 130 pages: all are women, of different ages, classes and ambitions, different in assertiveness, none "heroines," but they all share frustration with the patriarchal order. At one point the five gather together in the garden of one of them, Farokh Lagha, live there for one year, then disperse.

Farokh Lagha, a wealthy 51-year-old housewife, has lived for over 30 years in an arranged marriage. She dislikes her husband, recently retired, and waits impatiently for the rare times he leaves the house. Unable to move when he is around, she revives, finds movement and happiness when he leaves. In an impressive scene, Farokh pushes her husband to his death, in an act of self-defence, then pretends he accidentally fell down the stairs. Hatred and indifference in married relations is a significant theme in Parsipoor's work.

Zarrin Kohal is a 26-year-old overworked prostitute who has lived in a brothel since childhood. One early morning, a client comes and Zarrin can't see his head. Henceforth, all men appear headless to her. Overwhelmed by an observation she can't explain or share, Zarrin flees the brothel, changes profession, and joins the women in the garden.

Mahdokt, a maiden school teacher, is a prude who worries about hungry dogs in the street and dreams of knitting sweaters for orphans. When the school principal makes a pass by inviting her to a movie, she withdraws from teaching. Mahdokt dreams of becoming a tree, and in the garden is transformed into an exotic singing tree. Surrealism is another element in Parsipoor's writing.

The last two characters of *Women Without Men* are Faezeh and Mooness. The 28-year-old Faezeh loves her friend Mooness' brother. Tradition prevents her speaking of her love and Mooness, a 38-year-old spinster "too stupid and simple" to recognize the passion, fails to arrange the marriage. Here is a précis of one section of the novel that centers on Faezeh and Mooness.

On a sunny, summer afternoon, in the midst of political turmoil a few days before the U.S. overthrow of the independent Mossadegh government (in which General Norman Schwarzkopf's father played a role), Faezeh determines, despite the danger and the taboo of leaving the house, to declare her love to Mooness's brother, Amir Khan. To Faezeh's regret Amir is not there; and Parsipoor, with an incredibly humourous style, then portrays – in a conversation between Faezeh and Mooness – animosities and jealousies among women in-laws, derivative from the patriarchal structure of families.

Faezeh recounts how her sister-in-law accused her of not being a virgin, of having had an affair. An important theme in this book is exposing the taboo of virginity. In Iranian traditional culture, like most patriarchal cultures, virginity before marriage is mandatory for women. There also is a common belief that a woman's vagina is protected by a sheath, called pardeh. The pardeh is considered very fragile, and is supposed to be removed by intercourse on the first night of marriage. Since there are no polite words for women's genitals in Iranian culture, Parsipoor uses the word "virginity" for both the vagina and virginity.

Faezeh's sister-in-law had told her, "instead of cooking you should take care of your *pardeh*." Faezeh recounts to Mooness, "I told her, 'the vagina doesn't have a sheath.'" Faezeh's boldness in this conversation shocks Mooness. "'Virginity does have a sheath, my mother told me. If a girl jumps from a height, her sheath will be hurt. It might get broken.'" Faezeh replies, "'It is a hole. But it is narrow and it becomes wider.'" For 56 hours Mooness is sleepless. "Mooness was thinking; for 28 years she had looked out of the window at their garden, focused on virginity. Indeed, in the eighth year of her life she was told that a girl who is not a virgin never will be forgiven by god. And now it was two days and three nights that she knew virginity was only a hole. Something broke in her body. A cold anger filled her body. She remembered all those childhood days when she looked at trees with regret, wishing to climb just once, but for fear of her virginity she never climbed a tree. She didn't know why, but her body was ice cold."

In defiance of her brother's diktat not to leave the house, Mooness leaps to her death in the street below . . . then comes back to life, wandering in the midst of the coup-makers' blood-letting. Wandering in the bookstores near the University of Tehran, she discovers *The Secret Joys of Sex*, and after avoiding it for 12 days buys, then reads and rereads it. On returning to the house, Mooness is killed by her brother for her defiance, and for the second time she comes back to life, now as a monster who reads people's minds. In her third life she tells Faezeh: "There is something very dirty about you, but I have decided to leave this house and live with you. I want to form an anti-brother association, so that no one kills his sister."

From the Hebrew Press

Israel Shahak

FOR MORE THAN 200 YEARS JEWS HAVE BEEN DEMANDING EQUALITY IN EVERY
country in which they happened to live, with the notable exception of
Israel, the Jewish state. Israel always has based its institutions on the
denial of equality to non-Jews. This principle derives from the tenets of
Zionism which, from its very inception, long before the establishment
of Israel, staunchly opposed equality for non-Jews.

Recently, however, for the first time in Israel's history, there are
voices warning about the consequences of unequal treatment of non-
Jewish citizens of Israel. Remarkably, this opposition has emerged more
from the center of the political spectrum than from the Zionist left.

By voicing misgivings about fundamental inequalities in the Jewish
state, Israeli Jews have proven to be far more realistic than members of
the organized Diasporas, including their most prestigious and supposedly liberal publications. The same holds true in discussions about
repression and atrocities in the occupied territories, and about the
nature of the Jewish Orthodoxy. Much of what is written in Israel's
prestigious and large-circulation Hebrew papers would be characterized

elsewhere as "anti-Semitism" by all of organized Jewry and its allies.*

The situation with regard to land privately owned by Israeli-Arab citizens and located on Israel's territory was described by Gabi Baron under the title "The Mysterious Redeeming of Land." His article in the April 24, 1990, financial supplement of Yediot Ahronot covered the Heimanuta, a branch company of the Jewish National Fund (JNF), which itself is an offshoot of the World Zionist Movement.† The very terms "redeeming" or "redemption" [ge'ula] are borrowed from religion. In Judaism, they refer to the salvation of the individual soul, and also to the salvation of the Jewish people, to be reached when the Messiah comes and the Jews rule over the whole world. Consequently, the expression "unredeemed" carries a strong connotation of impurity and taint.

Misuse of these terms for quite mundane purposes can be dangerous, in the same way the misuse of sacred Islamic terms by secular Arab chauvinists, like Saddam Hussein, can be dangerous. As taught to children in Israel's Jewish schools, the "Redemption of Land" doctrine simply states that if a plot of land is owned either collectively or individually by Jews, it is "redeemed." If not, it is "unredeemed." It follows that "to redeem land," that is to transfer it from non-Jewish to Jewish ownership, is a foremost national obligation, whereas not to do so is a calamity to be averted.

In his article, Baron quotes JNF Land Development Director, Avraham Hilleli, as saying "the Jewish principle" dictates that "the JNF lands should be allocated for the exclusive use of the Jews." Heimanuta directors are quoted as adding that their agency seeks to acquire "every piece of land that is not yet owned by the Jews."

Like its parent body the JNF, the Heimanuta is now being financed from various government funds (some of them disclosed by Baron) which are not listed in the annual government budget. This money is

---

* The accusation of "anti-Semitism" is commonly used in North America to intimidate and inhibit non-racist criticism of Israeli state policies. This way discussion is confined, and the Israeli state and society are not discussed using the same criteria that are applied to other states and societies. [editor]

† Yediot Ahronot and Ha'aretz from which Israel Shahak quotes in this article are both large-circulation, Hebrew-language daily newspapers in Israel. [editor]

used by the Heimanuta both for "redeeming" the property of non-Jewish owners by purchasing it; or, apparently more often, for buying up Jewish property said to have been offered for sale to non-Jews.

Heimanuta even pays exorbitant prices for such property, only in order to prevent it from falling into non-Jewish hands. Presumably the Shabak, Israel's internal security police, and other government agencies report such prospective sales to Heimanuta. Each such land offering is then duly reported in the press, with the purpose of producing a wave of patriotic indignation. Some 10 or 15 years ago, the public indignation usually sufficed to avert a sale. But in the past decade some Jews were undeterred by journalistic indignation and even being branded as "traitors," as they defied the folklore that defined their actions as "unredeeming" already "redeemed" land. Nahum Barnea, in *Yediot Ahronot* of May 11, 1990, reported how Heimanuta also "secretly subsidizes apartments in Upper Nazareth for their Jewish tenants, so as to rule out Israeli Arabs from competing for them." Being illegal, such transactions assume the form of fictitious subletting. Since both Baron and Barnea stress the secrecy surrounding the operations of this company that they have described, one can surmise that it is involved in other subterranean activities as well.

Protests against such actions, couched in the strongest terms, have appeared periodically in the Hebrew press since about 1985. In the February 10, 1991, *Ha'aretz*, under the headline "An Amazing Resemblance to South Africa," Professor Uzi Ornan wrote:

> The Israeli Lands Authority (ILA) upholds all JNF regulations concerning the land under its control. This land can never be sold, or leased out. In this way, ILA officials can decide who can lease a plot, house, or apartment in a housing project. In so doing, the ILA applies a clear-cut "basic standard"...Whoever is registered as a "Jew" is fully eligible as a lessee in a greater part of the country, including its cities and settlements; but whoever is not so registered, is barred from owning real estate in most of the country's territory. In this way, the law and various regulations enforce what could be referred to as physical residential segregation, both of individuals and of whole communities, organized in separate "Bantustans."

As Professor Ornan and other Hebrew press commentators have long made clear, the area on which those racist restrictions apply amounts to 92 per cent of Israel's surface, or 94 per cent of the land within its pre-1967 borders.*

Two other discrimination problems are currently in the public eye. The first is discrimination against the Druze community. The second is the future effect on Israel, both as a state and a society, of persisting official discrimination.

The present focus on the Druze is quite symptomatic, since it has to do with "security." Although the religious segment of Jewish public opinion may take discrimination for granted, the secular segment seeks to justify it on the grounds that since the majority of the Israeli Arabs do not serve in the army, they shouldn't have the same rights as the Jews who do. The Arabs are considered disloyal, which explains their enforced exemption from army service in the first place. This means that the State of Israel, from its inception, has determined, with the help of its "experts," the communal loyalty of each non-Jewish community. Such populations have been granted rights, sometimes more generous, sometimes less, but never the full rights which accrue only to the Jews.

Both of these explanations for the existing discrimination, of course, are patently false. A population cannot be collectively responsible for anything. Traditionally, it was the anti-Semites who attributed collective responsibility to the Jews. In the second place, some Jews don't serve in the army on the grounds of health, religion, or because when they immigrated into Israel they were too old. However, they still get all their rights. Moreover, the Druze do serve in the army, and large numbers of them are recruited into the police, the prison service, and the like. Yet they are discriminated against. In the army, only recently have they been allowed to advance to the rank of colonel, but, by an administrative ruling, no higher. They also are discriminated against in all branches of the "security system."

As pointed out by Ran Kislev in *Ha'aretz* of May 10, 1991:

> The Druze have legitimate claims against the [Israeli] authorities.

---

* About 17 per cent of the population living within Israel's pre-1967 borders are citizens of Palestinian Arab identity. [editor]

Once a year, just prior to Independence Day, government officials visit them and speak about the "alliance forged in blood" between the Jews and the Druze and their "common fate."

Kislev notes that a government resolution was passed some years ago:

> to "put Druze villages on equal footing with Jewish development towns," but it appears that this resolution (like the majority of resolutions concerning the Arab sector) exists solely on paper. According to a government bill, the process of bringing conditions in Druze villages up to the level of Jewish towns should have taken five years. Now that four years...have lapsed, what has become all too obvious is not the municipal equality that ought to exist between Druze villages and neighbouring Jewish towns, but the similarity between conditions in Druze villages and those in Arab villages: the same dearth of development funds, the same dilapidated service infrastructure, and the same sewage running through the lanes of the villages.

When the Druze demonstrated in front of the prime minister's office, they got treatment, in Kislev's words, "more or less the same as other Arab protesters get: tear gas." Yet, since the Druze community is tiny, the funds which they ask for amount, in Kislev's words, "to no more than pocket money in relation to the overall budget." Since it is still not granted, Kislev expresses his suspicions gently, deeming it "inconceivable that someone in the government is deliberately making life difficult for the Druze, bringing the entire community, renowned for its loyalty to Israel, to the point of rebellion."

Druze protests have usually been led by retired officers who had served in the Israeli army for up to 30 years, often as deputy district governors (they cannot become governors) in the occupied territories, to find on their retirement that in addition to being denied the right to farm state-owned land in the vicinity of their villages, they may also still be regarded as "security risks." Since 1985, the Hebrew press has described some really bizarre cases, such as Druze being denied the right to work in weapons factories, after guarding the same factories during their reserve duty, or of others being fired from their jobs, ostensibly for "security reasons," but really in order to hire Soviet Jewish immigrants in their places.

In truth, the case of the Druze and of other even smaller minorities, such as the Circassians who are in the same position, shows that discrimination against all non-Jews is, in the Jewish state, a matter of principle which has nothing to do with security. If the Druze are granted equality in fact, the whole character of Israel as a "Jewish state" is bound to be affected. To maintain its official "Jewishness," the state must deny the Druze equal rights.

Kislev describes Israeli officialdom's "pecking order" in the treatment of Arab communities.

> Among the persons and institutions dealing with the Israeli
> Arabs, there exists an explicit scale laid down by the authorities
> according to which different groups in this sector are treated. . .
> The Druze are at the top, being more equal than others. The
> Bedouin come next, albeit much further down the scale, and are
> followed by the Christian Arabs. The Muslim Arabs are at the
> very bottom.

This type of formal stratification existed in Czarist Russia and similar pre-modern states. The Jews then were at the bottom of the "pecking order," or close to it. Israel is determined to treat its non-Jewish minorities the way the Jews were treated by the anti-Semitic regimes, and as other Eastern European or Middle Eastern minorities are treated by states or movements which have rejected the principle of equality of all citizens.

In *Ha'aretz* of April 11, 1991, Aharon Barnea starts from the assumption that there are two kinds of modern states.

> In a state of the law, of the type which has emerged as a model
> in the Western world, nationality is territorial, which means that
> all citizens of a given state are regarded as its nationals. This is
> the great legacy of the French and the American Revolutions.
>   But other types of states have developed as well, for example in
> Eastern Europe, where nationality has been conceived of

differently. In place of a territorial concept of nationality, its romantic-organic concept has become crystallized. . .

By its very nature, such a version of nationality engenders intolerance towards strangers, to the point of implying that members of other ethnic groups living in such a state cannot be integrated into the "spirit" or the "material substance" of the thus-conceived-of-nation, even if their ancestors had lived there for centuries.

Barnea explains that "the very character of the State of Israel, as a result of its claiming to be a democratic state on the one hand and the State of the Jewish People on the other," involves a contradiction which cannot but invite a calamitous outcome.

"I see the cunning of history at work in this instance," Barnea concludes, "for how else could one explain the current Jewish concept of nationality, if not by tracing its origins to the national-romantic model which Germany developed to such perfection?"

A statement as critical of Israel as this one, I would imagine, could not be published in any Western country without generating a concerted rebuke by the local organized Jewish community and its allies.

Yet the celebrated Hebrew writer A.B. Yehoshua also criticizes the inequalities which define Israel's character. In *Yediot Ahronot* of April 21, 1991, he first calls "preposterous" the stock arguments of all Israeli governments in favour of the exclusive Jewish right to come and live in Palestine.

People have the right to settle and reside in only one place. That is in the country in which they were born and lived heretofore. This right is natural and inalienable, not contingent on the will or legal charter of any regime. Anyone who violates this right, violates a basic human right. . . The Palestinians have the same rights in the Land of Israel as the French in France, or the Swedes in Sweden. . . The right to live in one's country of origin is not restricted to those Arabs who at present reside in the western Land of Israel [pre-1967 boundaries]. It also accrues to all Palestinians living abroad, regardless of where they were born, in the same way as a Russian Jew has the right to live in his historic country of origin – i.e., Israel – even if neither he himself nor his recent ancestors were born here.

Such unconditional recognition of Palestinian rights, jointly with the Right of their Return to Israel as well as to the occupied territories, which in Israel on principle accrues only to the Jews, amounts to a veritable conceptual revolution which subverts the present legal foundations of Israel as a Jewish state. It is enough to compare Yehoshua's doctrine with the standard Israeli claim that the Palestinian expellees from the territories, or those who have for several years resided abroad without reporting to the Israeli consular authorities, automatically forfeit their right to return to the land of their birth.

Other commentators argue that Israel's legal foundations in racism and ethnic discrimination not only hurt its non-Jewish citizens and adversely affect the state's future, but also threaten the interest of its Jewish citizens, especially the new Jewish immigrants from the U.S.S.R.

Bo'az Evron writes in the April 4, 1991, *Yediot Ahronot*:

> The new Jewish immigrants are, in fact, refugees fleeing a country fast falling apart...Israeli and Zionist emissaries have left no stone unturned in prodding the nations of the world to deny entry to Jewish refugees, so as to force them to settle in Israel. If the choice were theirs, 97 per cent would "drop out." But this means that the nations of the world, at Israel's prodding, have consciously embarked upon a policy of discrimination against Jewish refugees. Incontestably, it is an anti-Semitic policy which in a different context could not fail to provoke outrage. Only because the gates have been locked, and [Soviet Jews] have nowhere else to go, can we celebrate the "immigration miracle."
>
> If they were guided by the best interests of these Jews, the [Israeli] government and the Jewish Agency would seek to open all the doors in the world to everyone wishing to leave the U.S.S.R....But who cares about the best interest of these Jews? They concern [Prime Minister] Shamir and [Housing Minister]

Sharon only insofar as they can populate the settlements, or serve as a pretext for grabbing more land in the West Bank, or become soldiers in future wars.

Here the great secret of Zionism in the past few generations stands revealed. Long ago, Zionism ceased its concern for what is good for the Jews. Quite the contrary, Zionism is interested in seeing to it that the Jews suffer, so that they will leave their homes and come to Israel. This is why each glimmer of anti-Semitism fills the hearts of Zionists with relief. Zionism needs Jews in order to boost the Jewish population and military strength of Israel, not for their own sake...As human beings, they are of no concern to either the State of Israel or the Zionist Movement.

Part 4: HARD CHOICES

Hard Choices

We spoke to ourselves, we spoke to our fellow citizens, and to kindred spirits across borders; we spoke to and against our governments, and there were a few who went to meet with the people and the government of Iraq. We spoke in many voices: with urgency and anguish, with anger and humour and reason, pleading, in horror and grief. Some with particular skills composed songs and poems, statements and speeches, pictures.

We did more than voice our individual thoughts and feelings. We combined with others, and together we tried to prevent, and later to halt, this war. In its aftermath, there are people who want their thoughts and feelings about this grotesque barbarism to be kept alive, who won't allow this atrocity called "The Gulf War" to be packaged away with a "celebration." We have not been heard enough and we will not be silent now: this is one shared sentiment of contributors to this volume.

But we also face some hard choices. Will we deepen our sudden, new awareness of the Middle East and its peoples, or will we allow our present curiosity to evaporate? Will we assist the Iraqi people

to recover from what we have done to them, work for the lifting of
sanctions, or will we gently turn away from their desperate plight?
Will we be a practical part of the difficult struggle for an
independent and peaceful life for the peoples of the Middle East, or
will we have recourse again to dehumanized stereotypes and thereby
justify our accommodation to the "new world order"? Will we now
understand environmental survival is integral with the struggle for
peace and social justice, or will we treat it as some greater good
disconnected from the roots of war-making?

In this concluding section, so that we are better able to make
our hard choices, Charlene Gannagé and Christopher Huxley
recapitulate who comprised the anti-war movement in Canada and
what we did. This is followed by a commentary by Mordecai
Briemberg on the limitations of the Canadian anti-war movement.

Jewish-Israeli peace activists face demanding choices, and so do
Palestinians who are struggling for their so long-denied national
rights. Discussions about their dilemmas are important as well for
activists on this continent, for at least two reasons. Firstly,
solidarity work here must be undertaken with full awareness of the
difficulties faced by those whose cause we accept as our own.
Second, the insights they bring to resolving their dilemmas can be
used creatively, though not mimicked, in efforts to advance our
own work for peace and justice among fellow citizens.

In his essay, "Crossing the Rubicon," Michel Warshawsky
assesses the actions of the Jewish-Israeli peace movement, and
under the spotlight of their present impasse, he advocates hard
choices that movement must make if it is to become effective.

Political debate among Palestinians currently is intense: about
the immediate U.S. intentions for the region, about the precise
connection between the Palestinian and pan-Arab struggles, about
the limitations and possibilities of any Middle East conference
organized by Washington, about maintaining the intifada and
building independent Palestinian institutions that will advance
practically the effort to achieve an independent, self-governing
Palestinian state.

We on this continent, where political culture hardly qualifies as the world's most sophisticated, too often insufficiently appreciate the subtleties of others' politics, such as the Palestinians'. The essay by Dr. Salim Tamari hopefully will enhance this appreciation. Dr. Tamari outlines two major Palestinian trends of thinking, and then expounds and applies the one he finds most convincing. His essay, therefore, should be read as one voice in an on-going, dynamic and complex debate, still far from conclusion.[1]

There are other hard choices, particularly for democratic life within the Middle East. Here too we have our own responsibilities. For the neo-colonial repression and wars our governments inflict upon Middle Eastern peoples not only directly create miseries, they cumulatively weaken secular alternatives and can contribute to a despair that, in its turn, is a seedbed for vengeance and intolerance. We must do our part here to break that cycle so antithetical to democratic life.

Notes

[1] Dr. Tamari's article was part of a round-table discussion in Jerusalem in mid-February 1991, organized by the Palestinian Academic Society for the Study of International Affairs (PASSIA). PASSIA's publication *Palestinian Assessments of the Gulf War and its Aftermath* contains other valuable material from this discussion. The weekly English edition of the newspaper *Al Fajr*, published in Jerusalem, has provided another forum for a range of opinions in the current Palestinian debates.

U.S. Marine Refuses

Jeffrey A. Patterson

Kaneohe Marine Corps, Air Station, Hawaii
On August 29 I was ordered to board a military transport plane
for deployment to Saudi Arabia. I refused. When my staff
sergeants attempted to push me on to the aircraft, I sat down in
the hangar. It was from this perspective that I watched friends
and co-workers being shipped off to the largest U.S. military
operation since Vietnam.

I enlisted in the Marine Corps nearly four years ago, right out
of high school in Hollister, California. I joined for the same
reasons that most do: training, educational opportunities, and
maybe some adventure. Somewhere within was a desire to serve
my country.

My outlook changed during deployments to Okinawa, South
Korea, and the Philippines. Exploitation and prostitution were
rampant around our bases and sexism and neo-colonial
condescension were the approved attitudes toward our hosts.

I had seven months left to serve when the Saudi deployments
began and I refused to go, seeking conscientious-objector status.
I felt that tens of thousands of lives were being threatened for
imperialistic economic interests. It would be inconceivable for
me to defend Saddam Hussein. It would be just as inconceivable
to overlook who made him.

After refusing deployment I spent three weeks in the brig until
a federal judge ruled against the military argument that I was a
"national security threat." I'm now awaiting a court-martial.

I will never take up arms in defence of this country in any

conceivable confrontation it chooses to enter. That is not to say that I will not fight for the people of this land, or any other land. But my weapons are ideas, commitment, and a sense of justice. And my battles are against injustice, inequality, and the placing of the Earth's wealth in the hands of the very few.

Preparing the Anti-War Movement for a New Era of Disorder

Charlene Gannagé and Christopher Huxley

ABANDONING ANY PRETENCE TO ITS MUCH EXAGGERATED REPUTATION AS international peacemaker, the Canadian Conservative government wasted no time in endorsing President Bush's deployment of military force against Iraq. Unqualified support from Canada bolstered the U.S. claim to be acting on behalf of the "world community" against Iraq's takeover of Kuwait.

Prime Minister Mulroney initially claimed that Canada's role was to support the United Nations blockade of Iraq. Once the U.S.-led coalition began bombing Iraq, Canada's role escalated from "sweep and escort" support of U.S. air attacks to active participation in air-to-ground attacks.

Recourse to military force rather than diplomacy has been consistent with the sorry record set by the Canadian government in responding to crises within its own borders. Examples include former Prime Minister Trudeau's deployment of troops in Quebec following his 1970 proclamation of the War Measures Act. More recently, the military was sent on to Indian lands near Montreal in the summer of 1990 and used against the Mohawk people of Kanesatake and Kahnawake.

As in these instances, Prime Minister Mulroney felt no obligation to seek parliamentary approval before giving the order for warships to sail to the Persian Gulf. By the time Parliament finally had the chance to debate the original decision, Canada's commitments had further increased.

Despite an overall lack of success in stopping Canadian complicity in the slaughter of countless Iraqis, anti-war forces in Canada were able to mobilize a significant segment of public opinion against the war. At key points leading up to and during the war, protests were organized, including demonstrations of over 20,000 in Vancouver, 5,000 in Toronto and 20,000 in Montreal.

Social movements including solidarity and anti-racist groups, the student movement, the women's movement, the peace movement and progressive currents in the labour movement formed broadly based coalitions to oppose Western military intervention in the Gulf. The New Democratic Party (NDP) took an anti-war position, even though most other social democratic parties in the Western alliance failed to mount any significant opposition, with some endorsing the war, like the Parti Québecois in Quebec.

This essay provides an overview of the opposition to the war by different sectors of Canadian society. We look at several of the actors, their activities, and the controversies which continue to preoccupy those who participated.[1]

Spontaneity and imagination marked the early protest, as when some of the first initiatives were taken by women in the Maritimes. But hesitation and confusion developed in the course of the conflict. At least five stages make up the history of the war against Iraq. The first extended from the dispute between Iraq and Kuwait, leading to the invasion of Kuwait by Iraq, the U.N. condemnation of this takeover, and the imposition and enforcement of comprehensive sanctions. During most of this time the anti-war movement was non-existent or inchoate. The second stage involved the escalating military build-up by the U.S.-led coalition. This catalyzed the anti-war movement from individual anxiety to collective action, and was followed by the third stage, the systematic bombing assault on Iraq. The anti-war movement reacted and remained vibrant. But when Iraqi Scud missiles reached

Israel, in the fourth stage, certain perceptions of the conflict, if not its reality, were changed and sectors of the anti-war movement wavered. In the fifth stage, U.S.-led land, naval and air forces massacred what was left of a hungry and demoralized Iraqi occupation force as it fled Kuwait. At this point the anti-war movement already was in decline.

At the time of writing, even larger numbers of Iraqis, particularly children and the elderly, are dying from epidemics and malnutrition, the consequences of both the earlier bombing and the continuing sanctions against Iraq. Meanwhile the complex, destructive, environmental consequences continue to unfold. And yet, the anti-war movement has practically disappeared from the political map. It is important not only to chronicle the real expressions of protest, for these were seriously downplayed by the media, but also to identify the factors which prevented the development of a more effective anti-war movement. The process of rethinking and remaking a movement for peace and justice becomes more urgent as we enter a dangerous era of world instability, one in which the Canadian government could support the U.S. in further military ventures.

The peace movement

Although commonly referred to as a "peace movement," much of the energy of Canadian anti-war mobilizations during the 1980s was grounded in an understanding of the Cold War as a super-power rivalry that posed the danger of cataclysmic nuclear war between the U.S. and the U.S.S.R. This view of the threat to world peace largely ignored conflicts involving Third World countries, almost as if the U.S. war against the Indo-Chinese people had been forgotten. The Canadian peace movement's failure to offer any concerted response to the Israeli invasions of Lebanon, the most extensive in 1982, underscored this reluctance to take positions on regional conflicts.

Compared to the record of the Canadian peace movement since the end of the Vietnam war, the mobilization opposing the war against Iraq represented a significant shift in orientation. There are two reasons for this change; first there is the demise of the Soviet Union as a super-power, whether measured by declining economic strength or by that country's unwillingness any longer to enlist its resources in support of regional struggles. This development raised widely held hopes for world peace and a "peace dividend" – the transfer of military expenditures to social needs. So the new military aggression against the latest Third World bogeyman surprised unprepared peace activists. Disappointment quickly gave way to anger at what was seen as an attempt to steal the fruits of what was heralded as the end of the Cold War.

The second reason for the Canadian peace movement's new found willingness to try and prevent this latest war in the Middle East was the prospect of its ominous global ramifications. Whatever the overestimation of the Iraqi army, all reports pointed to a major build-up of conventional and non-conventional, even nuclear weapons. The speed with which the military forces were amassed added to the sense of urgency. The alarm over the possible consequences of this war were expressed in Canada more immediately than ever had been the case in the opposition to the war against Vietnam. And once Prime Minister Mulroney committed Canadian forces, the first time since Korea in an offensive overseas campaign, there was apprehension about possible Canadian casualties. This sense of unease was heightened by widespread doubts over Mulroney's kneejerk subservience to U.S. foreign policy.

A revitalized peace movement attempted to mobilize large numbers of people across the country to prevent war with Iraq. Having exhausted all parliamentary avenues to stop Canada's military participation, the Canadian Peace Alliance (CPA) announced a nation-wide campaign in November. The CPA "action agenda" covered all possible contingencies in event of war, including civil disobedience at the offices of government departments and Members of Parliament, embassies and consulates. Local peace groups were urged to form coalitions with organizations committed to social justice, including religious groups, war veterans, student coalitions, trade unions and women's organizations. CPA mandated its membership to pass resolutions, lobby all levels of government, and participate in public protests to prevent the war. In Ottawa and elsewhere peace activists occupied or obstructed government offices. Arrests at Litton Industries, a military-related plant in Toronto, were reminiscent of anti-war protests during the Vietnam era.

The peace mobilizations included a new voice: the environmentalists, who called for the development of new energy sources to reduce the Western world's oil-driven imperative to interfere in the Middle East. Greenpeace released a report indicating the extent of environmental damage and loss of human life if the United States triggered its regional arsenal of 1,000 nuclear weapons. A major advertisement sponsored by Canadian Greenpeace deplored Canada's support for a U.N. resolution authorizing the use of military force, and called for peaceful diplomatic efforts to resolve the conflict. The ad in *The Globe and Mail* was endorsed by religious leaders, women's movement activists, academics, trade union and community leaders, as well as prominent NDP figures. Montreal's anti-war movement was headed by the Coalition Contre la Guerre dans le Golfe Arabo-Persique and, in conjunction with trade unions, mobilized under the banner "Échec à la Guerre."[2] The coalition building extended to small communities, and in Baie Comeau, Quebec, home-riding of Prime Minister Mulroney, over 1,000 residents signed petitions against the war. A small contingent of Canadians travelled to Iraq, part of an international brigade of 73 anti-war activists who camped two kilometres from the Saudi Arabian border.[3]

The Canadian Arab community

Experts from the Canadian Arab community played a highly visible role as leaders and opinion makers in efforts to help shape a Canadian foreign policy independent from that of the United States. In Peterborough, Ontario, a symposium on the Arab world offered presentations from Canadian Arab scholars, including Atif Kurbursi, Elia Zureik, Aida Graff, as well as the opportunity to hear a recital of Arab music and poetry. The question of "linkage" between this latest crisis in the Middle East and the still unresolved Palestinian question presented an important challenge to the peace movement, and Canadian Arabs often spoke to explain this challenge. Members of the Palestinian diaspora living in Canada pointed to the hypocrisy of the U.N. for failing to enforce its own resolutions, dating back to 1967, calling for an Israeli withdrawal from the occupied territories.

And there was a range of opinion on the crisis in the Gulf. Some organizations, like the Arab-Palestine Association, defended Iraq's

historic claim to Kuwait, while others, like the Canadian Arab Federation (CAF) and the Canadian Arab Anti-Discrimination Committee,
opposed the occupation of Kuwait and stressed the need to arrive at a
resolution by diplomatic, not military means. CAF favoured diplomatic efforts by people in the region, through the Arab League.
Canadian Arab spokespeople participated in coalition actions, where
the common goal was to prevent or halt the war, and when allowance
was made for the expression of a wide variety of opinions about possible
solutions. This does not mean the Arab community was united against
the war. For example, one group of Canadian Iraqis organized demonstrations to counter those of anti-war protestors, citing the bitter experience of those who had opposed Saddam Hussein's dictatorship.

The Canadian Jewish community

The anti-war movement was gathering momentum until the media
reported that Iraqi Scud missiles had hit Tel Aviv. This, combined
with the on-going demonization of Saddam Hussein and the exaggerated accounts of his military power, made it easier to portray Israel as an
innocent victim.[4] This emphasis on Israeli popular fears of attack
served to mask the far more devastating destruction of Iraq by U.S.-led
forces, and to mask the Israeli human rights abuses in this period against
the Palestinians living on the West Bank and in the Gaza Strip. More
Palestinians lost their lives under Israeli-imposed curfews and repression than Israelis were killed by Iraqi Scud attacks.

In Montreal, Toronto and Vancouver the Canadian Jewish community proceeded to mobilize the largest demonstrations of explicitly pro-
war sentiments held during the conflict. It is important to record that
the Canadian Jewish community was not monolithic in its support for
war. The United Jewish People's Order participated in a teach-in
against the war, featuring Chris Giannou, a Canadian doctor who
worked for several years in Palestinian refugee camps in Lebanon,
including during Israel's 1982 invasion. Toronto Jews for a Just Peace
(JJP) co-sponsored anti-war teach-ins with the Toronto Disarmament
Network, and on the anniversary of the intifada in December 1990, JJP
and the Toronto Disarmament Network held day-long workshops.

Vancouver JJP members individually participated in the anti-war coalition Middle East Peace Action, and Jewish Women Against the Occupation organized a march in Toronto to the U.S. consulate and co-sponsored teach-ins. Even so, once Israel was perceived to be under attack, it was more difficult for these same forces to sustain their coalition activities against the war.

Students

For the first time since the Vietnam war, students mobilized across the country. The Canadian Federation of Students (CFS), representing 400,000 students from 75 student unions, helped coordinate a nation-wide campaign against the war. A positive development in British Columbia was the formation of a single, cross-institutional body of high school, community college and university students.

The B.C. wing of CFS invited Svend Robinson, NDP external affairs critic, to address their annual meeting. Students conveyed to him their demands for the government: to apply a foreign policy independent from that of the U.S., one that emphasizes the role of negotiator and peacekeeper in international affairs; to use Canada's role in the U.N. to address all violations of international law, including U.S. invasions of Panama and Grenada, and the continued occupation of Palestinian and other Arab lands in the Middle East; to restore all funds cut from special programs to pay for the war; to increase funding for research on and use of alternative energy sources, making Canada more self-sufficient in energy production; to recall all Canadian troops from the Gulf.[5]

In response to local university initiatives, the Ontario Federation of Students helped coordinate a province-wide coalition, and on several campuses students mobilized in 1960s style teach-ins. Campus coalitions were formed in the Toronto area, two of which also participated in a city-wide coalition. Young people across the country set up peace camps despite the freezing cold. A grade 11 student in Edmonton told a reporter she and her friends intended to be at the camp as long as there was war.[6] Student organizations in Canada recognized the need to make international links with student organizations in other countries concerned over the crisis in the Gulf. Correspondence provided by the

DENISE KOURI

High school students in several Canadian communities were prominent in opposition to the war against Iraq. These students demonstrated January 16, 1991, in their hometown of La Ronge, in northern Saskatchewan.

British Columbia office of the Canadian Federation of Students reveals the range of their communications which included the United States Student Association in Washington, D.C., the International Student Association in Prague, Czechoslovakia and the Asia-Pacific Students Association in Hong Kong.

The initial wave of high school student participation in anti-war activity took many by surprise. High school students organized demonstrations, candle-light vigils, and spoke on local radio programs. Peter Coombes, coordinator of Vancouver's peace movement coalition End the Arms Race said that 40 per cent of the hundreds of calls they received came from young people. John Murray, Yellowknife coordinator of Nuclear Free North reported that 85 per cent of the turn-out for one of their rallies never had been involved in the peace movement before. Most were high school students. In Winnipeg students were prominently involved in a march against the war, and in Prince Albert, Saskatchewan as well.[7]

The women's movement

The women's movement was one of the first centers of opposition to the war. Marion Mathieson and Betsy Carr of the National Action Committee on the Status of Women (NAC) called for an immediate withdrawal of troops as early as August 21. Mathieson said that "Brian Mulroney seems bent on entangling Canada in the risk of a war which is about money, greed, profits; and the macho flexing of muscle. It is about a new international order with the U.S. in control of the oil fields of the Middle East." A resident of Sydney, Nova Scotia, Mathieson also expressed concern for wives and families of naval military personnel: "Their distress is understandable and clearly shows that sending peacekeeping and surveillance personnel and equipment into a potential war zone is an irresponsible use of Canada's human, military and diplomatic resources."

In November 1990 Judy Rebick, NAC president, spoke out at a Toronto rally in favour of the withdrawal of troops. In February Rebick said: "We are alarmed at the values of a government that can find all kinds of money to fight the war but not find money to house the homeless and feed the poor."[8] NAC invited the Arab Canadian Women's Network to participate in their discussions about reaching out to Canadian Arab women.

Maude Barlow, representing Canada's Voice of Women (VOW), participated in an international women's peace initiative. With activists like Margarita Papandreou of Greece, she went to the Middle East to meet with Middle Eastern women. VOW wanted women in Arab countries to gain an international hearing. VOW spoke of the need for women to be equally represented in decision-making in the Arab world. Grace Hartman, national VOW president and former president of the Canadian Union of Public Employees, said: "We want to say to our sisters in the Middle East that we do not want your children to die. We do not want anyone to die."

Starting in the mid-1980s, the Toronto International Women's Day (IWD) activities began to focus on developing an anti-racist women's movement. In March 1991 the Toronto organization adopted the theme: "Women say stop the racist war from Oka to the Gulf." Native and Canadian Arab women helped build the march and rally and spoke at the event. Arab women were not always as prominent at IWD events in other cities. Sunera Thobani, of the Vancouver Indo-Canadian community has written:

> Do we have to remind our white "sisters" that women and children were hit the hardest in this barbaric assault [against Iraq]? Canadian women of Middle Eastern origin have faced a barrage of racism over the Gulf Crisis. They have been viewed with hostile suspicion and constantly reminded that they belong to the race of the evil Arab/Muslim devils that the Super-Devil Saddam embodies. The silence of the IWD rally [in Vancouver] over this racism and this violence was deafening.[9]

DON KOSSICKI

Organized in a broad coalition in Saskatoon, Saskatchewan, more than 1,000 people demonstrated on January 26, 1991. The coalition included people who had been active the previous summer and fall in solidarity with the native people in Quebec around the town of Oka. The Canadian government had sent the army to repress their struggle.

The Trade Unions

Following the occupation of Kuwait, many trade unions supported sanctions against Iraq. As the conflict escalated to the prospect of combat, the Canadian Labour Congress (CLC) lobbied the government for a peaceful diplomatic solution to the crisis. As Canada's commitments increased, the CLC expressed a dual concern: for the well-being of the Canadian military and for the image of Canada as a "peacekeeper."

The CLC was sharply criticized for not calling for withdrawal of troops. The best that could be said is that the CLC made some efforts to encourage a peaceful resolution, in contrast to the U.S. trade union federation the AFL-CIO, which changed its position to one of support for the U.S. military.[10]

In Quebec the unions were more forceful than the CLC in opposing the deployment of the military against Iraq. As well, individual CLC unions, like the United Electrical Workers, the Canadian Union of Postal Workers and the Public Service Alliance (representing civilian employees in the Department of National Defense), called for immediate withdrawal of Canadian troops. However, after the start of the bombing of Iraq, when the Saskatchewan Federation of Labour demanded the withdrawal of Canadian troops (January 22), the CLC reprimanded them for their stand, smearing it as "pro-Hussein."[11] Some prominent trade union leaders, including Bob White of the Canadian Auto Workers (CAW) and Linda Torney, president of the Metro Toronto Labour Council, called for the withdrawal of Canadian troops at anti-war rallies. White expressed his solidarity with young people who demonstrated for peace: "It's not un-Canadian to be for peace; it's not un-Canadian to oppose war. It is un-Canadian to blindly follow U.S. foreign policy that leads to war."[12]

During the past decade, the Canadian trade union movement has moved away from its traditional pro-U.S., pro-Israeli Middle East policies. The Ontario Federation of Labour in 1982 recognized the PLO as the sole, legitimate representative of the Palestinian people. The CLC followed suit in 1988, calling for the withdrawal of Israeli troops from the occupied territories and for an international peace conference.

When union leaders or union locals did take positions it was usually in opposition to the war. But for the most part, union activity did not go beyond passing motions. In no cases were on-the-job actions organized. There were, however, some notable attempts by local union leaderships to involve their memberships in community-wide expressions of anti-war activity. For example, in Hamilton, Ontario, a local anti-war event attracted two thousand, including many local steelworkers. In London, Ontario, another two thousand people marched to oppose the war in one of the largest demonstrations seen in that city in years.

The New Democratic Party

Given the initial breadth of popular opposition to Canadian military involvement in the U.S.-led war plans, including within establishment circles like the Liberal Party, it is not surprising that NDP leader Audrey McLaughlin clearly and consistently opposed the build-up for war. What is more significant is that once the war was launched by the United States, with Canada's participation, she did not falter in her opposition. The Liberal Party opposition collapsed the moment bombs were dropped on Iraq. But throughout the conflict, prominent NDP figures spoke against the war, including Stephen Lewis, former ambassador to the U.N., and Gerry Caplan, an influential strategist.

The NDP position was restated in the parliamentary debate on January 17, 1991, by Dan Heap, MP for the Toronto riding of Trinity-Spadina: "We of the NDP opposed this war before the bombing of Baghdad, and we oppose it now. We say to pull our troops out of the theatre of war and find better peacemaking roles for them; to plan with the United Nations for a peace conference, including an Arab-Israeli one; and to start now to provide urgent medical, food and other help to the refugees and displaced persons of war."[13]

A private delegation of three Members of Parliament (NDP, Liberal and Conservative) travelled to Baghdad in November without government endorsation to secure the release of Canadians. In an unprecedented move, Svend Robinson, NDP external affairs critic, met with PLO Chairman Yasser Arafat, and received his assistance in securing exit visas for five Canadians being held in Iraq. Robinson deplored the Canadian government's endorsation of the U.N. resolution giving the

U.S.-led coalition authorization to use unlimited force as "a betrayal of Canada's traditional role of peace-keeping through the U.N." He went on to state: "Our foreign policy appears to be written in the White House or out fishing with George Bush."[14]

McLaughlin had the support of her party's rank and file. An emergency resolution at the Ontario NDP convention in March affirmed support for her stand against Canadian participation in the Gulf war, and at a summer national convention in Halifax, McLaughlin greeted cheering delegates by reminding them that hers was the only party in Parliament to oppose the war. Less publicized was the unanimous endorsement by the British Columbia NDP of a Social Credit Party motion in the legislature praising the Canadian military for the "honour and distinction" with which they had fought in the Gulf. The NDP speaker on the motion added a further embellishment, praising the military for its "valour."[15] In the major anti-war rallies in B.C., no provincial NDP speakers came forward, though provincial leader Mike Harcourt did attend a Canadian Jewish community rally in favour of the war.

The federal NDP continues to address the root causes of the conflict in the Middle East. Addressing a U.N. non-governmental organization conference on the question of Palestine, in Montreal in June 1991, Svend Robinson urged the international community to state clearly its opposition to the policies of the Israeli government toward the Palestinians. He warned against rewarding Israel economically, saying it has "one hand outstretched for $10 billion in aid from the U.S., while its other hand is clenched in a fist suppressing the rights of Palestinians."[16]

Towards a new anti-war movement

Public opinion polls in November 1990 provided some background for understanding strengths and weaknesses of anti-war organizing. In the polls, more women than men were opposed to war, and more Quebecois than other Canadians. Support for the use of the military increased with income, while on the question of a blockade to enforce sanctions, 62 per cent agreed or strongly agreed. Before the mid-January start of bombing, there was majority sentiment against the war, and this was an encouragement to the anti-war movement whose strengths seemed greatest then, even if the media grossly underplayed the organized opposition.

Once the bombings began, however, nationalist sentiments, which initially had fuelled a desire to dissociate Canada from U.S. policy and to withdraw "our" military from danger, were turned to opposite purposes. Pro-war voices raised the call to rally behind Canadians in combat. Pro-war sentiments began to fill the media, complete with pictures of yellow ribbons and diary accounts of navy wives. The media sanitized the war with references to "smart" bombs with only "collateral damage." Television viewers had no countervailing images of war's real horrors to regalvanize their anti-war sentiments. The backdrop of popular anti-war sentiments faded and the organized anti-war movement felt more isolated. In April, following the end of the bombing, 63 per cent of Canadians said they thought Prime Minister Mulroney had done a good or very good job during the war. Only 31 per cent thought he had done a poor or very poor job. Some 40 per cent of Canadians felt the war was not worth the human and environmental costs.

During its formation, the anti-war movement debated whether or not to support U.N. sanctions, with only a minority calling for both the complete withdrawal of foreign troops and Iraq's withdrawal from Kuwait. Few understood the extent to which the U.S. was sabotaging any possibility of meaningful negotiation with Iraq. Few appreciated the gross, propagandistic, exaggeration of Iraqi military capacities. The speed of the war-making, along with the anti-war movement's confusion over sanctions, have left it demobilized after the ceasefire, while tens of thousands of Iraqis are suffering and dying from the effects of the earlier bombing and the continuing sanctions.

During the year-long free-trade debate leading to the last federal election, Canadians were forewarned that economic integration with the U.S. would include military integration. The current free-trade negotiations of the U.S., Mexico and Canada will bring further pressure for Canada to align its foreign policy with the U.S., especially in Latin America.

Building the new anti-war movement on the basis of international

A Statement Against War From Concerned Citizens of Japan

[Eighty-four Japanese citizens initiated a project to place a full-page ad in The New York Times. *It appeared March 18, 1991. The initiators said the ad was supported financially by numerous others who were identified as representing "many diverse professions, including industrial workers, farmers, writers, religious leaders, musicians, painters, photographers, physicians, nurses, housewives, students, scholars, lawyers, journalists, members of parliament, local officials, public servants, soldiers of Japan Self-Defence forces, teachers from primary school to university level, business executives, shopkeepers and social workers." Here are excerpts from the ad.]*

International conflict cannot be resolved by military force

We are a group of Japanese citizens who are deeply concerned about the Gulf crisis and its aftermath. The battle itself is over but our concern is undiminished. As there are certain things we would like Americans to better understand, at this juncture, we have chosen to state our views in this manner.

Iraq's invasion and annexation of Kuwait was unjust, misguided, brutal, and opposed by the majority of the world's people. Many peaceful ways of bringing it to an end were proposed and were in the process of being enacted. All these efforts were swept aside, however, by the massive military intervention of the Multinational Forces and their swift victory. The majority of American people seem to believe that this war was just. In the mood of this apparent "success" the idea seems to be spreading in the United States and infecting some other parts of the world that justice can be won with military power, that might makes right. This growing perception concerns us deeply. . .

As the U.S. Constitution is the foundation of American society, so the Japanese Constitution sets down our most cherished national values. Under this Constitution no human has been killed by Japanese military forces in forty-five years. As citizens, we will not allow our government to suspend our Constitution for political expediency. . .

Japan went to war in 1931. At first, it seemed to the Japanese that it was a just war to establish a "new order" in China, Korea and other parts of Asia, and that victory was certain.

In reality, war lasted fifteen years and the "new order" brought only misery and death to the people of Asia. In the end, the devastation came home. We suffered carpet bombing and fire bombing of our cities. The only nuclear bombs ever dropped on humans were dropped on us.

The Japanese learned from the war the horror of killing and being killed. We thought Americans had learned a similar lesson from the Vietnam War. But the mood in the United States today reminds us greatly of the mood in Japan in 1941. We hope that Americans learned from Vietnam that war isn't horrifying only when your own people are killed. Yet the air and ground attack, which was launched despite the fact that the Iraqi government had expressed its willingness to negotiate its withdrawal from Kuwait, killed hundreds of thousands of people – not only Iraqi soldiers but also civilian non-combatants. We urge you not to listen to those who say that the Gulf War should erase the lessons of Vietnam. The lessons of both these wars are the same. . .

Now the Japanese government has promised to pay the U.S. $9 billion for the war. There is strong opposition to this as well.

We do not want to contribute to any more killing. We do not

want Japan to move closer to translating its awesome economic power into military power.

We are surprised at the short memories of Americans who see no danger in this. Our neighbors in Asia are less forgetful. . .

We, who have contributed to make this statement possible, are united in the rejection of military force as a way of settling international conflict – and in the hope that the spirit of the Japanese Constitution will be seriously considered and adopted by all nations.

We ask all Americans to try and understand our position.

During the Vietnam War, strong links developed between people in the anti-war movement in Japan and the U.S. We feel a similar empathy with those Americans who opposed U.S. involvement in the Gulf War. To them we express our heartfelt support and commitment.

– Concerned Citizens of Japan Room 305, 4-29-12, Sendagaya, Shibuyaku, Tokyo

Iraqi Woman Buying Vegetables

Sima Elizabeth Shefrin

When the war started I felt confused by the television reports, shaken in my pacifist convictions, and unable to think clearly about the whole situation. Not until I started attending candlelight peace vigils did I regain my perspective, and was able to remember that regardless of the issue, it was not acceptable for Canadians and Americans to be killing Iraqi people.

"Iraqi Woman Buying Vegetables" was originally a fabric appliqué, which Bill Horne adapted as a silkscreen print to raise funds for Jews for a Just Peace, to send in humanitarian aid to Palestinian families in the West Bank and Gaza.

BRENDA HEMSING

Support by Any Other Name Still is Support

Mordecai Briemberg

IN THE SUMMER BEFORE THE WAR AGAINST IRAQ, THE CANADIAN ARMY WENT
into action at Oka, Quebec, to obstruct the aboriginal people's path to
self-determination. The military's sophisticated and effective use of
public relations, to cloak their repressive action in moral rectitude, was
stunning.

In the Gulf war too we witnessed similar sophisticated and effective
use of military public relations. Again our civilian media-marionettes
kept in lock-step with the military march. This was epitomized by the
sanctification of the Schwarzkopf briefings.

But the generals dressed in designer camouflage and medals were not
alone. Amidst the loud roll of the kettle-drums were the penny-whistle
notes of some "peace campers" and "progressives," endorsing the war
against Iraq. Persuasiveness and moral dignity did not characterize their
minor contribution. Should we therefore forget them? I think not, for
their stance, or so it has struck me, illuminates vulnerabilities within
the movements that did oppose this bloody annunciation of the "new
world order." For that reason the performances of a Gwynne Dyer, a
Fred Halliday, an Ivan Klima, Bill Arkin and others still warrant consideration.

Gwynne Dyer is the CBC's favourite "military analyst," a figure whose folksy manner and anti-war reputation among the Canadian peace movement only added lustre and credibility to his endorsation of this slaughter. Dyer was the featured speaker at Vancouver's first major public meeting on the impending war, organized by End the Arms Race, the coalition that maintains the annual, internationally known "Walk for Peace."

Prior to, on, and since that evening, Dyer has trumpeted the resurgence of the U.N. and the victory of international law and justice. In a June 1991 public appearance in Vancouver, Dyer incorporated this into a message of a world-wide dawning of a new age of "democracy," "growing non-violence" and the "collapse of patriarchy." Such phoney good news needs (and gets) a demagogic sales pitch on the platform. But it would not sell at all if it did not address psychological dispositions: to measure the world by the audience's own condition (comfortable), to think well of oneself (well-intentioned and opposed to evil), of one's society, Canada (peace-loving by "nature" and a "peacekeeper" by tradition). What satisfaction then, to be confirmed in all this and to be told it is part of a global, effortless new goodness.

The thrust of Dyer's message is echoed in an article on the U.N., which appeared in the Canadian *Peace Magazine*'s post-bombing special issue on the "new world order."[1] The thesis Jack Yost develops there, with minor caveats, is: "Through the crisis in the Gulf, a significant turning point may have been reached in the development of international law..." U.S. Ambassador Thomas Pickering is quoted at length and uncritically, from his speech to Veterans of Foreign Wars. Gwynne Dyer, in his promotion of the U.N.'s new shining path, more astutely downplayed Mr. Pickering. Dyer's television documentary feature, broadcast on CBC's newsmagazine *The Journal* on June 24, 1991, relied rather on the U.N. ambassadors of Canada, the United Kingdom, and the Soviet Union particularly, to mouth the lines about "international law and cooperation." The history of sabotaged negotiations and the use of double-standards in the U.N., both examined in previous articles, make such a phrase pure rhetoric.

Certainly aspiring and mobile social strata are more receptive to this false "good news." Over the last decades this strata has not been without heavy influence on a peace movement that focused far more on potential nuclear war, the danger of nuclear attack on one's own city, than on the many imperial-fuelled actual wars against Third World peoples, with the conventional massacre of millions. But this centering of the moral universe on one's personal vulnerability transcended class, and continued to characterize the peace movement's efforts against the Gulf war. Expressions of concern for "our" young men and women in uniform, dire predictions of "our" body-bag count: these nationalist appeals were believed to be effective tactics to win more adherents to the anti-war camp. But once the shooting began, these rationales were turned into their opposite – they became reasons Canadians supported the war.

Perhaps this centering of the moral universe on one's own situation also helps explain the over-estimation of popular anti-war sentiments in the months before the bombing of Baghdad. In retrospect, part of these popular uncertainties about war appear more clearly as expressions of worry about one's own vulnerability to Saddam Hussein's profoundly mythologized military arsenal. Canadians went to ground, literally: air travel declined, and 20,000 kilometres away from the Middle East a small army-navy surplus store in Windsor, Ontario, had a run on gas masks.

To pander to, rather than to challenge this narrowing of our moral universe proves self-defeating. One need look no further than the response of the mainstream Israeli peace camp to the war against Iraq to see how profoundly unreliable was their shrunken moral universe. Let us recognize that: "Israel was the only country that openly and unambiguously pushed for (the Gulf) war," in the words of Israeli Major-General (retired) Matti Peled;[2] that Israel used the war to impose its longest and most severe mass house imprisonment of the Palestinian people; that more Palestinians were killed as a result of Israel's curfew than Israelis were killed by Iraqi Scuds. In these very circumstances, the mainstream Israeli peace movement's ethnocentrism led it to endorse the war, condemn the European and North American anti-war movement, and in one prominent case call for the use of atomic weapons against Iraq.[3] Actual war poses the moment of truth for peace movements.

In this regard we also must recollect the ease with which the

Canadian anti-war movement accepted the misrepresentation of Israel as an endangered, innocent victim, easily dismissing magnitude in its visceral alarm at Israeli civilian deaths – compared with Iraqi civilian deaths, and all the while excluding from moral concern the repression of Palestinians. This monocular vision of the Middle East through the guilting lens of Euro-centric, anti-Jewish atrocities made the Canadian peace movement seriously vulnerable to the campaign of exaggerated demonization of Saddam Hussein, a campaign that drew upon our culture's reservoir of generalized anti-Arab racism. Perhaps the behavior of the End the Arms Race coalition in actively excluding Arab-Canadian speakers from the largest anti-war rally in Vancouver was the most egregious example of endorsing this racism, but was it the only manifestation country-wide?[4]

Certainly Saddam Hussein is a villainous dictator, like so many the West supports, whose main victims are his own people. But the anti-war movement had difficulty maintaining a distinction between this and the war-makers' propaganda that Saddam Hussein was an exceptional demon, a Hitler who threatened the world. Nor did the anti-war movement distinguish clearly between the deeply felt, legitimate grievances of the Arab world and Saddam Hussein's opportunistic appeal to those grievances. We abandoned Arab peoples who out of desperation responded to Saddam Hussein's rhetoric, rather than supporting their legitimate rights. In short, we did not strongly enough reject the false choice between George Bush and Saddam Hussein and independently endorse negotiations on the major issues of regional injustice which would have undercut both Washington and Baghdad's manipulations.

Fred Halliday was one figure who promoted this false choice between Saddam and Bush, and chose Bush. That surprised many because Halliday had been respected as a political progressive. A professor of international relations at the London School of Economics, he is expert about the Middle East, and in addition to his extensive progressive publications has been a contributing editor to the excellent, informative and critical, English language journal, *Middle East Reports*. The other editors of that journal took a very different stand from Halliday's.

Halliday wrote: "Simply put: if I have to make a choice between imperialism and fascism, I choose imperialism." Halliday tells us that

Ba'thism "is a linear descendent of European fascism, taking from it its racism, its use of terror, its cult of the leader and of supposed deliverance through war."[5]

Halliday evaded listing any features of his lesser evil, U.S. imperialism, perhaps because he would have had to include the same ones: racism, use of terror, deliverance through war, if not cult of leader. On U.S. National Public Radio Halliday declared: "I think that the United States, which has encouraged democracy in some other parts of the world, has a curious blind spot so far as the Middle East is concerned, partly because of oil, partly because they think it's just not worth the trouble." Alexander Cockburn pithily commented that "this conversion to the democratic mission of the U.S. round the world resembles nothing so much as Salman Rushdie's sudden discovery of the divine truth of Islam. . .Halliday has a lot less excuse."[6]

In a vein similar to Halliday, yesterday's Czech dissident playwright, Ivan Klima, voiced his vindication of Washington's war. He wrote a thin, two-character play, "No Blood for Oil." In it Klima counterposes an old-worldly male and a good-hearted woman protester. The woman, with totally naive simplicity protests under the slogan "no blood for oil." The man, a passerby, endorses the war and repeats Washington's public rationale. As the play proceeds the man's presumed political sophistication patronizingly disorients the empty-headed woman who, at the play's end, is left in utter confusion.[7]

A related phenomena among erstwhile critics of imperial war is a post-bombing trend to accommodate to the reality of a United States "victory." Bill Arkin is Director of Military Research at Greenpeace and main author of Greenpeace's post-bombing 171-page report on the Gulf war.[8] Yesterday (1974-78) Arkin was a U.S. Army Intelligence analyst and, like Dyer, has been welcomed as a friendly authority to Canadian peace movement platforms. At three prominent points in the Greenpeace report a summary statement, like the following, is made. Obviously intended for quotation, it indeed appeared in press reports:

> . . .Some could even argue that the allies made a real effort to get their unfortunate calling over as quickly as possible.

Much of this behavior could be seen as paving the way for positive new standards for humanitarian and military conduct. Through the repudiation of civilian attacks, albeit perhaps only in the context of an otherwise highly successful war, the US and its allies tacitly behaved in accordance with provisions of the Geneva Protocols, and may have also accepted certain de facto constraints, such as those of the Inhumane Weapons Convention.

Iraq's gross behavior, particularly its devastation of the natural environment, serves as a sad contrast.[9]

If you thought there was something intentional in the reduction of Iraq to a pre-industrial state, the Greenpeace authors plead rather that "the allies misunderstood the force of the application of their own weaponry."[10] Beyond such foolishness, there are obscenities in the report: "Surgical war had finally arrived, and the patient was skillfully carved and disemboweled."[11]

But the style in which the report is written is more complex and deserves a comment, for it epitomizes one way of retreating from the precipice of dissent. Buried within the high-profile, pro-Washington generalizations and framework, and hidden amidst tortured grammar, are multiple, low-profile details of damning, anti-war information. The report shows the skillfulness of a chess player: the major moves are intended to adjust Greenpeace to the new realities by flattering the war-mongers, who are the power-holders, while hesitations and criticism of the anti-war critics can be directed to a line of sacrificial pawns scattered here and there in the report. The Greenpeace report was written for a conference that would promote the creation of new international conventions to protect the environment *during* war-making, in an effort to be a "loyal" opposition.

In this new world order of a militarily unrestrained single superpower, with atomization of the organized century-long secular challenges to imperial order, with no well-recognized focal points of resistance, with no empowering, humane vision of compelling historic possibility, the Hallidays, Klimas, and Arkins abandoned reason and decency, to harmonize with the aggressor. What is significant is that they are not alone.

Jim Christie, president of the World Federalists of Canada, just wrote a scathing exposé of Bush's war verbiage about the dawn of world peace. The "rule of might" prevailed, not peace, writes Christie. But then this conclusion: "Perhaps, in the end, we shall have to settle for some time for a Pax Americana. It might be argued that the world could do worse." Could do worse? This is not an argument that echoes from beyond the graves of the dead millions of Vietnam, Indonesia, East Timor, Mozambique, Angola, Chile, El Salvador, Iraq...

Taken by surprise when Washington proclaimed its new world order and brought it to birth in blood, peace forces are far from equipped to detect its vulnerabilities, particularly as the expunging of a dissenting history of this century gathers momentum. As we begin to search for those vulnerabilities we must not acquiesce in the rewriting of history, or the reorganization of our own memories, so that they trail in the shadows of fashionable cant about "victory." When half of Americans surveyed believe that 100,000 or fewer Vietnamese were killed by the U.S. military – equivalent to estimating the Nazi genocide of Jews at 300,000 instead of six million – it is an act of political importance to keep a straight record and a clear memory of imperialist wars, including the most recent.

Notes

[1] May/June 1991, vol.7, no.3.
[2] *Challenge: A Magazine of the Israeli Left*, Tel Aviv, vol.2, no.2, p.3.
[3] See Michel Warshawsky's article "Crossing the Rubicon," below.
[4] See the letter from Middle East Peace Action Coalition, *New Directions*, July 1991, pp.4-5.
[5] "The left and war," *New Statesman*, March 8; subsequent issues of the *New Statesman*, March 22 and March 29, contain exchanges between Halliday, his critics and a supporter. Halliday also wrote "The War the Left Lost" in *Marxism Today*, April 1991, criticizing other opponents of the war.
[6] See Alexander Cockburn's column in *The Nation*, April 1, 1991, for further response to Halliday's viewpoint.
[7] *Index on Censorship*, April/May 1991.
[8] Arkin, William M., Damian Durrant, and Marianne Cherni, *On Impact – Modern Warfare and the Environment: A Case Study of the Gulf War* (Washington, May 1991).
[9] *Ibid.* p.145.
[10] *Ibid.* p.147.
[11] *Ibid.* p.8.

Crossing the Rubicon: The Israeli Peace Camp Faces New Challenges

Michel Warshawsky

FEWER THAN TWO THOUSAND WOMEN AND MEN SHOWED UP FOR THE "PEACE chain" organized by Peace Now to mark the 24th anniversary of Israel's occupation of the West Bank and Gaza. The expensive, giant advertisements which beckoned from the pages of the daily newspapers did not bring out the multitudes we have become accustomed to see at Peace Now demonstrations. Is it true that "the masses have become tired," as some of the movement's leaders claim? Or, worse still, have they moved rightward, becoming supporters of government policy, even if not wholeheartedly? Or, maybe they are "ready for battle" and all that's missing is the right gimmick to bring them back into the streets.

It seems to me that the explanation for the Israeli peace camp's present slump, unprecedented in the past decade, is to be found elsewhere altogether. The reason is not supposed fatigue of the mass of supporters, or an extreme change in political position, nor some technical-organizational problem. Rather the slump derives from the Israeli left's inability to offer a persuasive and mobilizing vision with which to face the challenges of the current political situation and government policy. A number of fundamental characteristics of the Israeli left, which encompasses the mainstream peace camp, constitute powerful obstacles to its becoming an effective opposition, able to restrain government actions and change official policy.

A left without distinctive principles

"We don't want the territories because they are a cancer, a demographic threat, and as far as I'm concerned, let the Arabs kill each other."

The supreme values championed by the Zionist left* are identical with those of the right, and left and right compete with each other over their fulfillment: Zionism, Jewish exclusivity, national interest, and state security in the narrow military sense of the term. All other values, including human rights, peace, the right to self-determination, and democracy, are subordinated to and conditioned by these supreme values.

The Zionist left is in favour of withdrawal from the occupied territories because it guarantees a Jewish majority in Israel. The Zionist left opposes repression in the occupied territories because it corrupts the souls of Jewish youth. It is for a peace policy because rejectionism is spoiling Israel's relationship with Washington; opposed to torture, except if it is vital for state security. The universal values of human rights, democracy, and the right of self-determination are, in the eyes of the Zionist left, conditional rights, means rather than ends, tools for the ensurance of the supreme values of Zionism and the interests of the Jewish people, not universal rights. The quarrel between right and left has become a technical argument over the most effective ways for achieving their common objectives. There is no education in values because there are no alternative values, only alternative ways of realizing the same values. There is no alternative vision, but only the same ethnocentric vision, which is indifferent towards anyone who is not a member of the tribe, and indifferent toward what does not contribute to the tribal welfare.

---

* When I refer to the Zionist left it obviously is a generalization. Within it are many men and women dedicated to struggling for human rights.

If the quarrel with the right is over the techniques for achieving maximum security for the Jews and over how to ensure a Jewish majority, and if values such as respect for human beings, the rights of the other person, and freedom for the other nation are not taken into account, then the techniques advocated by the right – repression and transfer – are more convincing in their effectiveness than a policy of compromise and concessions. If every Arab is our enemy, if every Palestinian is a threat to the maintenance of a Jewish majority, then transfer is preferable to a border fence, even an electronic one.*

An opposition despite itself

"The Arabs are the enemy, Arafat disgusts me – but peace is made with enemies."

In the eyes of the Zionist left, the essential division is not between right and left, between the violation of human rights and the respect for human rights, between nationalistic values and universal values, but rather a division *along* national lines. Their fundamental loyalty is to the nation and the state, and all other loyalties are subordinated to that. Ally and enemy are not defined according to values, but according to national identity. The Arab is an enemy by virtue of being an Arab; the right-wing Jew is a brother, one of the family, part of the tribe, towards whom one has a fundamental loyalty, even if his methods are unworthy of support.

Even if there is 100 per cent agreement between the world view of a member of the Israeli left and a specific Palestinian, the Palestinian remains an enemy while the Jew with extreme right-wing opinions will be thought of as an erring brother. There is no room in Zionist left thinking for the concept of solidarity with the Palestinians. At most, they carry on a "dialogue" with the enemy. Solidarity is reserved for members of the tribe, for members of the family.

This way of thinking leads the Zionist left to be ambivalent about its status as an opposition. If nationality, family, tribe are the primary ref-

* "Transfer" is the Zionist euphemism for their historic policy of uprooting and removing Palestinians from the land where they live and forcing them to flee elsewhere. [editor]

erence groups, national unity and "national consensus" are the natural state. Being outside the consensus is a deviation, the split is viewed as an aberration, unhealthy, and hopefully will be temporary. The Zionist leftist does not want to be in opposition. He does not blame the right for championing immoral, racist, and war-mongering values, but rather, for thereby causing a split in the "national consensus."

In the eyes of the Zionist leftist, war is first of all a sign and an opportunity to return to the warm and natural embrace of national unity, reason to put an end to the abnormal status of opposition. So the left Zionist gallops back to the bosom of the "national consensus" whenever the first signs of war, real or imagined, appear on the horizon. The hugs between Yossi Sarid from Ratz and Benyamin Ze'ev Begin from Likud are not opportunistic, but rather an integral element of this world view, the other face of Sarid's unceasing declarations about the disagreeable nature of carrying on a "dialogue with the enemy."* An opposition which announces from the start that it does not want to be an opposition, whose loyalty to the whole exceeds its sense of autonomy, does not have a chance of convincing the majority of people to turn their back on the government.

Up in the balcony: shooting and protesting

"Always with my government against our common enemy. . ."

If the basic division is between Jews and Arabs, between Israel and the Palestinians, and one's fundamental loyalty is given *a priori* to the nation, the Zionist left cannot wish for a victory of the "other side." The enemy must lose because his victory is a loss for "our" side. And it makes no difference what the concrete meaning of victory and loss are. The triumph of the intifada may bring Israeli-Palestinian peace, and its defeat may bring the annexation of the occupied territories, mass transfer, and war with the whole Arab world. And yet, in spite of this, the Zionist left does not want the intifada to triumph, and in practical terms will not work for such a victory.

* Yossi Sarid is a major figure in the parliamentary party Citizens Rights Movement, considered on the left of the Israeli political spectrum.
  Benyamin Begin is the son of former prime minister Menachim Begin, and like his father is on the far right of Israeli parliamentary politics. [editor]

The Zionist left stands, as it were, in the middle, between the two clashing camps: between Shamir's government – which builds settlements, orders the shooting of children, is responsible for the cruel oppression of the Palestinians in the occupied territories and sabotages every chance for negotiations – and the struggle of the Palestinians of the West Bank and Gaza, which the same Zionist left defines as legitimate. It does not support Shamir, but it does not want the triumph of the only power capable of foiling the plots of the Shamir government. It stands on the fence and protests. The truth of the matter is that it shoots, along with Shamir, at those whose struggle it defines as just; for it serves in the military in the occupied territories and persistently opposes those who refuse such service.* And having finished shooting, the Zionist left goes up on the balcony and protests the wild behavior of the Israeli actors, and yells to the Palestinian actors not to give in to the provocations of their opponent, to show restraint, and to take the beatings and insults without complaint.

As already mentioned, the Zionist left is not interested in a victory by the enemy, and it behaves as if the contest is between itself and the Israeli right, and that the Palestinians' intervention just ruins the job because, from then on, the left no longer can wish for the defeat of its government. Hence the Zionist left's refusal to refuse; hence the unconditional loyalty to the decisions of the government and the Knesset [parliament]; hence the automatic response to every call to arms.

An opposition which is not prepared to mobilize all its strength to bring down the government, out of fear of "aiding the enemy," cannot convince anyone that its actions have any point. It ends up driving its original supporters to despair, to not knowing why they are acting, and to feeling that their struggle hasn't a chance.

Protest but not resistance

"We must respect the law and the decisions of the democratically elected government."

The unwillingness on the part of the Zionist left to take sides, or

---

* There is a movement in Israel whose members refuse military service in the occupied territories. It is called "Yesh Gevul," meaning "There is a limit." [editor]

more accurately the fact that it does not line up on the side of the intifada, inevitably leads it to line up beside the Israeli government. This
also is the root of the mainstream peace camp's satisfaction with just
protesting.

It is not coincidental that two issues have divided, and still divide,
the mainstream from the radical wings of the peace camp. The first is
refusal to do military service in the occupied territories, and before that
in Lebanon. The second is open violation of the Anti-Terror Ordi-
nance, the Israeli law which prohibits meetings of Israeli citizens with
PLO representatives. On these two issues, significant portions of the
Israeli peace camp have chosen not to be satisfied just with protest, but
to confront the law, the government, with a kind of declaration of civil
disobedience: "Your war is not our war, your laws are not our laws." We
also can add to this various acts of support for the Palestinian population, like bringing food convoys to refugee camps, and defying the military curfews on Palestinian communities in order personally to express
solidarity.

The unwillingness, on the part of Zionist leftists, to pay the price of
risking their careers and imprisonment, is not simply a matter of
spoiled, middle-class activists. No less important a deterrence is the
stigma of social punishment that symbolizes being outside the community. Social legitimacy for these leftists is not merely a matter of image,
but has intrinsic value.

Above and beyond the argument over whether one step or another is
tactically opportune, the direct challenging of unjust laws entails a
willingness to confront the regime, to make a statement of withdrawal
from the community, with readiness to pay the price. It is no wonder
the Zionist left sees this as a line which is not to be crossed, since it sees
belonging to the community, and the proclamation of that belonging,
as one of the mainstays of its outlook and its political message. But an
opposition which declares from the start that it doesn't intend to go
further afield than protest, and sees any confrontation with the system
as out of the question, is declaring itself to be an opposition which is
neither willing nor able to halt the course of political forces against
which it is fighting. Such an opposition cannot mobilize or inspire over
the long haul, as it announces from the start that all of its activism is
doomed to failure.

Identification with the establishment

"We built the state. We are the pilots and soldiers from elite units. They are the camp-cooks and drivers..."

Not only does the Zionist left owe its fundamental loyalty to nation and state, it also sees itself as *part* of the state establishment, its institutions and symbols. The IDF, the Shin Bet, the Kibbutzim, the Histadrut belong to the Zionist left, and are its own flesh and blood.* In their eyes, Likud is something of a usurper, ruining what the Zionist left built with hard labour and, it believes, with tremendous success.

Being the establishment explains why the Zionist left scorns the "simple people," and accuses them of "ruining the state" because of their ignorance, and cultural and moral primitiveness.† The Zionist left does not believe itself capable of persuading the people, irredeemable primitives that they are, to take up the cause of social and political change; so it carries on its campaign not only exclusively within establishment institutions, especially the Knesset, but addresses itself specifically to those in the establishment who disagree with it, the right-wing politicians. Its identification with the institutions and symbols of the state, especially the Histadrut and the Kibbutzim, also explains why the lower classes, particularly Oriental Jews, don't see it as an alternative. For most members of the Oriental communities, these symbols and institutions are a kind of enemy from which they began to shake themselves free ten years ago.

A left which feels closer to a colonel from the right, to the head of the Shin Bet, or to Histadrut officials than to the common people, in whom they have no faith and with whom they feel no closeness, closes off the option of becoming a majority and of mobilizing the popular support required to topple the right-wing establishment from power.

* The elite units of the Israeli army (IDF), the internal security (Shin Bet), the agricultural and industrial collectives that have served as frontline military outposts (kibbutzim), and the trade union federation that owns major corporate enterprises (Histadrut) have been the social, political and economic base of the Zionist left in Israel, particularly the Labour Party. [editor]

† Such charges are made particularly by European-origin Jews against Jews who came from the Arab world, "Oriental Jews," who form a majority of the Jewish-Israeli population, and have been discriminated against systematically. See Shlomo Swirski, *Israel: The Oriental Majority* (London, Zed Books, 1989). [editor]

The United States: flag-bearer for the peace camp

"Yes to the American peace plan! Yes to Bush's war for peace!"

To the Zionist left, the major power for peace in the world is the U.S. administration. Its role is to resolve conflicts and to force peoples and states to overcome their particularistic considerations and to agree to a world order based on justice, fairness and rationality.

The pro-Americanism of the Israeli peace camp is not only a matter of an incorrect political evaluation of a specific situation. It is an expression of a general view which divides the world into good guys, the West, and bad guys, the communists and the Third World. The United States leads the "Free World," defends it, helps underdog peoples, and pulls stubborn regimes from their erring ways on to the path of reason and goodness.

Washington's policy has a central place in the strategy of the Zionist left. As Arabs are a vicious enemy, the Israeli populace primitive racists, who will stop Shamir and Sharon? Who will take action for a peace policy? The answer: Washington. The protest activity of the mainstream peace camp is aimed at heralding U.S. intervention and, if and where there is a need, encouraging it. The peace camp does not see itself as creating changes by itself, and neither does it look to the Arab states, nor to the Palestinians, nor to the Israeli people themselves as the active agents of change. From Washington, and from Washington alone, will go forth the "Word of Peace."

Peace Now arose in order to bring to bear pressure for the success of President Carter's efforts at Camp David, and Peace Now has directed all its efforts since 1988 to the advancement of the "American peace plan." Peace Now recognized the centrality of the Palestinian question only after the United States did. And only after the United States recognized the PLO, in November 1988, did Peace Now recognize it. If the United States does not intervene in this region on this issue, the Israeli peace camp will have no perspective to recommend to the public; and if the United States supports a military solution or a settlement which ignores the fundamental rights of the Palestinian people, the peace camp will line up for Washington's new line. In placing all the responsibility for efforts towards peace on the shoulders of the U.S. administration, the Zionist left is not only misreading the political map, it is teaching the general public an approach of passivity, for either the changes will come from Washington, or not at all.

These traits of the Zionist left and of the mainstream peace camp explain how they came to line up so enthusiastically in support of the latest Gulf war. And they explain how, in this war, they supported, through their silence, the war crimes committed by the Israeli occupation forces against the Palestinian population of the occupied territories.* These traits also explain why the Zionist left's current activity consists almost exclusively of applauding the Bush-Baker peace initiative. These traits explain especially why the peace camp has disappeared from the political map and slumped to the bottom of the stairwell.

One can say with a high degree of confidence, the Israeli left needs an *aggiornamento*, a new beginning, and critical examination of its political, philosophical and ethical foundations.

All of the limitations described in the first part of this article present, if one takes their mirror image, the alternatives required to get the Israeli left out of its present dead-end.

An Opposition by Choice: "Consensus" is not a value, and national unity is not an ideal. In other words, to be in opposition to the government, or even to the dominant way of thinking in the society, is not to be in some sort of abnormal or unhealthy state. The society is divided according to clashing interests and opposing perspectives. The left is supposed to articulate a specific set of interests and values, and to fight the opposing interests and the values which contradict its own. In terms of a left perspective, the meaningful divisions are not those determined by nationality, but rather by values. An enemy is not a member of the other nation, but rather the proponent of values which are in opposition to ours. An ally is not a member of the tribe, but precisely one who champions the same values we do.

Values of Its Own: The assumption underlying the concept of an opposition is that it has distinctive principles. As regards the Israeli left, this means crystallizing a comprehensive vision which makes a

---

* Prominent members of Peace Now not only supported the U.S.-led war, they called international press conferences to denounce the anti-war movements in Europe and North America. At one press conference the novelist Amos Oz even endorsed the use of nuclear weapons against Baghdad. [editor]

qualitative break with the values of the Zionist consensus, placing universal values of democracy, social justice, equality, and unconditional respect for human rights against the values of narrow nationalism. In the context of the Arab-Israeli conflict, it is particularly vital to present an alternative vision to the dominant perspective of presumed eternal and inevitable conflict and the alienation of peoples. In the progressive vision, the state is not a value, and a Jewish state cannot be an aim. The concept of security, in a left interpretation, is absolutely different from that of the right, and is based on a conception of coexistence, respect for rights, and togetherness.

Come Down From the Balcony: If the world is divided into ideological camps and not into national camps, there is no place for a neutral stance or for fence-sitting. Not only must the left as left not support any kind of national government, just because it is its government; it also must not content itself with the stance of critical observer. Any left worthy of the name must choose sides. In our case, it is not sufficient to criticize the government for its rejectionist policy. The left must champion the victory of the intifada as the only means of halting the race towards eternal conflict and barbarism in the region. An authentic left wants the intifada to be victorious, and works for this victory to the best of its ability, because this is the victory of good over evil, of right over wrong, of rights over might.

Resistance and Not Just Protest: From this we can conclude that the left must work to defeat the policy of the occupation, more specifically to pave the road for its defeat. The left must put an end to its policy of "restraint" which forbids going beyond protest and expression of opinions, and must in fact do just the opposite: mobilize strength and resources to prevent the continuing success of the policy of occupation. This will be achieved by creating a public opinion that is willing to: selectively refuse military service, violate the "anti-terror law" against meeting with PLO representatives, enter areas where military curfews threaten starvation or facilitate the terrorizing of the Palestinian population, demonstrate against the government precisely during periods of national mobilization for war. Indeed, what is required is a left interested in the defeat of oppression, which sees this as a sort of self defence, and which imposes no restraint on its efforts.

The People and the Establishment: The left must not belong to the world of the establishment, and anyone who sees himself as part of the establishment cannot be thought of as left. The left must belong to the world of the people, enduring what they suffer, sharing their longings, dreaming the same dreams, and especially struggling together for their interests. In order to become a true alternative in the eyes of the people, the left must change its symbols and banners. Instead of immigration, care for the residents of poor neighbourhoods; instead of the army, care for the fate and needs of the individual soldier; instead of "security needs," the needs for which the majority in Israel dream and struggle. And the left must see the Kibbutzim and the Histadrut for what they really are: an elite that has built its wealth at the expense of the Arabs, on the one hand, and the ordinary Jews on the other, and therefore they must be seen as adversaries rather than allies and role-models.

Anti-imperialism: Israel is in the heart of the Arab world, and this makes it impossible for any left worthy of the name to see itself outside the camp of those battling imperialism the world over. The left must divorce itself from pathetic, blind support for U.S. policy throughout the world, and instead take its place in the world anti-imperialist camp, and in the struggle against U.S. hegemony. In our region, this also means turning our back on a western orientation, and replacing it with an orientation towards the east: integration with the Arab region, and joining in its struggles for economic and cultural independence and political sovereignty.

An examination of these six points shows that the peace camp's emergence from its current state of crisis will be neither easy nor quick. It is a matter of a qualitative about-face, wherein a colonialist left becomes a democratic left. There is no assurance at all that the greater part of the left will manage to cross this Rubicon, and it is likely that only a minority will. Yet one thing is clear. If it is not able to do so, the traditional left will become an increasingly marginal part of the Israeli political picture, with no chance of becoming a viable alternative in the eyes of the great majority of the Israeli people. Without an alternative vision, the left is doomed to remain a loyal opposition within the establishment, to continue to shoot and weep, shoot and protest.

The Next Phase:
Problems of Transition

Salim Tamari

ONE OF THE NOTABLE ACHIEVEMENTS OF THE GULF WAR IS THAT IT COMPELLED the Palestinians to make a reassessment of their future political strategy. This at a time when their crowning achievement in the last decade – the Uprising (intifada) – had reached an impasse.

Just before the war I referred to this impasse as one leading to political paralysis: "the crux of the Intifada's predicament lies in the routinization of the daily aspects of revolt (centered around the commercial strike and street confrontations with the army), which can neither be escalated into a campaign of total civil disobedience – and complete disengagement from Israeli rule – nor transformed into a political initiative which can engage the enemy in negotiations on terms favourable to the Palestinians. The first option is hampered by the limited organizational potential of the movement which, at this stage, seems to have reached its uppermost capacity for popular mobilization (and to have retreated to heavy dependence on the 'direct action' tactics of factional 'strike forces'). The second option is beyond the political capacities of the internal resistance, given the existing balance of forces between the contenders."[1]

While the first of these conditions still holds true today, has even

338

been reinforced by events, the second condition, related to the new balance of forces, has been modified by the war. One can venture, at this early stage of *post bellum* arrangements, to suggest the following new adjustments.

(1) Israel, unable to perform its self-defined role as a strike force on behalf of Western interests, has been reduced from the status of a junior partner of the U.S. to that of a client state, much more susceptible to the effects of U.S. and Western European economic aid. Another significant consequence of the war is that it has refuelled the dormant Israeli debate on the Palestinian question and the territorial/colonial dilemma that had divided the Israeli polity at the beginning of the intifada.

(2) With the military blow directed at Iraq, the Arab states are no longer divided between "steadfast" states (Iraq, Syria, Libya and Algeria) and those, previously led by Egypt and Saudi Arabia, that represent U.S. interests. On the other hand, the leading Arab states that joined the U.S.-led coalition, particularly Egypt, Syria and Saudi Arabia, are in a position to exact concessions from the Americans for the purpose of restoring their Arabist credentials, and in striving to legitimize their anti-Iraqi campaign. Politically these concessions can only be meaningful if they were translated into pressure on the Israelis to make territorial concessions in the occupied territories.

(3) The definition of the "new world order" in terms of resolving the Arab-Israeli conflict is currently the subject of U.S.-European policy formulation. Its main ingredient is the absence of the Soviet Union (and the Third World bloc) as a decisive factor in balancing American intervention. But it is unlikely that a *Pax Americana* in the aftermath of the Gulf war can be confined to U.S. military hegemony in as much as the European Economic Community, Japan, the Scandinavian countries, and the Soviets have substantial interest in the area and are likely to resist American diktat of post-war arrangements. Nor is it in the interest of the Americans any more to act *or to be perceived to act* as the defenders of Israeli intransigence over a peace settlement.

(4) One of the most significant factors in the new framework is the future role of Jordan. Jordan represents the exception in the Arab world as having responded to the dual crisis of economic recession and legitimacy with a genuinely democratic experiment, and was virtually the

only country in the Arab East (aside from Yemen) not to bow to U.S. diktat. So far it has proved more resilient than the PLO in adapting itself skillfully to the defeat of Iraq, its major economic partner in the Middle East, and in designating itself as crucial interlocutor in the post-war settlement. Of utmost significance here is that Jordan is now seen by the Palestinians as having a joint role in any planned peace initiative, but one that cannot be implemented without the participation of the PLO.

My aim is to suggest that the intransigence of the Israelis over a territorial solution, and the length, complexity and protracted nature of the impending political struggle, require the Palestinians to focus on the modalities of the "transitional period," i.e. transition to sovereignty, with the same zeal they have focused so far on their long-range objectives. These modalities are related to the future of the intifada, and to the interim measures that they are willing to propose in any forthcoming peace negotiations.

Palestinian reading of the new map

There have been two varieties of Palestinian reactions to post-war realities. One was the feeling that the conduct of the war vindicated the original view which saw the campaign as aiming at removing Iraq as the main obstacle to establishing U.S. imperial hegemony in the Middle East, and that consequently the Palestinians should now resist the imposition of U.S.-Israeli solutions which may or may not have the blessing of the United States' Arab allies.

Inside the occupied territories this perspective calls for the escalation of the intifada,[2] and for non-cooperation with initiatives floated by the U.S. administration and its Arab allies. It views the coming period as a phase of resistance to imposed solutions until the existing balance of forces shifts in favour of the Palestinians. At the heart of this outlook is the assumption that a radical transformation of neighbouring Arab regimes, especially those in Syria and Egypt, is a prerequisite for rectifying the existing imbalance created by the defeat of Iraq. Internally this tendency advocates tactical, and in some cases long-term, alliances with Hamas and other Islamic currents. We see here a political atmosphere reminiscent of the vision that prevailed immediately after the 1967 war.

The second tendency shares with the first one the need for resisting attempts at creating an alternative Palestinian leadership, currently waged by the U.S., Saudi Arabia, and Syria.[3] But this perspective does not see the war as providing a *carte blanche* for the Israelis to impose any solutions.

On the contrary it sees the war as having created new opportunity for political initiatives which must be seized fully by the Palestinian leadership. Writing recently in the Jerusalem press, Ghassan al-Khatib noted that one of the main achievements of this war accomplished exactly what the U.S. has refused to acknowledge: *an organic linkage between the Gulf war and the issue of Palestine.*[4] This linkage, he proceeded, calls for the need to develop the momentum of the new international legitimacy acquired by U.N. resolutions, particularly Security Council resolution 242, and U.N. resolution 141. This requires that Palestinians transcend the phase of vetoing political initiatives that they deem to be politically unsatisfactory, and move towards initiating their own political positions that resonate with the new relations of power.[5]

The determinant factor favouring which of these tendencies will prevail depends to a large extent on the ability of the Palestinian movement to launch an initiative that galvanizes the main factions of the PLO around a new minimum program, one that will reassert in principle the November 1988 resolutions of the Algiers Palestine National Council (PNC), while transcending the political deadlock that is currently facing the intifada. The inability of the movement to move clearly in this direction will not relegate the Palestinian movement to oblivion, as the pundits keep reminding us, but will take the initiative from the hands of the national movement and shift it in the direction of Hamas on the one hand, and the Arab states on the other.

The future of the intifada

Within the occupied territories there is a general feeling that the war constituted a watershed for the uprising of December 1987. Just as the

November resolutions of the PNC were a turning point in translating the political demands of the upheaval into a concrete political program, the Gulf war is seen as a fundamental break with the initial strategy and tactics of the intifada, indicating the need for rethinking those strategies. After three years of rebellion there is a general malaise in the Palestinian streets affecting people's attitude to the daily routine of the intifada: the commercial strike, the street confrontations, and the obligatory monthly circulars. The severe curfew imposed by the Israelis on the West Bank and Gaza during the first two months of 1991, led to the destruction of the winter crops and the pauperization of the general population, in particular farmers, daily workers and small merchants. An additional blow was added by the loss of remittances and direct aid from migrants and governments in the Gulf.

There is no doubt that the vast majority of Palestinian people in the occupied territories are behind the intifada and its political objectives. Events have shown that in all regions tens of thousands are still mobilized to resume the battle when national issues, or regional issues of land confiscation and deportation of activists, are involved. What is being questioned here are those tactics whose efficacy has been depleted.

What the Palestinians need today is a reprieve; breathing space that allows them to rebuild their economy while waging a protracted political struggle of disengagement with Israel. In order to accomplish this dual objective I would suggest that the most crucial formulation here is to define the nature of the transitional period during which negotiations will take place. *It is precisely because this period is likely to be prolonged, complex and protracted, involving successes and retreats, that we must have a positive definition of the transitional period.* By "positive" I mean a concrete program for the modalities, forms, and preferably, periodization of power arrangements during the transition, rather than defining it as the passage of time required to reach nationally declared objectives.

The following are concrete suggestions for these forms and modalities:

(1) *Early forms of resistance have turned into their opposite.* The current forms of resistance, routinized by the intifada, must be reformulated in a manner that serves the daily needs of the people, and not their adversary. What was a successful and imaginative weapon in 1988 and 1989

has turned into its opposite today. The commercial strike which initially indicated a struggle between the army and the resistance as to who controls the street, has already made its point. With the passage of time it has become a debilitating gesture of bravado, and a net drain on the economy. It is time for the United Leadership to initiate new measures ending or replacing the commercial strike with more imaginative actions, such as a boycott of commodities, rather than be forced into futile confrontations with merchants that will erode credibility.

The need for the United Leadership to intervene at this level assumes also its ability, and the need, to control and discipline unruly elements in its midst who have succeeded, since the beginning of 1990, to divert the mass struggle into factional and narrow forms of street action without any clear political objectives.[6] While the general public has maintained its support for the intifada, these elements threaten to disrupt the umbilical cord that links the leadership of the rebellion to its mass base.

(2) *Normalizing daily life in times of rebellion:* In this regard the Islamic tendency has been more successful and imaginative than the United Leadership. While there is general agreement that educational programs and school attendance should be maintained and protected during the intifada, in practice only during strike days initiated by Hamas and Islamic Jihad is school attendance observed. The damage to education is bad enough because of Israeli curfews, and does not need to be compounded by the national movement. The Palestinian movement must seek to "normalize" daily life while struggling against occupation, perhaps inspired by examples set by the Lebanese people. Revival of academic life, cultural innovation and social activities, must not be seen as domains isolated from the arena of resistance. Even the rituals of joy, such as weddings and seasonal festivities, which have been subdued during the intifada, must be restored and incorporated into the rituals of rebellion.

(3) *The alternative economy:* The critique of shortcomings of alternative economic models instituted during the intifada already is underway.[7] During the three years of intifada civil disobedience an experimental program for an alternative economy developed, though it was more form than substance. The successful aspect of this phase was to instill in the people the notion that economic disengagement with

Israel is possible, through the boycott of commodities and taxes, and through innovations in local enterprises. Now begins the arduous task of actually developing local production and marketing networks without heavy reliance on substantial injections of aid from abroad. A modicum of a plan is needed to coordinate growth of private industries with those enterprises and cooperatives initiated by grass-roots movements. This in turn assumes and requires the formulation of a new minimal consensual program among the main factions of the United Leadership.

(4) *A new minimal program:* The political consensus formulated by the factions of the Palestinian movement during the intifada was crowned by the political program of the 1988 Algiers PNC and its peace initiative. While it is essential to continue the adherence to this initiative, the program itself has to be redefined in light of the consequences of the Gulf war and the new political alignments in the region. Without a new minimal program the Palestinian movement will fall back to its segmented, partisan components, each fighting for its own platform. Disunity here is fatal to the extent that it will allow external forces and the Israelis to deal with the Palestinians as "political tribes," or worse, to transcend the Palestinian movement altogether and adjudicate a separate deal with Palestinian "notables."

The elements of the new minimum program, in my view, must include the following: (a) promoting the early forms of civil disobedience while strengthening the local economy; (b) establishing procedures for consensus building which allow for dissenting opinion to articulate its position without disrupting accords arrived at by a majority; (c) establishing institutional channels to arbitrate interfactional disputes and establish acceptable ways to resolve them; (d) maintaining a democratic forum for the continuous examination of strategy in light of ongoing political developments; (e) coordinating activities around this minimum program with political tendencies (e.g. Islamic currents) which are unlikely to join ranks with the Palestinian peace initiative; (f) maintaining an open dialogue with all adversaries, including the Israelis, on the basis of the Palestinian peace initiative.

An international mandate?

It should be obvious that the implementation of this minimal program is going to be prolonged and protracted. The current weakness of the

Israeli opposition, and United States hesitation to apply substantial pressure on Israel in favour of territorial concessions, mean that it will be years before serious negotiations between Israel and the Palestinians bear fruit. For this reason the Palestinian side must propose interim measures which will ensure the protection of the population of the occupied territories and the survival of their cultural and economic institutions while negotiations are going on.

Two decisive features distinguish these interim measures from the autonomy scheme proposed in 1989 by the Likud government, and then retracted by Yitzhak Shamir. One is the provisional nature of the measures, and the other is the recognition, at least by the international community, that the end result is the evolution of the occupied territories toward sovereignty.

Components of this transitional period must include at least some of the following features:

1. Freedom to plan and invest, including the entry of funds, for the economic growth of the territories;
2. Freedom to nominate and elect candidates for local, municipal and village councils, professional and trade union offices, and freedom to nominate and elect representatives at the national level;
3. Freedom of movement within the regions of the West Bank and Gaza and between them, including the city of (Arab) Jerusalem;
4. Cessation of all punitive measures against educational, cultural and research institutions, and against the press;
5. Freedom for planning, zoning and development of infrastructure for municipal and village councils, to be restricted only by ecological and inter-regional planning considerations;
6. Cessation of all colonial settlement activities and freezing the growth of existing Israeli settlements until their fate is determined by a negotiated settlement;
7. The withdrawal of Israeli armed forces, and armed settlers, to regions outside municipal and village councils in the West Bank and Gaza.

These suggestions are not new, and several of them have already been raised in the first political platform attributed to the intifada leadership, the so-called 14 point platform of January 14, 1988. The first item of this platform called for adherence to the Fourth Geneva Convention relating to the protection of civilians in times of war, and the annulment of the Emergency Laws, inherited from the British Mandate.[8]

The tasks of maintaining security and internal order during this interim period, including the security of Israeli civilians in the occupied territories, is a logistical problem of some proportion. Within Palestinian political circles there is a preference that these tasks be vested in an international force acceptable to both Israel and the Palestinians. Initially such an international presence will in all likelihood be rejected by the present Israeli government, and probably by the Labour opposition, not only because of the difficulty of arriving at a mutually agreeable force, but because it implies the (partial) suspension of Israeli sovereignty and control over the territories, *prior* to the conclusion of a final settlement. But its attractiveness lies in that it will relieve the Israelis from the daily tasks of a brutal rule over an unwilling population, with all the political and moral liabilities that entails and without having to relinquish sovereignty immediately.

Perhaps the most concrete arrangement for translating these measures in the transitional period would be to establish a United Nations Mandate over the territories, to be collectively administered by a corporate body designated by the international community. What makes this proposal a pressing issue today is the brutal collective measures undertaken by the Israeli Military Administration during and after the Gulf war. Most notable among them were the prolonged curfews preventing farmers and workers from going to work; the use of curfews to collect taxes and fines from citizens; and extreme measures limiting the movement of people from one district to another, *even after the curfews were lifted*. This includes the liberal use of green identity cards, equivalent to South Africa's pass cards.

The fact that these measures were not lifted after the war, and in many cases were expanded and supplanted, indicates that they are intended to serve ends other than the proverbial security of state and public order. In my view they have two main objectives: to break the institutional patterns of the intifada by establishing an extensive network of permits and control mechanisms which will render every citizen dependent on the state's dispensation of daily needs; and second, to create economic hardships of such magnitude that the population at large would welcome any measure of political liberalization as an alternative to sovereignty.

But these measures have not worked and are unlikely to succeed. What makes Palestinian society so resilient to these draconian steps is a simple agrarian base, and strong social bonds of communal solidarity steeled by a tradition of stubborn resistance. On the other hand, it is only through such an interim agreement described above, involving the gradual devolution of Israeli control and ensuring the protection of civilian life and institutions, that the preconditions for substantial negotiations can proceed. The Gulf war has created a new international situation which makes it difficult for Israel to avoid economic and political pressures if it chooses to be part of this new order. On the Palestinian side, a great amount of fortitude, flexibility, and vision also is required: first to maintain an internal unity that is capable of resisting the impending pressures to circumvent the PLO, and second in order to pursue the strategic line of struggle that is needed during the transitional period suggested here.

Notes

[1] "The Uprising's Dilemma: Limited Rebellion and Civil Society," *Middle East Report*, May-August 1990, pp.4-8.

[2] Circular No.68, Unified National Leadership (UNLU), March 1, 1991. It is clear from the debate over the meeting with U.S. Secretary of State James Baker, however, that the leadership is divided over this issue.

[3] It is significant that Khaled al-Fahoum, a leading figure in the pro-Syrian Salvation Front, did not posit the Front as an alternative to the current leadership of the PLO after the war. He merely suggested that the Palestinian National Council (PNC) should be convened and new elections be carried out to replace Yasser Arafat. (Interview broadcast by the BBC World Service, March 9, 1991). During the war itself none of the constituent parties of the Salvation Front distinguished itself from the Syrian stance, unlike the Popular Front for the Liberation of Palestine and the Democratic Front for the Liberation of Palestine, both based in Damascus, who identified themselves with Iraq.

[4] Ghassan al-Khatib, "After the Gulf War: A Palestinian Agenda" (in Arabic), *Al Quds*, March 5, 1991.

[5] *Ibid.*

[6] For a detailed analysis of the undisciplined side of the uprising see Muhammad al-Manasra, "On the Negative Features of the Intifada" (in Arabic), *Sawt al Watan*, Vol.1, No.B, April 1990.

[7] Three forthcoming studies deal with "alternative economy" and suggest creative adjustments: Izzaat Abdul Hadi in a major work on cooperatives (to be published by the Beisan Institute, Ramallah, Summer 1991); Samir Hleileh on the development strategies of grass-roots movements, *Afaq Filistiniyya* No.6, Spring 1991; and Samir Abdullah, on the domestic economy debate, monograph to be published by the Arab Thought Forum, Summer 1991.

[8] For an analysis see Ale Jerbawi, *The Uprising and Political Leadership in the West Bank and Gaza* (in Arabic), (Beirut, Dar at-Tali'a, 1989) pp.70ff; for a listing of the 14 points see *PASSIA 1990 Yearbook* (Jerusalem, 1990), p.209.

The Unknown Soldier

"*The concept that war is horrible* is altogether different from the stunning practical realization of horror we have willed. The first is easy to live with; the second is hard to forget."

Harold Evans, former editor of the *Times of London* wrote those words in defence of the publication of a startling and macabre photo, March 3, 1991, in the British Sunday paper *The Observer*. The publication of the photo had caused a storm of controversy.

A young American photographer, Ken Jaracke, took the photo as fleeing Iraqi conscripts, many Kurds and Shiites, tried to escape Kuwait. They were trapped and methodically slaughtered in the final hours of combat, in what U.S. pilots called their "turkey shoot." The Iraqi whom Jaracke photographed still was in the cab of a truck, his upper body visible and facing forward.

"Evidently he'd been trying to crawl out through the windshield when the truck was hit," said Jaracke.

However, Americans and Canadians never saw this photo. "I figured it never would get published in this country [U.S.]. In fact when the Associated Press in Dhahran transmitted the picture, some editor in New York took it off the wire," explained Jaracke.

"I think people should see this. This is what our smart bombs did. If we're big enough to fight a war, we should be big enough to look at it."

One American group, *Refuse and Resist*, projected the image onto the side of the U.N. headquarters in New York, and onto the walls of CBS, ABC and NBC, in an action funded by Kurt Vonnegut and others.

Tony Harrison, a British poet, looked at the photo and this "armature half-patched with clay," this "icon framed," spoke to him. Reprinted here is Harrison's poem, "A Cold Coming." (The English publisher Bloodaxe Books have reproduced the photo on the cover of *A Cold Coming*. This publication includes two war poems by Tony Harrison, "A Cold Coming" and "Initial Illumination.")

A Cold Coming

Tony Harrison

'A cold coming we had of it.'
T.S. Eliot, *Journey of the Magi*

I saw the charred Iraqi lean
towards me from bomb-blasted screen,

his windscreen wiper like a pen
ready to write down thoughts for men,

his windscreen wiper like a quill
he's reaching for to make his will.

I saw the charred Iraqi lean
like someone made of Plasticine

as though he'd stopped to ask the way
and this is what I hear him say:

"Don't be afraid I've picked on you
for this exclusive interview.

Isn't it your sort of poet's task
to find words for this frightening mask?

If that gadget that you've got records
words from such scorched vocal chords,

press RECORD before some dog
devours me mid-monologue."

So I held the shaking microphone
closer to the crumbling bone:

"I read the news of three wise men
who left their sperm in nitrogen,

three foes of ours, three wise Marines
with sample flasks and magazines,

three wise soldiers from Seattle
who banked their sperm before the battle.

Did No.1 say: God be thanked
I've got my precious semen banked?

And No.2: O praise the Lord
my last best shot is safely stored?

And No.3: Praise be to God
I left my wife my frozen wad?

So if their fate was to be gassed
at least they thought their name would last,

and though cold corpses in Kuwait
they could by proxy procreate.

Excuse a skull half roast, half bone
for using such a scornful tone.

It may seem out of all proportion
but I wish I'd taken their precaution.

They seemed the masters of their fate
with wisely jarred ejaculate.

Was it a propaganda coup
to make us think they'd cracked death too,

disinformation to defeat us
with no post-mortem millilitres?

Symbolic billions in reserve
made me, for one, lose heart and nerve.

On Saddam's pay we can't afford
to go and get our semen stored.

Sad to say that such high tech's
uncommon here. We're stuck with sex.

If you can conjure up and stretch
your imagination (and not retch)

the image of me beside my wife
closely clasped creating life..."

(I let the unfleshed skull unfold
a story I'd been already told,

and idly tried to calculate
the content of ejaculate:

the sperm in one ejaculation
equals the whole Iraqi nation

times, roughly, let's say, 12.5
though that .5's not now alive.

Let's say the sperms were an amount
so many times the body count,

2,500 times at least
(but let's wait till the toll's released!).

Whichever way Death seems outflanked
by one tube of cold bloblings banked.

Poor bloblings, maybe you've been blessed
with, of all fates possible, the best

according to Sophocles i.e.
"the best of fates is not to be"

a philosophy that's maybe bleak
for any but an ancient Greek

but difficult these days to escape
when spoken to by such a shape.

When you see men brought to such states
who wouldn't want that "best of fates"

or in the world of Cruise and Scud
not go kryonic if he could,

spared the normal human doom
of having made it through the womb?)

He heard my thoughts and stopped the spool:
"I never thought life futile, fool!

Though all Hell began to drop
I never wanted life to stop.

I was filled with such a yearning
to stay in life as I was burning,

such a longing to be beside
my wife in bed before I died,

and, most, to have engendered there
a child untouched by war's despair.

So press RECORD! I want to reach
the warring nations with my speech.

Don't look away! I know it's hard
to keep regarding one so charred,

so disfigured by unfriendly fire
and think it once burned with desire.

Though fire has flayed off half my features
they once were like my fellow creatures',

till some screen-gazing crop-haired boy
from Iowa or Illinois,

equipped by ingenious technophile
put paid to my paternal smile

and made the face you see today
an armature half-patched with clay,

an icon framed, a looking glass
for devotees of 'kicking ass',

a mirror that returns the gaze
of victors on their victory days

and in the end stares out the watcher
who ducks behind his headline: GOTCHA!

or behind the flag-bedecked page 1
of the true to bold-type-setting SUN!

I doubt victorious Greeks let Hector
join their feast as spoiling spectre,

and who'd want to sour the children's joy
in Iowa or Illinois

or ageing mothers overjoyed
to find their babies weren't destroyed?

But cabs beflagged with SUN front pages
don't help peace in future ages.

Stars and Stripes in sticky paws
may sow the seeds for future wars.

Each Union Jack the kids now wave
may lead them later to the grave.

but praise the Lord and raise the banner
(excuse a skull's sarcastic manner!)

Desert Rat and Desert Stormer
without scars and (maybe) trauma,

the semen-bankers are all back
to sire their children in their sack.

With seed sown straight from the sower
dump second-hand spermatozoa!

Lie that you saw me and I smiled
to see the soldier hug his child.

Lie and pretend that I excuse
my bombing by B-52s,

pretend they have the burnt man's blessing
and then, maybe, I'm spared confessing

that only fire burnt out the shame
of things I'd done in Saddam's name,

the deaths, the torture and the plunder
the black clouds all of us are under.

Say that I'm smiling and excuse
the Scuds we launched against the Jews.

Pretend I've got the imagination
to see the world beyond one nation.

That's your job, poet, to pretend
I want my foe to be my friend.

It's easier to find such words
for this dumb mask like baked dogturds.

So lie and say the charred man smiled
to see the soldier hug his child.

This gaping rictus once made glad
a few old hearts back in Baghdad,

hearts growing older by the minute
as each truck comes without me in it.

I've met you though, and had my say
which you've got taped. Now go away."

I gazed at him and he gazed back
staring right through me to Iraq.

Facing the way the charred man faced
I saw the frozen phial of waste,

a test-tube frozen in the dark,
crib and Kaaba, sacred Ark,

a pilgrimage of Cross and Crescent
the chilled suspension of the Present.

Rainbows seven shades of black
curved from Kuwait back to Iraq,

and instead of gold the frozen crock's
crammed with Mankind on the rocks,

the congealed geni who won't thaw
until the World renounces War,

cold spunk meticulously jarred
never to be charrer or the charred,

a bottled Bethlehem of this come-
curdling Cruise/Scud-cursed millenium,

I went. I pressed REWIND and PLAY
and I heard the charred man say:

Oh no, he's back again.

Let's pray
that this
time is the
last time.

© GANNETT OUTDOOR GROUP

8341

GANNETT OUTDOOR

RECESS

SUNSET
CAR
RENTAL
650-3752
WEND FROM $59.95
100 MILE FREE

CHRIS GAINOR

This is one of many examples of billboard propaganda put up by newspaper owners. The Gannett Group, responsible for this billboard on Sunset Strip, Hollywood, owns 88 daily papers in the U.S. The photograph was taken February 1, 1991.

JOHN TAMBLYN

"Because there was and there wasn't a city of Baghdad" was a billboard exhibition by Jamelie Hassan. It was sponsored by Artcite Gallery of Windsor, Ontario. The billboard appeared in Windsor and London, Ontario in the late summer of 1991. The original image came from a photograph Hassan took of a Baghdad mosque in 1979 when she was studying in Iraq.

Resources

Though many references for further reading can be found in the individual essays in this volume, there are a number of publications which provide invaluable information on current developments in the Middle East. If these publications are not presently in your local library, request they subscribe.

Al Fajr: published weekly in English-translation from Jerusalem, this newspaper concentrates on Palestinian developments in the West Bank and Gaza and includes news, discussion and cultural reports. (*Al-Fajr*, 2025 I Street N.W., Washington, D.C. 20006, U.S.A.)

Israeli Foreign Affairs: published monthly by Jane Hunter in the United States, based on comprehensive monitoring of the media and informed sources, it provides far and away the best documented and most comprehensive news in English about Israeli foreign relations. (*Israeli Foreign Affairs*, P.O. Box 19580, Sacramento, Ca. 95819, U.S.A.)

Middle East International: published bi-weekly in London, this is the most comprehensive news magazine in English on Middle East politics. Contributors are well-informed, professional journalists from many of the countries in the region, as well as from Europe and North America. Its cartoons are excellent. (*Middle East International*, P.O. Box 53365, Temple Heights Station, Washington, D.C. 20009, U.S.A.)

Middle East Reports: published bi-monthly in the United States, this magazine provides readable analytical and background articles on Middle East politics, economics, women, culture, health and other matters. Contributors are critically minded academic experts from many countries. The magazine includes excellent photographic material. (*Middle East Reports*, Suite 119, 1500 Massachusetts Ave. N.W., Washington, D.C. 20005, U.S.A.)

Near East Cultural and Educational Foundation (NECEF) Newsletter: this publication is particularly useful for information on Canadian government policy and Canadian solidarity activities in the Middle East. In addition to publishing educational material in Canada, NECEF is a federally charted charitable foundation for humanitarian work in the Middle East. It has an excellent network in Canada and internationally for obtaining information and speakers. (NECEF, 106 Duplex Avenue, Toronto, On. M5P 2A7, Canada)

News From Within: published monthly by the Alternative Information Centre in Jerusalem, it provides news and analyses of Jewish-Israeli society and politics from a dissenting viewpoint. (*News From Within*, P.O. Box 24278, Jerusalem)

For a daily chronology of the war against Iraq, and for key sections of statements and documents issued at the time, consult the **Journal of Palestine Studies**, issue 77 (Autumn 1990) through issue 80 (Summer 1991). This periodical also is an excellent source of documents related to the U.S. Middle East conference currently in progress.

Contributors

Bob Bossin is a song writer and one of the founders of the Canadian folk group Stringband. He also has written one-person shows and performed them internationally.

Mordecai Briemberg teaches English as a Second Language at Douglas College in New Westminster, B.C. He is a member of the board of directors of the Near East Cultural and Educational Foundation of Canada.

Elaine Briere is a photographer and human rights researcher. She is coordinator of the East Timor Alert Network in Canada.

Dr. Louise Cainkar is executive director of the Human Rights Research Foundation and director of the Palestine Human Rights Information Center, both in Chicago, Il. She has made extended visits to Iraq and Kuwait to assess civilian casualties.

David Chiu is a biomedical engineer who teaches at the British Columbia Institute of Technology. He went to Kuwait after the end of the bombing on behalf of the World Health Organization to investigate the state of medical equipment there.

Barbara Coward teaches English as a second language at Douglas College in New Westminster, B.C. She was active in the college committee to oppose the war against Iraq.

Susan Eisenberg is a Boston-based poet and playwright, union electrician, performer and teacher. Her first poetry collection, with a foreword by Denise Levertov, was published in 1984: *It's a Good Thing I'm Not Macho* (Whetstone Press).

Dr. Norman Finklestein teaches international relations at Brooklyn College, New York, and is a specialist on Israeli-Palestinian issues.

Dr. Charlene Gannagé is Canada Research Fellow and assistant professor of sociology at York University, Ontario. She is a member of the Arab Canadian Women's Network and has been active in the Toronto Coalition for Troops Out of the Gulf.

Dr. James A. Graff is a professor of philosophy at the University of Toronto. He is president of the Near East Cultural and Educational Foundation of Canada and a member of the international coordinating committee of U.N. Non-Governmental Organizations on the Question of Palestine. His book *Palestinian Children and Israeli State Violence* was published 1991.

Mason Harris has been teaching in the English department at Simon Fraser University since 1966. He teaches a course on anti-utopian science fiction based on Orwell's *1984*, and has an avid interest in Orwell's critique of the use of language to invent false versions of reality in the political journalism of the 1930s and 1940s.

Tony Harrison is a poet and playwright in England. Penguin has published his *Selected Poems* and they, along with Faber and Bloodaxe, have also published his plays. His television work includes a defence of Salman Rushdie, "The Blasphemers' Banquet."

Jamelie Hassan is a Canadian artist of Lebanese ancestry. She has studied in Rome, Beirut, Windsor and Baghdad and has exhibited widely. *Inscription*, a catalogue of her recent work with an essay by Gayatri Chakrovorty Spivak, was published in 1990 by the Dunlop Art Gallery, Regina, Sk.

Marwan Hassan is a novelist. Cormorant Books has published *The Confusion of Stones: Two Novellas* (1989) and *The Memory Garden of Miguel Carranza* (1991). He is presently at work on a novel entitled: *Nobody Knows Bloor-Yonge Station*.

Amir Hassanpour is a professor of communication studies at the University of Windsor. He is from Kurdistan (Iranian part), and was active in the Kurdish national movement from the 1960s to the early 1980s. Soon after the overthrow of the Shah he contributed to a short-lived effort to build a Kurdish university in Iran. He is a specialist in Kurdish language, culture and history.

Jane Hunter is a journalist specializing in Israel's foreign policy. She publishes the monthly magazine *Israeli Foreign Affairs* and is author of several books, including *Israeli Foreign Policy: South Africa and Central America* (South End Press).

Nasib Samir el-Husseini is a political science lecturer at the Université du Québec in Montreal and a research worker at the Centre d'études arabes pour le développement (CEAD) in Montreal.

Christopher Huxley is associate professor at Trent University Ontario, where he teaches sociology and comparative development. In 1988 he accompanied Charlene Gannagé on a fact-finding tour of the West Bank and Gaza Strip. He was active in the Peterborough-based Citizens for Peace in the Gulf.

Dr. Hanna E. Kassis is a professor of religious studies at the University of British Columbia, where he specializes in Islamic-Christian relations and also teaches Arabic. He was born in Palestine and is Christian.

Michael T. Klare is professor of peace and world security studies at Hampshire College, Amherst, Massachusetts. He is author of several books on U.S. military policy, and is defense correspondent for *The Nation*.

Don Kossick has been an organizer in Saskatchewan for the last 20 years in the farmers, labour and international solidarity movements, and worked building the Saskatchewan coalitions to oppose the war against Iraq.

Anton Kuerti is a concert pianist, living in Toronto. He also has been a candidate for parliament on behalf of the New Democratic Party.

Raymont Legault is active in Quebec with the Palestine solidarity organization SALAM. During summer 1990 he worked to build support in Quebec for the rights of the Mohawk people of Kanewake and Kanesetake.

Rick McCutcheon is the coordinator for the Canadian Friends Service Committee in Toronto.

Carel Moiseiwitsch is an artist whose work appears in European and North American publications.

Emile Nucho was born and raised in Lebanon and emigrated to Canada in the late 1950s. He completed his studies in Canada and the U.S., receiving an M.A. in Islamic Studies at McGill University. He is an active member of the Unitarian Church in Vancouver.

Marion Qawas is a Canadian who has been active in the Palestinian community here and in support of Palestinian national and human rights for 20 years. She helps produce the only Palestinian radio program in Canada, "Voice of Palestine," broadcast weekly on Vancouver's community radio station CFRO-FM.

Dave Rogers is a song-writer in England.

Dr. Suzanne Rose is a specialist in Amerindian linguistics. She also trained as a physiotherapist and spent a year in the Sudan, developing community health care curriculum for war-displaced women. She has campaigned against uranium mining, nuclear warship visits, and military shows, and has worked as an anti-war campaigner for Greenpeace Vancouver during the war against Iraq.

Leon Rosselson is a song writer living in England, and frequently performs internationally. He has recorded many albums, cassettes and CDs for Fuse Records. His most recent CD, *Wo Sind Die Elefanten?* (Where Are the Elephants?), includes "General Lockjaw Briefs The British Media."

Shahla Sarabi is an Iranian woman presently living in Vancouver. She is an avid reader of the literature of her homeland and closely follows events there.

Dr. Israel Shahak is a retired professor of chemistry at the Hebrew University Jerusalem, and chairman of the Israeli League for Human and Civil Rights. Dr. Shahak is a survivor of the Warsaw ghetto and Nazi concentration camps. He regularly produces English translations of the Israeli Hebrew press.

Elizabeth Shefrin lives in Vancouver and has curated shows of images of Nicaragua, Chilean arpilleras and the story of Chinese settlement in Vancouver. Her own art reflects a variety of political, feminist, and multicultural concerns, including an on-going exploration of her Jewish heritage.

Sandy Shreve is a poet and office worker in the women's studies department at Simon Fraser University. A collection of her poetry, *The Speed of the Wheel is Up to the Potter*, was published in 1990 (Quarry Press). She is active in the Vancouver Industrial Writers Union.

Heather Spears is a Canadian writer, now living in Denmark. She won the Governor-General's Award for poetry in 1989, and she has just finished her first novel, a work of science fiction. Heather Spears has done drawings of babies in hospitals (*Drawings From the Newborn*, 1986), Palestinian victims of the intifada (*Drawn From the Fire*, 1989, and *Massacre*, 1990), and often sketches for Danish newspapers.

Dr. Salim Tamari is a professor of sociology and anthropology at Bir Zeit University on the West Bank, an educational institution closed by the Israelis since the beginning of the intifada nearly four years ago. He is a contributing editor to *Middle East Report* and editor of the Bir Zeit research periodical *Afaq Filistiniya*.

Michel Warshawsky was born in France in a Jewish orthodox family who sent him to Israel for religious studies. He became active in opposition to government policies and has served several prison terms, for refusing military service in the West Bank and Gaza and for making printing facilities available to Palestinians. He is director of the Alternative Information Centre in West Jerusalem, which publishes the monthly *News From Within*.